evidence of my existence

evidence of my existence

my existence

jim lo scalzo

OHIO UNIVERSITY PRESS

*in association with the Ohio University School of Visual Communication
and the E. W. Scripps School of Journalism*

Ohio University Press, Athens, Ohio 45701

www.ohio.edu/oupress

© 2007 by Ohio University Press

Printed in the United States of America

Ohio University Press books are printed on acid-free paper ⊗ ™

14 13 12 11 10 09 08 07   5 4 3 2 1

Library of Congress Cataloging-in-Publication Data

Lo Scalzo, Jim.
  Evidence of my existence / Jim Lo Scalzo.
    p. cm.
  ISBN-13: 978-0-8214-1772-0 (hc : alk. paper)
  ISBN-10: 0-8214-1772-X (hc : alk. paper)
  ISBN-13: 978-0-8214-1773-7 (pb : alk. paper)
  ISBN-10: 0-8214-1773-8 (pb : alk. paper)
  1. Lo Scalzo, Jim. 2. Photojournalists—United States—Biography. I.
Title.
  TR140.L67A3 2007
  779.092—dc22
  [B]

                                                    2007026552

for gabriel and serena

You love me and

I love you and

all the rest is

background noise.

author's note

I'm not an advocate of the "creative nonfiction" or "autobiographical novel" style of memoir writing, which gives the author liberty to stretch truths for his convenience, to change the chronology of events for dramatic effect, and to exaggerate an emotion in order to convey a desired mood. I believe that memoirs, as the name suggests, should be based on memory. Time may alter the exactness of the information conveyed. But to alter it purposefully is to betray the medium—no less an offense than a photojournalist staging a picture.

Every scene, every conversation, every moment written in this book happened and is recounted to the best of my memory. As a recitation of memory, this work should be regarded as my opinion, as one side of the story. Additionally, while much of the dialogue is not verbatim—I don't tape my life's conversations, of course—it is written here as best I can recall.

While it may seem counterintuitive not to include photographs in this book, the size and weight of its pages are not conducive to displaying photography. The publishers and I chose to keep the book a work of writing and to exhibit imagery related to the text on the book's Web site: www.usnews.com/loscalzo-book/.

To protect people's privacy I have changed most every name and in several cases additional identifying traits.

acknowledgments

Portions of this book were previously published elsewhere: parts of "Burma" appeared in the January/February 2004 issue of *National Geographic Traveler* under the title "Favorite Places"; parts of "Arizona" appeared in the *Washington Post* under the title "Along the Byways of the Navajo Nation"; much of "Morocco" appeared in *U.S. News & World Report* under the title "Overexposed," copyright 2004 U.S. News & World Report, L.P., reprinted with permission; and much of "Brazil" appeared in *Brazil: True Stories,* edited by Annette Haddad and Scott Doggett (San Francisco: Travelers' Tales, 2004) under the title "Upriver Chapter."

A thousand thank-yous to my readers, the charitable literati who waded through my early manuscript and offered suggestions: Sean Shesgreen, Sarah Maza, Chris Usher, Adrienne Dearmas, James O'Reilly, and Stacey Schultz. And especially Julianna Baggott, who found time between writing books of her own to help me craft this one.

I also want to share my gratitude with the photo department of *U.S. News & World Report* for giving me opportunities befitting a much finer photographer, with the staff of Ohio University Press for being so brave and generous in publishing this work, with my parents for everything, and with my wife, Deirdre, for being the love of my life.

texas

I want to tell you about a picture. I want to tell you because she's in the frame. It was taken on a drive from Columbia, Missouri, to Big Bend National Park, a drive she and I made back in journalism school. She had never heard of our destination but was eager to go, volunteered her car. We drove south for 1,200 miles, camped alone in the desert, and prayed that her rusting Nissan wouldn't crap out when it was time to head home. I fell in love with her there, among the javelinas and the prickly pear. You can look at a person a hundred times without actually seeing her—but change your environment and the skies suddenly clear.

On the drive down I had night duty, the midnight-to-morning shift. I took the wheel when we hit Oklahoma, and she dozed off next to me, her legs up on the dash, my birding book folded open on her lap. I smoked cigarettes to stay awake and listened to whatever radio I could get, which at that hour, in that lonely part of the world, was the invectives of AM evangelists. Somewhere south of Wichita Falls in a landscape populated only by oil wells, I pulled over to take a piss. It was 5 a.m. and I left the car running, thinking the sudden lack of noise might jar her awake. I also left on the radio, apparently; when I stopped tramping through a field of winter wheat, had a go at my belt, I could hear a voice behind me babbling on about being saved.

I turned around to see if this monologue had awoken her. There was a single lamppost not five feet from the car, and it was throwing a peachy chemical light through the windshield and onto her legs and feet, which were still crossed on the dash, and onto her right hand, draped limply out the window. My seat was illuminated as well, noticeable only for being empty. Though the sun wasn't up, there was the slightest orange band on the horizon. And that was just enough light to silhouette the oil wells, bobbing up and down like those long-necked birds that drink Dixie cups of water. The car's headlights were on.

Though I didn't record it with my camera, and though I have witnessed countless other images of her in the fourteen years since, images of her sleeping at that exact hour of the day, of her alone in our bed as I step out gently, quietly, for days, weeks, months on assignment, it is that picture of her in Texas, in that beat-up car on that lonely road, that most often comes to mind.

one

iraq

In the first few weeks of 2003, D.C. went dark. A midwinter rainstorm parked itself a hundred yards above the city, concealing the top of the Washington Monument, causing streetlights to come on at odd hours, and leaving me, like many Washingtonians, feeling cold, dank, and testy. I was running around town in my usual pretrip panic, trying to buy or borrow all the things I needed to cover what appeared an inevitable invasion of Iraq (the satellite phones and power inverters and chemical weapons–protection suits), while still making it to my daily photo assignments.

Something needed to give, and I decided an upcoming assignment in Alexandria, Virginia, would be my last before flying to Baghdad. I was there atop a metal ladder and about to photograph a gaggle of computer geeks when Deirdre rang me on my cell. I hit the receive button and heard her crying before I brought the cell phone to my ear. "There's no heartbeat," she said. A half dozen faces were staring up at me, smiling, waiting. I pinched the cell phone between my head and my shoulder and held down the motor drive. This wasn't happening.

We were just a month into Deirdre's second pregnancy, after the first was lost to a miscarriage, and thus newly liberated from two years of conception hell—the calendars, the Clomid, the doctor's appointments at George Washington Hospital, where I was made to manually produce far too many samples. The room for that activity locked from the inside, thankfully, and had mood lighting, a lame, vintage porno tape, and a splotchy couch that was as much of a biohazard as anything the Americans might find in Iraq. With the lab results came a lecture, Deirdre and I sitting like dejected schoolchildren in the doctor's office, the doctor telling us that my count was too low, that my sperm lacked Olympic swimmers. We wouldn't be able to conceive on our own, the doctor had said, even though we had once before.

Not two weeks later, just after New Year's, Deirdre's pregnancy test stick displayed twin blue bars. I had half a mind to walk back into the doctor's office and pin that plastic rod to her forehead. No hard feelings, of course. It's just that telling a man he can't give his wife a child is akin to telling him he is a waste of biomatter. We just wanted a family and we thought we'd finally made one.

But now this: me racing back to our house, then clutching my wife in the midday darkness of our family room, the rain coming and coming. We sat there for hours, let our sorrow take root and grow around us like a hollow tree. We pretended that I wasn't going anywhere, that this stupid war wasn't happening, that we were alone in the world. And in the morning when a nurse wheeled Deirdre into surgery at GW Hospital, when she disappeared down the fluorescent green hallway for her second D & C and I forced myself to resurrect my long mental to-do list, I could feel myself driving an ax into the trunk of our creation. It was enslaving me, my preparation psychosis, directing my actions and emotions from just off screen, like a puppeteer. Deirdre's doctor poked her head into the waiting room and told me to sit tight, that Deirdre would be out in an hour. I fled through the front door instead.

Sixty minutes. That was enough time to hit the Jordanian Embassy to pick up my visa ("We don't have. Sorry. Tomorrow"), Penn Camera for a spare firewire card reader ("Nope. Try our store in Rockville") and the *U.S. News* offices in Georgetown to pick up my laptop ("Ain't finished"). Fuck! For a month I had pleaded with our in-house tech support not to wait until the last minute, to configure my computer to communicate with my sat phones well ahead of time so I could deal with unforeseen problems. In return, their Mac guy, an otherwise congenial fellow who has since left the magazine, had labeled me a nudge and made only reluctant, unsuccessful attempts at the task. Inadvertently made my computer worse, in fact. The last time he handed my laptop back it had a seizure, flashing on its screen a series of multicolored disco lights before sending a week's worth of notes, e-mails, and contest entries into the ether.

Now I was fed up and brokenhearted and running out of time and I had given him this day as his deadline to fix everything and fix it right, for Christ's sake, and when I ran in to pick up the computer and saw it at his desk in the same spot I had left it, found the man seated not two feet from my shiny black laptop but paying it no mind, found him in fact with his feet up, reading a copy of *The Lord of the Rings,* I wanted to brain him. I wanted to kick out his chair and bring the laptop down on his skull, repeatedly, until blood flowed from ears.

"Not finished? What the hell?"

He gazed up at me, slowly and with his eyebrows raised. "Excuse me?"

"You've had all month."

"Yeah, well . . ."

"Jesus, man, I need my laptop."

He shrugged his shoulders, threw me a look that said, "You're shit out of luck, pal," then returned his attention to his novel. I hovered over him and he didn't look up. Still I stood there and finally he offered, "I'm on my lunch break."

"Your lunch break? Well I'm going to Baghdad and my wife just had a miscarriage AND I WANT MY FUCKING LAPTOP!" I whisper-screamed this last part inches from the poor guy's ear. He displayed a Zen-like level of restraint, tightening his jaw and staring through the pages of his paperback. This infuriated me further still—being outclassed by a person who was simultaneously screwing me over—though by now I was ten minutes late and I stormed off without my computer, sped back to the hospital without having accomplished a goddamned thing, and there was Deirdre waiting for me in recovery. My lovely wife slumped in a wheelchair, her body drained, her heart broken, her cheeks stained with tears. I raced her home and put her straight to bed, then retreated to the spare bedroom, nearly tripping over all the things I had gathered for Baghdad but had yet to pack. I walked to the window that overlooked Garrison Street and slid it open. It was still raining and I felt like I was drowning.

I hated myself for this, for not giving her a child, for being bound to an ever more involved itinerary. For leaving her again. "I'm not gonna tell you not to go," she had said on the way home. She was a woman of few words and even fewer demands; it was the first time I can remember her lobbing such a plea. Tossing it out there and seeing how I'd respond. Putting the ball in my court. For years we had lived separate lives, me photographing, her writing, each cultivating our careers and reuniting when we could. Though I was the one who did most of the going, who had set this agenda and placed the miles between us. She pretended to be fine with it, and for too long I had pretended to believe her. "I'm not gonna tell you not to go." The weight of those words hit me in the gut. Then I let them fall to the floor, left them lying there between us, unacknowledged.

I couldn't bag Iraq, not after the magazine had paid for my plane ticket, and paid for my hostile environment training (which prepares civilians for working in a war zone). Not after I had been so brazen about getting my visa, faxing my application to the Iraqis right after Hailey told me we weren't sending a photographer to Baghdad. Hailey was my boss, the magazine's director of photography, and for years we had butted heads over precisely these kinds of moves. Over my impetuosity. And my temper. And my difficulty accepting direction (her words from my latest performance review). Applying for a visa behind her back wouldn't help matters any. So I hadn't felt the need to burden the woman with that information, with the details of yet another independent and improbable pursuit.

Iraqi visas were near impossible to get. When the Ministry of Information in Baghdad signed off on mine—the luck of the draw,

I guess—Hailey, to my great relief, took the high road and didn't make an issue of it. Got approval from the editor of the magazine for me to go. And really, we needed somebody there. The prep for battle, the vowed resistance, the weapons inspectors racing against the clock. And what if there was a coup? What if the Shiites turned on Hussein, or his fellow Baath members? What if the war never happened and Hussein proclaimed victory?

I couldn't bag Iraq. Not after sticking my neck out like that. And not with all those freelancer shooters out there, young, hungry, and talented, waiting to use such an opening to gain a foothold in the mag world. My staff position at *U.S. News* & *World Report* was one of the most coveted jobs in the profession. And the rarest. The big three newsmagazines, *Time, Newsweek,* and *U.S. News,* employed just four staff photographers—one at *Time* and three at *U.S. News.* We were the last of our species, and if I was ever wary of our extinction it was because I had watched too many other photographers lose their jobs.

U.S. News was under increasing fiscal constraints, outsourcing nearly all of its photographic needs. It didn't use to be that way, and I was living proof—made the seventh staffer at age twenty-six, a dream job, fresh out of grad school and with no magazine experience. But even then I was a hard traveler. And if I didn't earn the position, I like to think I earned my keep, shooting hundreds, perhaps thousands of assignments. I hit fifty states by the time I was twenty-eight, fifty countries by the time I was thirty-three. I amassed hundreds of comp days and spent them on the road, shooting more photo projects. Wanderlust was my existence, the very reason I became a photojournalist, and I'm sure it's what saved me while others were downsized.

Sixteen years on the road: eight for *U.S. News* and eight on my own before that. The benefit to my career was undeniable; so was the toll on my personal life. Here I was still childless, a phantom to my immediate family, a blur to my wife, her pathological tolerance worn thin. And the physical effects. I was only thirty-five and yet felt like an old man. I was exhausted. Worn out. Fried. My back hurt constantly—years of carrying too much gear. And I couldn't sleep worth a shit. All those time changes, the overnight flights and early calls, the Ambien and Xanax to get to sleep and the Dexedrine to stay awake. My gut hurt too, having played host to an extensive collection of microorganisms, the hideous little creatures that inhabit the shitholes of the world. If you believe, as the Hindus do, that the body is just a garment, one you shed in the transition from this life to the next, then those shed by me and other footloose photographers won't be worth the trade-in.

I had never been seriously injured on assignment—and I wish it weren't so, as at least I'd have an excuse for my condition, could point to some sympathy-inducing trauma rather than a laundry list of inglorious battle scars. I *had* been spit on a lot: by Mennonites (Missouri), heroin addicts (Pakistan), and the KKK (South Carolina). I'd had hepatitis (the Navajo Nation), two bouts of amoebic dysentery (India, Burma), and four cases of giardia (Nepal, Peru, Afghanistan, Cuba). I'd been shot with rubber bullets (Seattle), been knocked on my ass by a water cannon (Quebec), and inhaled more pepper spray and teargas than I care to recall. I'd tumbled into freezing water (Antarctica) and open sewers (Iran, Bolivia) and gotten frostbite on one of my toes (Alaska). I'd been punched in the stomach (Afghanistan) and slapped in the face (Egypt). I'd been chased by a lunatic with a machete (Haiti), a car full of crack dealers (Virginia), and an elk in estrus (Wyoming). My hands and feet had been invaded by botfly larvae (Brazil), and my intestines by foot-long tapeworms, called *Ascaris lumbricoides* (India). These monsters enter your body through the soles of your feet and travel up your legs to your gut, where they grow and procreate. And procreate. And procreate. How did I find out I had them? Let's just say I know more about giving birth than most men.

Obviously, mine was not a distinguished existence or an illustrious career. But then I've never been my own idea of a photographer. I wasn't dashing or urbane. I had no panache. I didn't wear a Leica around my neck like jewelry. I didn't sit in smoky cafés saying things like "The closer you get to death, the higher the f-stop." I didn't live in a loft with thirty-foot ceilings and elegant black-and-white prints adorning exposed brick walls. Well-traveled, yes, but still unrefined. I didn't shower every day, I thought every headache was a sign of cancer, I laughed out loud when I saw somebody trip, and I had an irrepressible urge to lay into people I didn't like. Not just the casual villains of the photojournalist—that writer who refers to you as "my photographer," that art designer who turns your picture into a postage stamp, that tech guy who doesn't give a rat's ass if you *are* heading to a war zone, because he's got a book to read—but everyday people, the ones whose venial sins I endured on my way home from work, the ones driving too slowly or flicking cigarette butts out their window. The ones clogging Connecticut Avenue by parking in the right lane *after* 4 p.m. The ones in the Hummers.

My misanthropic eruptions—which I had long ago accepted as the pure and natural byproduct of the East-Coast, type A, get-out-of-my-way personality—were forever horrifying Deirdre, a quiet and contemplative type. Take our camping trip to West Virginia. No sooner had we put up our tent than I wanted the heads of the yahoos in the next site, the ones ruining our quest for a little peace and quiet, keeping us up until 3 a.m., howling like animals, throwing beer cans, setting off firecrackers, blaring cracker music: Alabama and Skynyrd. The next morning we packed up early to relocate. The sun wasn't yet up, and as we were leaving I eased our vehicle downhill slowly, silently, in neutral and with the lights off, brought it against the offender's oversized tent, my front bumper kissing their nylon. She dug her fingers into the dashboard. "What are you doing? What are you doing?" I flicked on the high beams and brought my hand down on the horn, that ferocious Jeep horn wailing as if the missiles were about to land, as if Armageddon were upon them. I revved the engine too—let them think I'm coming in. The tent shook, there was panic. Still I held down the horn. Out jumped a man in his tighty whiteys, disoriented and hung over, wincing, trying to block the high beams with his hand.

"Show some consideration!" he screamed, his panic bringing me profound joy. It still does.

Though Deirdre laughed about it later—one of the reasons I love her, her ability to find humor in my hangups—titling the incident my "redneck rampage" for the sake of dinner party guests, I knew that pretending to run people over wasn't good for our relationship. That my friends were serious when they'd ask what Deirdre saw in me. She's *smart,* they'd add indelicately. And how could I be offended—I wondered it myself. The drama, the distances, the phoned-in affections. The unfulfilled promises of being around more often. She *was* smart. Tough. Beautiful. Successful. Covered Congress for the Washington bureau of the *St. Louis Post-Dispatch*. Could have had any man she wanted—even back in J-school—yet for some reason she had chosen me. The life I gave her in return was no romance novel but a frenetic travelogue, a collection of journeys, some humorous and some horrifying. And if the protagonist was finally growing road-weary, it had less to do with a loss of desire than with these familial, and physical, failings.

A life defined by place, by where I'd been and where I was going. It presented an absurd paradox, this existence, my wanting to be on the road and yet hating the consequences. But how to stop moving? Travel was a compulsive craving. An addiction. Heroin. The buzz it offered was euphoric, the escape ephemeral, the hangover cold and distancing. Once home I'd buy an armful of travel guides from the Borders up the street, plant myself on my porch, and research the next fix, any fix. It didn't matter if I wasn't going there. I was the only person I knew who read *Lonely Planet* guides for places he had no plans to visit. How was the exchange rate in Lesotho, or the black market in Yemen? What was the best beach in Tonga, and how much was it to fly to the Seychelles? The variables were infinite, and so were the opportunities, all open to me as a photojournalist, the dream job of every wanderlust. If Odysseus were alive today he'd carry a Domke camera bag instead of a bow and arrow; Ibn Battuta, two Canons instead of the Koran.

It's what I had wanted since childhood, when I'd seek solitude in the pages of my parent's *National Geographic* magazines.

To escape my inadequacies and fears and neurosis and venture on my own to a new and exciting destination. To savor like a deep breath the people and places of a path all my own. My happiness was dependent on it still. More than my picture-making, my family, my wife, my existence. The ugly, insatiable truth was that all those blessings took a backseat to my need for new environments. Place meant everything.

▢ And now Iraq. If the gear arrayed on the floor of the spare bedroom was any indication, this would be unlike all the other journeys. I had collected three silver chemical-protection suits— which looked like the recycled wardrobe from some 1950s alien-invasion flick—two gas masks, two jugs of decontamination spray for chemical and biological warfare agents, countless germi-cidal disposable wipes ("proven effective against tuberculosis," the label promised), and a bottle of Cipro left over from the year be-fore, when I and dozens of other journalists got too close to Senator Daschle's office just after it was contaminated with an-thrax. There was a twenty-five-pound flak vest and a Kevlar hel-met. And then all my camera and computer gear, the sat phones, a dozen different chargers. The camping equipment. My clothes. Way too much shit. "I'm not going," I declared aloud. Then I started to pack.

By the morning of my departure I'd managed to cram all 195 pounds into two Pelican cases, a camera backpack, and an over-sized computer bag. With some effort I hauled the bags down-stairs, then went back up for a final walk-through. The newfound cleanliness of the spare bedroom left a lump in my stomach. This was it. I sat on the bed and stared at the wooden floors, which hadn't been visible for weeks. After some time Deirdre walked in and sat down next to me, and I cried because I already missed her and because I was scared. I wanted to go and I didn't want to go and I knew she didn't understand. I cried because it's hard to turn your back, no matter how sore, on a lifetime of desire.

two

north carolina

The Outer Banks of North Carolina are a thin and vulnerable strand of sandbars, arching southeast into the Atlantic for a hundred miles before reversing course suddenly, at Cape Hatteras, and drifting southwest to rejoin the mainland. The scenery is dramatic, with undulating dunes and muscular surf, though its immunity from putt-putt golf, parking-lot pools, and other boardwalk blight, long the landscape of much of the mid-Atlantic seaboard, has weakened in recent years.

In the early 1970s, before the well-heeled of Washington DC built their summer dachas on its dunes, before eateries with lewd names—Dirty Dick's Crab House, Try My Nuts Nut Company—cluttered its roads, before airplanes towed billboards above its shores, the Outer Banks were a place apart. There were few distractions, and its roads were not well maintained. The only convenience store I can recall was a single-story, pink cinderblock job named Wink's. The only beach company a colony of ghost crabs. My family visited the Banks every July, seven dark-haired souls pressed into a wood-paneled station wagon, destined for a crappy little cottage called Whitehouse. My anticipation of this annual pilgrimage approximated something closer to obsession than excitement. I loved the Banks' smell, dry and sun-baked, like threshed wheat. I loved its sounds—by day, the water-sprinkler rasp of spur-throated grasshoppers, by night the quivering chorus of green tree frogs. I even loved the way it looked on a map, like a necklace of land draped over the ocean, so exposed that a single tsunami could wash it forever beneath the sea. I loved the aloneness it afforded.

My home outside Washington was the hive of the neighborhood, the place where every kid within a five-block radius seemed to gather to eat lunch, play Wiffle ball, torment each other with squirt guns. Living in the neighborhood playground afforded me the shortest commute to the goings on. But on the down side, it meant precious little private time, something I craved even in my single-digit years. Strange though it seemed to the rest of my posse, I would flee for afternoons at a time into the woods behind my house. There was a creek I could follow through miles of semi-interrupted forest, and it rewarded its lone explorer with the thoroughly unimpressive display that is the suburban Maryland ecosystem. In terms of fauna, this consisted mostly of squirrels, crows, and crayfish.

If the wilds of greater Washington were a slight bit tame, a slight bit too familiar, then those of the Outer Banks seemed of another world—as exotic even as the destinations that appeared in the glossy, yellow-bordered magazines my parents received once a month in the mail. During the anxious months of winter, when I was stuck indoors, I'd often fan the magazines out on the floor of my bedroom and work through them chronologically. I didn't care much for the cultural exposés, the pieces on Afghan horsemen and endangered Philippine jungle tribes. It was the spreads without people that caught my fancy. Staring at all those lonely landscapes, I felt something rising in me, a sort of preface to sexual desire, a lust more instinctive than that generated by the photographs in the *Penthouse*s my brother hid in the basement. In those pictures I was fearful to make a connection, to go beyond looking. The fantasy of inclusion was overruled by self-consciousness, by embarrassment, by the tried-and-true mores that are supposed to emanate like pure white light from good Catholic boys. Within the pages of *National Geographic,* however, the fantasy was accessible. I allowed myself to be in them, to feel the rocks and smell the trees and move wherever I wanted, freely, immodestly, because in the middle of nowhere nobody was watching. Being alone outdoors excited me.

And being alone indoors terrified me. Literally. I was afraid of ghosts, Jodie (the red-eyed devil-pig from *The Amityville Horror*), and that shrieking, wild-haired fetish doll from *Trilogy of Terror,* the one who pierced Karen Black over and over with his jungle spear, then buried his teeth into her neck. It was a peculiar phobia for a child, to be terrified in one's home rather than in the woods surrounding it. And it was due, I'm sure, to my siblings' puerile penchant for scaring the living bejesus out of me— throwing me in a dark closet, say, where one of them was already hiding, waiting to pounce. Or dangling me by one leg over a flushing toilet. Or tying me to a chair in the basement and leaving me there with the lights off.

One winter the four of them, all older, conspired to convince me I was sharing my bedroom with a family of poltergeists. In the night I became certain the child-ghosts were pulling the sheets off my bed one tiny tug at a time, so slowly it would take a speeded-up film to notice, and that I could hear them snickering about it. My siblings put my anxiety to the tune of the then popular Foreigner song "Cold as Ice." At dinner they sang: "Jimmy's room has pol-ter-geist, and he's willing to sac-ri-fice his sleep." Come spring, when I could return outdoors, alone, the demons vanished. The natural world was a place of refuge, a sanctuary from familial pranks, an environment for which I had already developed an irrepressible longing, a hyperawareness. And come summer, when my clan vacationed in the Outer Banks and I headed out on my own, in the opposite direction of the beach, toward the naked, skin-colored sand dunes that surrounded the Currituck Sound, I was comfortable enough to remove my clothing, which seemed an intrusion on my aloneness, an unnatural, unnecessary appendage, and float on my back in the tepid, shallow water.

▢ I was eleven when my parents gave me a Polaroid camera for Christmas. It was rectangular, close to a foot high, and the only setting it offered was a peculiar plastic switch with the numbers +1 +2 and −1 −2 inscribed above and below it. I used it to make that season's happy snap of the family standing before the Christmas tree, and then lost interest in the machine. I was beginning a distracted, pain-in-the-ass phase which my parents would summarize forgivingly as my "attitude problem." All at once I loathed sixth grade, after-school Bible study, piano lessons. I talked back to teachers, tore up bad report cards, got into fistfights, smoked cigarettes stolen from my friend's mother's purse. I spent an increasing amount of time alone in the woods. That summer, the last of the 1970s, our annual pilgrimage didn't include my oldest sibling, the howls of his high school pack drowning out parental demands to attend the family vacation. This meant my mother had to stay home too and guard the house against teenage sleepovers, impromptu swill fests, and other nocturnal predations.

I brought the Polaroid with me to the Outer Banks, an impulse move to make some courtesy snaps for her. And when my father and sisters headed for the beach, I headed for the sound, camera in tow, imagining myself on the job for the *Geographic*. Seeing the images right away was what caused the epiphany, them coming to life in my hand, a minute-long fade-in from white to blues and browns and greens, to herons and horseshoe crabs and the reflection of the sun on the water. Instantly, I was a creator. And I had an ally, one that justified my escapist behavior. It offered evidence that what I was seeking wasn't strange at all—it had appeal. Value. I kept staring at an image of the sound with sea oats in the foreground and the setting sun in the background. It was the same scene you'd encounter in any of those sad beachfront art shops, the ones where every square inch of wall space is crammed with oil paintings in oversized wooden frames. Only I created it in seconds. It seemed like cheating, and I liked that. The images weren't the product of any particular skill—anyone can push a button. They were a product of the journey, which for me had always come naturally.

From then on at home I excused my walkabouts as "photo safaris." While they didn't result in any pictures I can remember, they did deepen my certitude that the twin pillars of my early well-being—my wanderlust and my picture making—shared a single existential tenet: place means everything. In order to reveal what matters in the world, you have to put yourself square in front of it. Photography is about being there, as the saying goes. It is about recognizing as curious the environs around you and exploring them for yourself. It is about walking through the woods behind your house at eleven years old, with no other mission than to reveal to your peers, your friends, your loved ones that the world outside their door is full of pretty things.

three

india

"Hold it steady!" the Sikh screamed again, and this time I clutched the metal rungs of the gurney and knelt beneath it. Still the gurney swung from side to side. "Bloody hell." The Sikh was sweating now, pumping hard with his right arm, trying to saw through a man's leg. A man who had leprosy. A man who was awake—his only anesthesia a rolled-up towel stuffed into his mouth. He bellowed and writhed with such primal desperation I thought his heart would give out. Or my stomach.

I was thankful I could no longer see him. I stared at the drops of blood on the floor. The flecks of fatty tissue. The black soot from the nearby coal plants. The Sikh's feet mixed these ingredients into a deep brown roux, his flip-flops leaving a peanut-shaped ring where they had just been. What was he doing in flip-flops? No gloves or gown or mask was bad enough. But flip-flops? I didn't know the guy; he was one of the doctors of dubious pedigree the leper colony paid to perform operations. Every Wednesday a different surgeon arrived, young and smiling and carrying an armful of medical books, eager to try his hand at major surgery.

Before the operation the Sikh had administered a spinal, or at least tried to administer a spinal. No one seemed to think it worked. Especially the patient, who protested the Sikh's snipping through his skin and arteries with an anxious and rising monologue, like an auctioneer. And when the Sikh shaved the muscle from the man's thighbone he threw back his head and screamed. Then came the sound of sawing—not the familiar and satisfying hum of metal through wood but a metallic whine, like a steel wire passing through wet piping.

Finally there was silence, the sawing finished, the patient passed out. A gelatinous lump passed above my head. Just a knee, actually, the man's shin and foot removed sometime before. "Save that for the soup," the Sikh joked. He smiled and his teeth were blood-red, stained from a fresh wad of betel nut juice, the local chew. I stood up quickly, too quickly. The last thing I remember before fainting was the Sikh pulling the leper's skin flaps over an angry red stump.

Then there was a nun kneeling above me. I was flat on my back in the hallway and she was laughing and pressing a white stick beneath my nose. The stench of ammonia rushed into my brain, but still I wanted to lie there, to stay asleep. My whole body felt hot and empty, like a balloon floating above it all: the dressing room, that wretched leper colony, India. The State of Bihar, a place of legendary backwardness, with higher rates of poverty, illiteracy, violent crime, corruption, and disease than any other state in India. Not a good place for even a seasoned traveler, let alone a neophyte like me. I was still a teenager.

This was my first venture overseas, to photograph and volunteer at a leper colony outside of Calcutta. It wasn't going well: the heat, the gore, the toll of the food on my stomach. The terrific foreignness. Then being robbed of my camera gear. Amoebic dysentery. And still that residue of anxiety from two months before, from nearly being kicked out of college. "India's gonna be your penance," Schwartz had warned me. I finally felt chewed up enough to admit he was right.

☐ When I first stepped onto the campus of Loyola College in Baltimore, in full eighties rebel mode after four years of Catholic high school—leather jacket, hoop earring, perfect mullet—I was eager to begin shooting for the college paper, the *Green & Grey*. I was nearly alone in this desire, and before the end of the school year was handed a title nobody wanted, photo editor. My hopes of developing a more creative photographic style were promptly squashed beneath the burdens of volume and the thankless rigors of black-and-white printing.

Most of my time was spent in an unventilated, closet-sized darkroom, lit blood-red by a single bulb. I would mix batches of powdered chemistry into developer and fixer and stop bath, trying like hell to create something akin to a black-and-white print, but more often emerging with what looked like a dusty Xerox. Working with chemistry was such an antiquated process: the metal reels, the plastic tongs, the laundry line of dripping prints. I immersed myself in it anyway, often laboring through the night to get the photographs just right. That aloneness! I indulged it in the darkroom like an alcoholic on an all-night bender, emerging in the morning, a full twelve hours later, nauseous from the fumes and squinty-eyed from the dark. It gave me somewhere to be besides pretending to study in the library or prowling the sad, sticky pubs along York Road.

In matters scholastic I maintained my long and ugly tradition of profound indifference. While extracurricular projects had long distracted me, I did consider this one—slaving at the paper—a form of study, one that benefitted the entire student body (even if nobody actually read the thing), and in my own perverse logic this endowed my actions with moral purpose. It also removed much of the emotional burden from my new and ill-chosen shortcut through the academic requirements of sophomore year: cheating. I went through English lit without reading a single assigned book. The professor was on autopilot, giving students the same quizzes and tests he gave the previous semester, which one of my roommates kept and fed to me. For the year-end essay I tried to persuade another student, who was taking the same class but with a different professor, to share with me her paper on *Huckleberry Finn*. She refused. Then one afternoon I saw her in the computer lab, saw her stepping away from her terminal, and, yes, promptly used the vacancy to occupy her seat, copy the said paper from her floppy disk, and, a day later, hand it in as my own. Fuck it. And fuck them. I didn't want some literary lightweight telling me what to read. I was reading Marquez and Kundera and Camus, and they gave me Macondo and Prague and Attica, places I escaped to and made room for in my heart. Places that suffered, and for whose losses I felt the most terrible affection. Twain's Missouri was for pussies.

This wasn't a good side of me, I did realize, and decided to right myself that summer, alone, on the road. I would hitchhike my way across America, lose myself in the great parks of the West, the Grand Canyon and Zion and Yellowstone. When I revealed my plan to a Jesuit professor, he suggested another option. He said he knew of a leper colony in India run by Indian Jesuits, a place that could use a summer volunteer. I liked the idea of myself there, on the other side of the world: a *Geographic* photographer on assignment. I could volunteer during the day and photograph during my free time. I didn't hold any altruistic motives about volunteering—just thought it an easy way to integrate myself into the lives of those I would photograph.

There was the small matter of paying for the flight. I didn't have $1,500 and wrote a letter to the dean of the college, Father Joseph Sellinger, asking him bluntly for the money. When I returned from India I would write an extended piece for the *Green & Grey* on my experience, my letter promised, and would put together a photographic exhibit on the patients for the student art gallery. At the very least it would generate some press attention for the school. His response came just before finals—a telephone invitation to meet him at his residence.

Father Sellinger was a large Irishman, red-faced and white-haired, with a bulbous Mickey Rooney nose and a disarming smile. I liked him instantly, his air of self-assuredness, his immodest, green-eyed gaze; a man influential enough to have the college's business school named after him, yet gracious enough to think my request was funny. "How much do you need again?" We were sitting in his living room office, his black shirt and white collar a stark contrast to the colorful college trinkets that adorned his quarters: the mugs and pennants and paperweights. Through a window behind him I could see students walking to and from class.

"Fifteen hundred dollars."

"I'll give it to you," he said, his decision seemingly made before I arrived. "But it's coming out of my own pocket, so keep it quiet." I promised I would, and then promptly told half the school. How could I not? To have someone take a gamble on you—your parents, yes—but a total stranger? The dean of your college? Such blind trust was humbling. And I felt eternally grateful. The guy had never even met me and yet somehow knew that India was what I needed, that the experience would affect my life in immeasurable ways. Days later, when I got caught cheating, Father Sellinger's gesture left me feeling all the more loathsome.

The majority of my grade in basic philosophy, a class I hadn't bothered to attend in weeks, was based on the final exam: two questions chosen from a list of ten, all of which were provided to the students ahead of time. The professor was a new guy named Schwartz, and he bore the telltale signs of a latent flower child: overgrown beard, long hair tucked behind his ears, too-small John Lennon glasses. And the avant-garde approach to learning—a gesture that was lost on me. Instead of memorizing the answers, or, more simply, learning them, I wrote them out longhand from the book with a second piece of paper tucked beneath the main one. This created a set of answers that were imprinted though uninked: ten invisible cheat sheets that would accompany me into the exam, arranged numerically in my backpack, and from which I would pluck the appropriate pages, re-trace, and hand in. That was the plan anyway.

On exam day I successfully yanked the prewritten pages from my pack, only the lighting in the room was so flat I couldn't read my indentations. I maneuvered the sheets this way and that, trying to see the lettering. Soon enough the ex-hippy caught the vibe and was lingering above my desk—a position that gave him a better view of the indentations than the one I had. He reached his hand into the curious pile of papers on my desk, pulled out one of the answer sheets, and held it up to the fluorescent lights, wincing, as if inspecting a bill that might be counterfeit. "Gather your things and wait for me in my office." That walk of shame from the classroom, the other students staring, smirking, whispering that I was busted—the humiliation made my head spin.

Drifting across campus, which was abuzz with the school's out-for-summer energy of high-fiving students and backslapping parents, I felt as if my body was caught in a rip current, pulling me on a trajectory that no struggle could reverse. I was screwed, kicked out of school for sure. And right after the dean of the college endowed me with his own money to fly to India. There was no more trip, no more newspaper, no more future. In two days my parents, angry and disgraced, would pick me up from the dorm, and I'd climb into the back of their station wagon, the same one we used to take to the Outer Banks, and wave good-bye to my roommates, my girlfriend, my life as I knew it. When I reached Schwartz's office, I sat in a plastic chair across from his desk and cried into my hands.

He arrived with another cheater in tow, a woman who I knew only from a distance, one with a Long Island accent. She took issue with this impromptu arraignment and let him know it with the tone and indignation of a privileged eleven-year-old. That blathering twit, the aperture of her mouth looking big enough to hold a softball, motoring on about proof, about getting her parents involved, about having people fired. When she ran out of things to say, she turned on her heels and marched out the door. Schwartz's face was scarlet, and I was mortified for him. This is the thanks he gets for passing out the exam early— having to deal with people like her, like me. I broke the silence. "I'm sorry."

"What were you thinking?"

"I don't know." He stared at me long and hard, tapped a pencil rhythmically against his desk. I changed my tune. "I do know. I didn't care about your class." He raised his eyebrows in mock surprise. "And I don't take instruction well."

"You like to do things your own way."

"Yes."

"To be lazy."

"I'm not lazy."

"Cheating is lazy."

"Not when you're spending all your time at the college paper and you're working your ass off and don't have time to deal with classes."

"You're a victim? That's ridiculous."

"Maybe, yeah. Okay. I made a bad choice but I'm not lazy. And I *am* interested in philosophy. I swear. Just not what your class was covering. And I *am* reading literature, just not the books I'm told."

"So you cheat in other classes?"

"Yes."

"That doesn't bother you?"

"No."

"Because when I walked in here it looked like you were crying."

"Well, I got caught and Father Sellinger just gave me his own money to go to India and work at a leper colony and what if he finds out and I'm expelled?"

"*You're* going to India?" I nodded. "The dean is sending you to India and this is how you repay him?" I couldn't bear the thought of it, the grand humiliations that lay ahead. Yet neither could I bring myself to plead for mercy.

"If you're gonna expel me, can you wait until September?"

"'Cause you wanna go to India? What a lark. I've been there and I'm telling you, man . . . *You?*" He pulled back his long hair, as if about to tie it in a ponytail, then let it go. "India's gonna be your penance." He told me to get my sorry ass out of his office.

Those weeks in Washington before I departed for India, working at Colorfax, a one-hour processing place on I Street downtown, not knowing if I would see my junior year, if that lame job would be the highpoint of my photo career. The anxiety was crippling. The guilt, that most useless of human emotions, coming as it does after the fact, a cold stone in my gut.

It was late May and there were cicadas everywhere—a harmless swarm known as Brood X. Every seventeen years they crawl from Washington's soil by the tens of millions and take flight, sputtering into buildings, cars, each other. The novelty of their arrival had the local news all atwitter. Strangers on the street wore expressions of exaggerated horror, ones that said they were secretly happy for this bizarre and shared experience. Near Dupont Circle vendors sold cicadas dipped in chocolate. In the suburbs kids chased them down with tennis rackets, plunked them over neighbors' houses. What a fate, to spend seventeen years beneath the Earth's surface drinking sap from tree roots and then to reappear finally, above ground for a two-week orgy, only to get whacked by a brat with a Wilson.

He didn't report me, Schwartz, nor even fail me. When the report card arrived at my parent's house and I tore it open, saw a "D," I didn't utter a word, didn't betray the slightest excitement. I stuffed it into my pocket, walked into the woods behind the house, and breathed in lungfuls of relief. These chance verdicts to which we owe our careers. And these unlikely characters. I vowed that his amnesty would not be wasted, that it would be the fulcrum on which my life suddenly, abruptly, righted.

The depth of my good fortune still sinking in, I noticed long, diagonal slits in the branches of a dogwood tree. And in those slits little grains of rice. Cicada eggs. In a few weeks a new brood would hatch into nymphs, fall to the ground, burrow beneath the soil, begin their lives, their lonely journeys, not to reappear above ground for another seventeen years: the summer of 2004. My journey, too, was just beginning. And though there was no way for me to know it back then, it would continue for precisely seventeen years, would come to an end the very week those cicadas reemerged, tired and a bit worse for wear, poking their little brown heads into the bright light of day.

☐ The first thing I noticed were the crows. They weren't all black but had gray necks and chests. And there were hundreds of them. I could see them through the oval window the moment I landed in Calcutta: swirling in the sky and hopping along the tarmac, a murder far larger than those in D.C. As I stepped onto the runway my attention was soon diverted. For a few moments I thought another plane was blasting us with its engines, so intense was the June heat. Yet other passengers were crossing the tarmac without concern. It couldn't be like this, could it? It felt as if a pair of sweaty hands was covering my mouth. The air made my eyelids sticky. And it had a rancid tang, like something was burning, something that used to be alive. Cowshit, I later learned.

I followed the flow of passengers into the terminal, the domestic terminal, as I had transferred to an Indian Airlines flight in Delhi sometime in the night, a transfer that seemed so distant, from another lifetime. And now crowds. People. Faces. Bumping into me. Staring. Spitting on the floor, a blood-red juice that dribbled down their chins. Outside, too, a throng of people was gathered, pressing against the windows and looking in. They were not waiting to greet loved ones, this crowd. Even I could see that. They were living there, right there on the sidewalk, in little structures made with sticks and black garbage bags. They left cooking pots scattered about and little fires that produced lots of blue smoke. Unlike the chubby actors I had seen in *Gandhi,* the extent of my preparation, these beings were not gleaming with inner pride. They were thin. Some held naked babies. What clothes they wore were in shreds. Their teeth protruded at strange angles. Their faces were hollow. They looked cadaverous. And I didn't feel sorry for them, those poor and desperate people, gawking at all the lucky souls with shoes on their feet and food in their stomachs. With places to go, I didn't feel sorry for them one bit. I felt threatened.

When my backpack appeared on the luggage carousel, it was wide open. A shirtsleeve was hanging out and dragging alongside. I didn't say a word, zipped it back up and went for the door, pressed through a mob of taxi and rickshaw drivers. They shouted at me all at once, everyone screaming, tugging on my shirt. Someone tried to pull off my backpack, tried to carry it for me. I yanked it away and he laughed. "This way. This way," he said, pointing into the distance. When he pointed I noticed he had two thumbs, the second one little and lifeless, growing out of his wrist. I rushed away from him, from all of them, avoiding eye contact. Several gave chase, so I walked faster. Soon I was alone, sitting beneath a billboard near the airport exit and wiping the sweat out of my eyes. I felt dizzy and out of it, as is if every moment that preceded the last had happened days before, not seconds. I didn't want to go back and I definitely didn't want to go forward, into Calcutta, to catch a train to Bihar. I wanted to disappear.

Navigating the throngs at Howrah Railway Station deepened my culture shock. Families were living there too, right on the platform. There were beggars waving deformed children in my face, beggars pleading for something to eat, beggars trying not to let me pass, grabbing my arms, my bags, my feet. I hated them touching me: their breath and stink and sweaty desperation, all so foreign and wildly determined. It was my first time dealing with Third World aggression and I felt always on the verge of losing it, of pushing back and screaming "Get off!"

Someone helped me find my train, my seat in cattle class, the berth so crowded I had to sit hunched and cross-legged on what appeared to be a luggage rack. Throughout the three-hour train ride a parade of people appeared at the head of the berth, begging, selling tea, offering massages. At one point a man appeared wearing nothing but a white cloth. His nose was missing. So were his fingers and toes. He held out two hands. They looked like oven mitts. Someone threw a cup of tea at the man's bare feet, and he jumped to avoid being burned. There was laughter.

The train arrived in Bihar late in the afternoon, in a dusty shithole called Dhanbad. My berthmates seemed surprised I was getting off, as were those waiting to board the train. One waved "no" with his finger and motioned for me to get back on. Outside the train station the rickshaw wallahs pounced. There were more than in Calcutta, encircling me, pleading to be chosen, and behind them an instant crowd of onlookers, craning to see.

On hearing me tell a driver I wanted to go to Nirmala, a man with severe acne scars pushed his way through the crowd and offered me a ride. He worked there, he said. At Nirmala. And he had a motorcycle big enough for two. He pulled me by the arm, and for some reason I didn't resist. The drivers said not to go with him; they would take me.

"Don't believe them," he assured me. "They'll steal from you." We sped away, weaving through the clutter of buildings and bystanders. I had been traveling for three days straight, and glimpses of India seemed to buzz by incoherently, as if in a dream.

Cows lay motionless in the street as trucks and buses thundered past at unstable speeds. A skeletal man with shiny bronze skin labored to pull an entire family in his rickshaw. A naked child stood by himself on the side of the road, an arm's length from rushing traffic, sucking on his fist and pissing where he stood. After twenty minutes the clutter began to dissipate. Dhanbad thinned to an occasional building, then yielded to a quilt of lime-green rice fields.

The road we followed was on a small ridge, and soon we were looking down on a complex of yellow buildings. It was surrounded on all sides by a ten-foot-high brick wall. We coasted to the gate and were let in by a uniformed guard with a bow and arrow slung over his shoulder. Little white trucks with hand-painted red crosses on their sides were parked in a dirt driveway. Giant trees adorned the rich grass that surrounded most of the buildings. Myna birds flitted about, and barefoot girls balancing baskets of squash on their head walked by and smiled effortlessly. On a distant verandah I could see a group of men in bandages playing cards.

The motorcycle driver, whose name was James, told me to wait there, and he returned a few minutes later with a paunchy man in a stained white robe. He introduced himself as Father Bhat, and yes, he had gotten my letters. Was expecting me. He had James lead me to a guest room, more of a bungalow, really, which had a wooden desk and a bed draped with a long, green mosquito net. James pointed out the kitchen and told me I should grab dinner before they carried the food to the hospital. James told me I could work with him if I liked. He was a bandager and they started at eight in the morning.

◻ Leprosy is a bacterial infection, contagious though difficult to catch, and completely curable through a prolonged treatment of antibiotics, known as multidrug therapy (MDT). First introduced in the mid-eighties, MDT has wiped leprosy from much of the planet, a remarkable feat given that nobody is yet certain how the disease is transmitted. Most scientists speculate it moves in respiratory droplets, made airborne when a victim coughs or sneezes. Once inhaled, the bacterium can take up to five years to incubate, to take root in one's nervous system and wreak havoc. Sensory, motor, and automatic nerves are impaired, causing hands and feet to lose their sense of feeling, to stiffen inward, claw-like; eyes no longer blink properly, lose their ability to flush out irritants that can cause infection and blindness; glands stop producing oil and sweat, causing skin to dry and crack.

Those *Ben-Hur* horrors we associate with the disease, the rotting flesh and falling limbs, are not products of leprosy itself, but of secondary infections caused by nerve damage. As hands and feet grow numb, they are prone to injury, to being burned, say, by grasping and holding onto a hot pot of tea. And when blisters appear, why get treatment? It doesn't hurt. In India, where so many walk barefoot, a person with leprosy may puncture the bottom of his foot, only to yank out the shard and keep walking because he doesn't know he has a disease that prevents him from feeling pain, or because he doesn't want anyone else to know. By the time he comes limping into the hospital, the infection from the nail has spread. His toes or foot may be lost or need to be removed.

Indians who seek treatment for leprosy may resolve their physical affliction only to create a social one. As known lepers, they risk losing their caste, their livelihood, their family. They are deemed *Dalits,* outcasts, the lowest of the low, the ones made to eke out an existence on the margins of society, as prostitutes, as sewer cleaners, as beggars. At the time of my visit they couldn't drink water from a public source. They couldn't go to public school. They couldn't ride public transportation. They couldn't marry off their children. They couldn't even take money from the hands of someone offering it. They had to pick it up off the floor.

In 1987, when I arrived at Nirmala and before the World Health Organization (WHO) began an intensive global elimination campaign, leprosy in India was rampant. WHO estimated there were about four million cases, though the directors at Nirmala said that figure was closer to fourteen million. Nirmala was treating about three hundred patients in their hospital and another four thousand outpatients. Three times a week medical teams drove to nearby villages in those white, rusting medical vans, offering free examinations and medication, trying to convince those with ulcers and infections to come to the hospital for treatment. And to convince everyone else not to run the poor souls out of town.

Those victims who braved retaliation by visiting Nirmala did so before the sun came up. On my first morning, I stumbled onto these outpatients, having awoken before dawn and wandered outside, the shapes of the compound just becoming visible through a thin blue mist. In the front of the hospital I noticed the outline of several people, then realized it was actually a long line of people, all sitting, wrapped like ghosts in white saris and loincloths. There was little chatter and nobody looked at me.

☐ The dressing room smelled pretty gamy for 8 a.m., despite having two ceiling fans at full spin and two broad open windows. A group of lepers crowded the door, some leaning on crutches, others holding the heads of children for balance. Two of their brethren were being serviced inside, each with a single foot propped up on a wooden block. James sat before one of the men, winding a bandage around his ankle and foot. The second dresser waved hello and gestured for me to watch him work. He was using office scissors to snip away some skin on a man's heel. His patient was all smiles, which was surprising because he had a hole in his foot the size of a golf ball.

"The blood is bothering you?" James asked. He was in his early thirties, a father of four, I later learned. One of his children was two years old and still didn't have a name. "No Name," they called her. His family lived with him at the colony.

"I'm fine," I said.

"Okay, okay," he said. "So I show you what you do?" James switched spots with his colleague. "You remove all the gauze that is in the ulcer, then you disinfect it." He dipped a cotton ball in a dish of iodine, then moved it in and around the hole in the leper's foot with the nonchalance of a dishwasher scrubbing out a glass. He did this barehanded. "It's important to file down the dead skin so the disinfectant can work. Then you restuff the ulcer with gauze and bandage him up. It's most simple."

They squeezed another chair into the room for me. And it was most simple, actually. They gave me the easy ones and I kept up without rushing. Since leprosy numbs your extremities, I wasn't overly worried about hurting anyone. And the patients seemed perfectly happy to let me clean and re-dress their wounds. My guess is they thought I was a foreign med student, not some summer volunteer looking for a photo project. On unwrapping one man's bandage, I saw that the top of his foot was eaten away. He only had one toe left, his pinky, and it didn't have too secure a hold. The other dresser handed me his office scissors. "Cut it off," he said. So I did, putting his toe between the blades, turning my head, and squeezing. There was a plunk in the metal pan below. The patient picked it out of the pan, put it in his shirt pocket, and there were laughs all around.

The infections were troubling to look at, of course. But it was the smell they emitted—sour and festering, like turned milk—that disturbed me most. When the dressers broke for tea, I wasn't feeling too well and stepped outside for air. The smell came with me, stayed in my lungs, my clothes, my hair. I contemplated working with a mask, but thought the dressers might take me for a wuss. I liked them and wanted them to like me. And the patients might find it insulting. I did need to photograph them.

The picture making proved easier than I expected; in the coming weeks not one patient objected. On the contrary, they wanted their portraits made, a consequence of their social status, perhaps. It was a form of attention, one that proved they mattered, they existed. I made environmental portraits mostly, with far too many subjects staring at the camera. Despite my novice approach, Nirmala was still a decent catch, newsworthy and hopeful. An opportunity to reveal the ugly truths of this disease through a single microcosm. And I had an ideal job, one that enabled me to interact with most of my photographic subjects, a brave and willing cast of hundreds.

The more I learned of their affliction, the more I believed theirs was a story that deserved to be told, a cause-and-effect that would drive me toward future news stories. This is what journalists do, I remember realizing. And it felt satisfying, like a form of service, the ability to pass information through pictures. The ability to inform. To reveal. To tell. It was empowering.

☐ One afternoon a man hobbled into the dressing room, tears flowing down his cheeks. His right leg was missing just below the knee, and the stump was wrapped in a shirt. He had a little girl with him, a dark beauty with oily hair and kohl-covered eyes. Her expression was wrought with concern; she stood in the corner and didn't speak. The dressers sat him down. James unwrapped the shirt and made a tsk-tsk noise with his tongue. The man's stump was dressed with mud and straw. They were rough on him, chipping at the mud violently and shouting at him in Bengali. He cried more. He was handsome, with greased back hair and a pencil-thin mustache. Not getting any sympathy from the dressers, he tried whining to me. I was glad I couldn't understand.

He had had a terrible infection in his foot, James said. When he realized it was from leprosy he was too scared to come to the hospital, scared for his future, his family. He paid a car mechanic to cut off the whole foot, and how he survived was anyone's guess. The leg got infected, and he thought it a good idea to cauterize the wound with mud. James said these kind of incidents happened all the time, and I soon learned it was true. There was the woman who had let maggots infest her foot, and the man who tore off a long piece of his turban and stuffed it into a hole in his testicles. And there was the boy at the teahouse out-side the hospital, a boy who kept his sleeves lowered though it was so hot. "To hide the patches," James said, pink patches on the skin being an early sign of leprosy. One afternoon he joined us for a smoke. We smelled something acrid and pointed out to him that his cigarette was burning his fingers.

☐ Halfway through my trip I was robbed: my clothes, my cam-era gear, my malaria pills. And shortly after, my sanity, the theft triggering an abrupt surrender of my emotional well-being. For weeks I had kept my head barely above the colony's pall—and now felt too consumed to continue. I slipped below the surface and drifted downward slowly, steadily, until landing on my back, in my bed, sick with dysentery, paranoid with culture shock, frightened to leave my room.

The theft happened on a crowded train. I had decided to flee the colony for a weekend to visit a Jesuit friend from Loyola, Fa-ther Sneck, who happened to be teaching English at a college on the other side of Bihar. The local train station was a mob scene, and I was thankful that a young stranger took me under his wing, bought me my ticket, escorted me to the right train. He even cleared a spot on the luggage rack for my backpack. I slung the pack above my head, draped one of the shoulder straps through the bars so I could keep an eye on it. I sat down directly beneath it, looked up, and it was gone.

I stood up and gawked at the empty space, as if having wit-nessed a magic trick. My bag wasn't there, but my brain kept telling me it had to be. I just put it there a second ago. I looked around the berth; every person was staring at me. "Where's my bag?" Silence. I looked down the hall for my helper, and there he was, standing just a few feet away in the train's open doorway, lighting a cigarette.

"Something wrong?"

"My pack is gone. Someone stole my pack."

"Oh, no." The train started moving. I looked outside and didn't see anyone running. I didn't know whether to jump off or stay on. I ran up and down the train, searching. Did he do it? Was it him? I snuck back to watch him without him noticing. He was still looking for my bag. If he tossed it to someone off the train, why didn't he get off too? He could jump off right now if he wanted. The train was moving slowly enough. And he was here alone, or so I thought. I didn't remember seeing him talk to anyone. But he got me the seat. An end seat by the hallway. He patted the spot for me to put my bag. He was standing right there. Fuck! I decided to stay on the train and keep looking, a lost cause.

As we rolled south, I plopped myself in the doorway of the train, my legs dangling outside, the tracks clattering below. It was raining, and for the first time the temperature felt cool, tolerable. That guilt again, reaching even greater depths than two months before. My arrangement with Father Sellinger, my side of the bargain, it was lost and I felt so ashamed. How could I face him, my parents, my friends at the paper? My exposed film was still at Nirmala, but I wasn't near finished, had spent too much time in the bandaging room and not enough behind the camera.

That night I became as sick as I have ever been in my life; I had caught dysentery somewhere along the line and was now purging from both ends. Father Sneck did cheer me up with a great find—a Pentax K-1000 that he borrowed from one of the professors. The camera looked like it had been dragged across India from somebody's rear bumper. There was a single 50 mm lens with a barrel so bent it wouldn't focus closer than seven feet. The camera meter was broken too, so I'd have to guess the exposure. And the rewind lever was missing, which meant to change film I'd have to bring the camera into a darkened room, take out the roll, and wind the film manually back into the spool. But the camera appeared light-tight, and the sound of the shutter seemed to change appropriately with the speeds offered on the dial.

Back at Nirmala my dysentery improved. I still had trouble holding down food and got nauseous when I stood up for extended periods. One of the visiting doctors put me on my own multidrug therapy: blue ones, green ones, white ones, none of which worked. I kept my morning job in the dressing room, though always felt on the verge of heaving. Or shitting. In the afternoons I was spending more and more time in bed, sweating into the rank, itchy pad that was my cushion, trying to save up the energy to go out and shoot in the early evening light.

One afternoon James knocked on my door, saying they were going to amputate a man's leg, the man whose previous doctor was a car mechanic. His young daughter, Meetha, had stayed at Nirmala with him and was now attending school with other girls on the hospital grounds. She was sweet and I had photographed her frequently. One night when the electricity was out and I was walking alone outside, I noticed her through an open window, sitting on his bed, in candlelight. She was showing him something in her schoolbook and the sight of them together, their lives dependent, their futures doomed, made my heart sink.

The operation was held in the dressing room, not the most hygienic environment. And the doctor, the Sikh, his thin guise of confidence, his blood-red teeth; I knew the moment I saw him that this would be a rough one. Then darkness. Distance. The floating above it all. When the nun snapped me out of it, helped me off the hallway floor, I felt a cold slap of air on my sweaty back. Embarrassed, alone, and homesick, I was an unwilling participant in an alternate reality. Why was I here? To skirt between two worlds, one of privilege and one of poverty, was a skill I had yet to acquire. Or appreciate. I walked back to my room and stared at myself in the mirror, thin, bearded, and haggard, my eyes red and sunken and my knees browned with blood. I couldn't take it anymore.

From that moment on, the door to my room was no longer a portal to long-held desires but a barricade against newly acquired Third World phobias. People staring and pushing, scheming and robbing, dripping with gangrenous sores. I couldn't go out there. Didn't want to see another person, feel the weight of their existence, face the dismal realities of their lives. Only to eat, to slip into the kitchen and grab some food, always the same damn food, *dal bhat* and *roti*s. The smell of it made me want to puke.

My dysentery wasn't helping matters. My stomach in knots, it kept me in bed for more hours each day. On occasion James came by to check on me, to invite me to his house for tea. I hated to answer the door, felt so foolish and feeble. The spoiled American who couldn't deal. Ours could have been a fine friendship and instead I couldn't deliver, left the poor guy standing there. "I'm sick, man," was what I would tell him before closing the door in his face. "I'm sorry." What a basket case.

And then I'd lie back down, lie down for what seemed a hundred years, swatting mosquitoes and watching tiny, translucent geckos dart cross the ceiling. Smelling my shit from the bathroom, a hole in the ground in an adjoining room. Listening to distant sounds: footsteps on the gravel, a generator starting, laughter from the schoolhouse. Day after day, night after night, not making pictures, not volunteering, not doing anything besides vowing never to set foot on that stinking, vile, cornhole of a subcontinent ever again. Ever.

☐ When I returned to D.C., having lost twenty-five pounds, most of my luggage, and all of my pride, I felt like an animal that had reluctantly shed its skin. Now that it was off, I needed some time to toughen my new self before reentering the world. And yet the following year I found myself back in South Asia. And again the year after that. The subcontinent wouldn't let me go, had seeped into my veins. I had survived the worst it could throw at me, like overcoming an illness against which I now had immunity. I was certain the poverty wouldn't bother me anymore. And it didn't.

On those subsequent ventures I crisscrossed India and Nepal, Pakistan and Afghanistan—and after graduating from college settled for six months in the dirty, dilapidated city of Kathmandu. There I let loose my inner flower child, skipping showers, smoking hash, and falling in and out of love with other backpackers. Yet every morning, no matter how tired or hungover, I arose before dawn, put my 20 mm lens on my Nikon F3, stuffed my pockets full of Fuji ASA 50 slide film, and pedaled across town in the dark, hoping to make some portfolio pictures at one of the city's many stupas or temples.

It was on one of those mornings, while photographing Bodhnath, an enormous Buddhist temple, that I caught eyes with another photographer. It was *Losar,* the Tibetan New Year, and Bodhnath's stark white stupa looked half submerged in a sea of burgundy robes. Tibetan women were passing out grogs of *tumba,* a strong mountain brew of fermented millet and hot water, and by 11 a.m. most of those in attendance, the monks as well as the backpackers, were shitfaced. Several lamas emerged from an adjacent monastery, wearing tall yellow hats that curled forward like plumage. They carried a framed portrait of the Dalai Lama and led a procession around the stupa, everyone cheering and tossing handfuls of *tsampa,* ground grain, into the air. Though it was drizzling, nobody seemed to mind.

The other photographer kept her distance, squatting on a higher ring of the stupa while the rest of us celebrated below. She was in her early forties and carried two Nikon FM2s around her neck. Her hair was clean, her clothes were clean, her gear was clean. She had wide silver bangles around her left wrist— the kind they sold in the upscale hotels. I worked the procession close with my wide angle, and after the event, while shaking the tsampa from my hair, she walked past me. "Who you working for?" I called out.

She stopped and looked me up and down. I was bearded and raffish, my clothes ragged and my gear covered in dust. "*U.S. News & World Report,*" she said, finally.

"Sweet. How does one hook up with *U.S. News?*" She gave a halfhearted wave, walking away before I finished my sentence. She turned around and walked away as if I were a dirty beggar with his hands out chanting "One rupee, one rupee."

four

maryland

In the spring of 1990, having seen just enough of the world to long to see the rest, I moved back into my parents' house, broke, depressed, and very unemployed, and began a demoralizing two-year-long job hunt, spent largely in their basement, churning out cover letters on an electric type-writer while the rest of the house, the neighborhood, and seem-ingly the entire country went off to work. I had made some de-cent portfolio pictures in South Asia, and at first I thought they would offer enough evidence of my skills to land me a job. Or at least some part-time work. But the photo world, a profession besieged by wannabes, isn't so easily impressed. And that makes finding a first job a long and bumpy ride.

I began by writing, calling, and otherwise pestering in per-son every major media outlet between D.C. and New York, gen-erating a phalanx of cold shoulders and raising nary an eyebrow. Of course, the picture editors at the *New York Times* and the *Wash-ington Post* had more pressing issues to deal with than meeting an untested aspirant. And I should have known that the fine folks at *National Geographic,* where I was lucky enough to get a portfolio review, wouldn't be impressed with such an ill-chosen selection of images: those of a *sadhu,* or Hindu holy man, naked save for the ashes of cremated people smeared across his face and belly, lifting a fifty-pound brick with his foot-long lingam. They laughed me out the door.

The only place that didn't tell me to take a hike was *USA Today,* where the director of photography advised me to try and come up with a new portfolio picture each week, no matter how difficult. It was by then midsummer and I felt sufficiently desperate to give his suggestion a whirl.

I made halfhearted early morning visits to all the tacky tourist spots that lent themselves to a *National Geographic*–style spread, as that was still where I hoped to work: Mount Vernon and the C & O Canal; county fairs in Maryland and ethnic festivals in D.C.; Civil War reenactments at Antietam and anti-whatever protests on the Mall. And it was all so fruitless. I grew up with these places—visited them on field trips and first dates and those godawful family outings for the sake of visiting relatives—I didn't find them interesting then and didn't find them inspiring now. And the idea of photographing solely to come up with a portfolio picture, as opposed to trying to get a portfolio picture while shooting a story for an employer or while volunteering for an organization or while exploring a new place for the first time, made all the unsuccessful tries, which in my case were all of them, feel like a further waste of time.

I resorted to sending query letters to all the community papers in the area, the ones that appeared in my parents' mailbox late in the afternoon and in free stacks at the Safeway. Soon I had a portfolio review with the *Montgomery County Journal*. One of the picture editors there, upon surveying my slides, responded that the images were nice indeed. But they offered little evidence as to how well I'd do in someplace like a dull suburban classroom. My response: "I didn't realize photographers put pictures of dull suburban classrooms in their portfolios." There was an awkward silence while she processed the fact that I was being a smartass, a silence I made no effort to break. And then I was out of options.

☐ Alone in my parents' house. No career, no money, no prospects. It was the lowest point in my life, and I vowed not to be a smartass at my next portfolio review. No more pictures of penises or snarky comments about suburban classrooms. The next review didn't come for another month, and it was at the request of the *Washington Business Journal,* where the sole photographer was stepping down. The editor looked at my pictures with feigned interest, then said he had to choose between me and a more experienced woman. He was giving both of us assignments to see how we'd do—a shoot-off for the position. I was familiar with the other person's work, wasn't overly impressed, and was thus convinced I had this thing locked.

My assignment was to photograph some government executive for the front page of the paper, and for a reason that must have been more apparent to me then than it is now, I dragged him over to the columned foyer of the Lincoln Memorial for the portrait session. It didn't work. He looked lost, like a displaced tourist at the Parthenon. Worse, I shot him as a vertical. Had I bothered to actually look at the paper I was trying to work for, I would have learned that the layout of the front page photo was always the same—horizontal. The verdict was instantaneous.

If finding that first photo job is a protracted Darwinian struggle to prove yourself more fit than the rest of the herd, I was as doomed as a zebra with a broken leg. But instead of being torn to shreds by hyenas, I was getting nibbled to death by varmints. I practically handed her the job. I let myself get taken by someone lower on the food chain, someone I should have trampled, because I was too stupid to review the product. In the wake of this loss—the most painful to date—I receded into the only level of my parents' house where I didn't have to see, speak to, or otherwise interact with another living person.

Basement life. The cool, cave-like humidity, the fluorescent lighting, the faux-wood panels. There were no windows to the outside world, unless you counted the TV, which was tuned to trash talk shows during the day and the growing Gulf crisis at night. I sat in front of the flickering blue screen for much of the fall and all of the winter, thinking about all the journalists on their way to Saudi Arabia while I cowered below ground night after night, waiting to hear my parents go to bed before I emerged, so that I didn't have to face them. They didn't pressure me to look for work elsewhere, to pursue a more probable career, to make money. Not once.

They knew I was happiest when I was traveling and that photography was the means by which I expressed that elation. And that someday photography might finance this wanderlust, give my life the motion it needed. Like any good parents, they wanted their child to chart his own happiness.

Still, perhaps because they were so cautious about confronting me about my repeated rejections, I could hardly face them. I was coming upstairs only to eat and sleep, the latter extending to unhealthy hours. And yet during the day I'd still drift off on the basement couch, made listless by that most awful trait of prolonged unemployment: boredom. I was going on two years of this and after getting hit by so many waves of rejection felt like a forgotten shipwreck, alone at the bottom of the sea.

five

brazil

Rising from a muddy delta a hundred miles south of the equator, Belem is the Amazon's link with the Atlantic. It is the largest port on the river, where oversized tankers fill their hulls with local fare before drifting back to sea. But for those like me wishing to head the other way, into the heart of Amazonia, the city offers a far more ambitious opportunity. From Belem it's possible to follow the river like a highway across the entire width of the rain forest, leapfrogging from village to village on small fruit and cargo boats until finally reaching Iquitos, Peru, 2,100 miles to the west.

From my parents' basement in Washington it seemed a novel idea—cross the world's largest jungle, photographing along the way, then write about the experience and sell it as a package to a travel magazine. Or the Sunday travel section of a newspaper. Even if I couldn't get it published, I'd still come away with some portfolio pictures. And it would liberate me from my un-

derground malaise. Though I had enrolled in the graduate photojournalism program at the University of Missouri—a last-ditch
attempt to jumpstart my career—there were still four months
to kill before moving to the Midwest and beginning my first semester. And that was just enough time to recoup my sanity, to
lose myself in a destination that was sufficiently vast and, equally
important, dirt-cheap to visit.

If negotiated properly, the entire river journey, including
stops in various towns along the way, would cost less than $350,
according to my *Lonely Planet* guide. And I was quite sure I could
finagle a free flight down. I typed up a letter to Brazil's international carrier, Varig Airlines, detailing my project, offering a rather
optimistic list of possible media outlets, and asking to fill an empty
seat on one of their planes.

It wasn't exactly ethical to seek such a freebie and then pur-
port to write an unbiased story, even if that story was an experi-
ential travel essay. Nor was sending my proposal on letterhead of
a company that didn't exist: "Nomad—A Travel Features Syndi-
cate." Hell, that part was probably illegal. I had designed the
letterhead on my friend's computer, and with his help even created a snazzy little logo from one of my India pictures: a silhouette of a man leading a camel by the reins. We placed the logo on
every sheet of paper, on every envelope. It looked perfect. There
was no question that Nomad was a purveyor of quality journalism. And at the time I didn't think twice about orchestrating
such a scheme, about creating a fake company to dupe an airline.
I was so desperate to travel that the mere thought of crossing the
Amazon pumped adrenaline through my veins, kept me awake at
night. It made me happy, an emotion I hadn't felt in years. I would

have stowed away on the damn flight if they hadn't sent me a free ticket. But they did.

☐ On my inaugural afternoon in-country, searching Belem's Ver-o-Peso fish market for the next vessel heading upstream, my cojones retracted slightly. There were dozens of rickety wooden vessels tied to moorings. And scurrying around these decks were hundreds of fishermen, short, tough, and tattooed, with bronze skin and intimidating stares. They were unloading baskets of crab and shrimp and turtles and impaling the pride of their catch, the sharks, sawfish, and pirarucu—the world's largest freshwater fish, at up to ten feet long—with giant bloody hooks, dragging them to the dock entrance, and hanging them for all to see. Asking these guys for a lift was suddenly more than I could muster. I decided to make pictures first.

Unlike many photographers who shoot primarily in the early morning and late afternoon, I like to work scenes in harsh mid-day light. The sky is at its bluest and because exposures are so fast, shadows achieve a deep, velvety blackness. The fish market, with all its shaded awnings, was ideal for such contrasts: a place to turn people into silhouettes and allow the colors of the environment, the brown river, the blue sky, the green bananas, to decorate the rest of the frame.

The scope of the market was hard to comprehend, let alone portray in a single frame. I walked past gray river eels, coiled like sausages, and giant stingrays flipped on their backs, their oily bellies glistening white in the sun; past bushels of clams and oysters and freshwater caimans, an alligator-like reptile, with hammock cords tied around their snouts; past piranhas by the hundreds, sardines by the thousands, and giant catfish, some more than six feet long, stacked like logs in a cord, their mouths buzzing with flies. There are more species of fish in the Amazon than in the entire Atlantic Ocean, and from the menagerie on display it appeared fishermen were pulling out each kind.

Gawking at the aquatic life, I didn't feel the hand rummaging through my camera backpack. I did hear things falling out, however, and was surprised to see my pen, my notepad, my *Lonely Planet* guide on the ground before me. I swung off my backpack, which was sliced wide open. I had been razored, the favored local larceny, though all my thief got was a pair of sunglasses. I went right across the street and bought a couple of the tight wife-beater undershirts all the men seemed to wear, a pair of flip-flops, a green bandana for my head. And a less conspicuous bag for my gear.

Feeling more confident in this gaucho garb, I made the rounds of the boats and was directed to a two-tiered wooden relic with a lower deck filled with bushels of onions and crates of Guaraná, a Brazilian cola. The upper deck was already crowded with thirty or so brightly colored hammocks, the beds of river travelers. The hammocks hung from hooks drilled into the ceiling and were occupied by bored, shirtless men with unlit cigarettes dangling from their lips. As I wove through the congestion, all eyes were on me. I caught glimpses of lewd tattoos, half-empty liquor bottles, the tip of a machete poking from a rucksack.

In the pilot house I found a wire-thin man with the name Raimundo stitched on a worn, red baseball cap. "Captain, yes," he said, pointing to himself, and we negotiated a fare—thirty bucks!—to Santarem, the next major port, more than five hundred miles upriver. Though the boat wasn't leaving until the following morning, he told me to crash here for the night to secure a space. I went back to my hotel to get my stuff and returned within the hour, slinging my hammock on the port side of the deck and shoving my backpack on a ceiling rack directly above me. Determined not to get pinched again, I used two flexible steel cables to lock my bags to the metal pipes.

The deck was cool and breezy, completely open on all sides except for a thin, white railing. My neighbor was friendly to the point of being annoying, a short and shirtless man whose sole apparent obsession was that I share with him his bottle of Hot Damn. It tasted like a lowbrow version of peppermint schnapps, like fireballs in liquid form. But what the hell. I was eager to endear myself to my fellow travelers—an ethnic mix of Indian and Brazilian called *caboclos*—to immerse myself in my new surroundings and shed the memory of my underground ennui.

We polished off the bottle, then promptly switched to *cachaça,* a thick, alcoholic sugarcane drink that he bought from another passenger. I'm pretty sure my stomach would have rejected these syrups even by themselves. But together they produced a less subtle reaction. When they returned to the world in a violent orange eruption, one laced with rice and beans, which I didn't remember eating, the taste left in my throat was so surprising, a simultaneous hot and sweet, that I kept right on heaving, long after my stomach had nothing left to offer. Then I plopped down on the floor of the boat's bathroom, a floor that sat directly above the engine—which was on to power the lights—and was thus hot to the touch, reeking of diesel fumes, and wet with something I prayed was water. I remained there the entire night, the other passengers peering at me through the door.

Extricating myself the following morning, I saw that Belem had been replaced with jungle—a tight, knotted weave of vegetation slipping slowly by in different shades of green. I collapsed in my hammock, my stomach mush, my ears ringing. My brain felt like it was swelling against my skull, like it needed to be tapped and drained before it exploded. And that's when I was lying down. When I stood I felt like one of those bobbing-head dolls you see in the back of cars, the horizon swinging this way and that. So I remained in my hammock and tried to focus on the shoreline, sprinkled with bird life. I also tried not to swing into the passengers around me. On these boats, "capacity" has no meaning. Nor does "speed." We were chugging along at a stately eight miles an hour. But I had more time on my hands than money, and in those parts there was no cheaper way to travel. Or more scenic.

The river was the color of caramel and wider than I had ever imagined. Though our boat was small enough to ply just offshore, I could barely see the forest on the other side. The volume of water flowing between those banks was hard to grasp— more than that of the Nile, Yangtze, and Mississippi rivers combined. At its mouth near Belem, the river dumps about fifty million gallons of fresh water into the Atlantic every second. So powerful is this surge that Atlantic fisherman allege they can fill their canteens with fresh water fifty miles off shore.

Throughout the day the great green wall off our port side grew ever higher. It seemed strained, like that of a dam trying to hold back a huge, crushing carnival of life, of trees and birds and monkeys, of one-third of the world's plant and animal species. That was thirty million species—all right there, crammed behind a fortress of leaves a hundred and fifty feet high and two thousand miles long. Yet the species I saw most often, at least at first, was *Homo sapiens.*

They lived in stilt homes along the riverbank. Upon hearing our motor, caboclo children would paddle out in dugout canoes, grab hold of our stern, and try to hitch a ride. Passengers and crew cheered them on, but our wake was too jarring and most of the young daredevils were left to laugh at their attempts. Vendors were a bit more persistent, and they leeched onto our hull with boats full of caiman, turtle, and river fish. Members of the crew bought their fancy and cooked them up on the lower deck with rice and beans. Everyone ate lunch there together at a large table—everyone but me, that is—then returned to their hammocks to nod through the hottest part of the day. By early evening I was finally up and around, mixing with the passengers who gathered on the bow to enjoy the end-of-day coolness. In this way I passed the next two days: playing dominoes, photographing the passengers and crew, and checking off various species of birds in my field guide.

We arrived in Santarem under the blaze of a midday sun. It was a dumpy backwater with lots of mosquitoes and little to see, so I stayed only long enough to find another vessel heading west. It was a banana boat, much smaller than the first, and the captain claimed he was pushing off immediately. He was pretty drunk for 1:30 in the afternoon, but then who was I to throw stones. Anyway, he seemed to have regained his composure by midnight, when our boat drifted from its dock and into the starry jungle night.

☐ On this leg to Manaus, I met a man with leishmaniasis. Everyone knows about the disease in the Amazon, speaks about it with the same hushed tones East Indians reserve for leprosy. It's a parasite transmitted from the bite of a tiny sandfly, and it can do hideous things to a face. There were no apparent signs on this traveler, an educated, English-speaking caboclo named Edilson, and had he not lifted his pant legs halfway through the trip to show me, I never would have noticed.

Edilson was a handsome old man who, minus the cigarette, brought to mind the molded portrait on our Indian-head penny: the long, braided hair, the steep nose, the omniscient expression. His voice was equally enduring, straining out story after story about a lifetime in the river basin. The guy had worked on the Trans-Amazon Highway, Brazil's attempt in the early 1970s to alleviate coastal population pressures, and that interested me greatly. The project was Biblical, both in its scope and in its failings. The idea was to build a nineteen-hundred-mile dirt highway from Belem to the Peruvian border, then lure one million poverty-stricken Brazilians into the jungle with promises of cheap land and future urban development. "A land without men for men without land," was the government's slogan. In the first three years less than six thousand families bit, and they were devastated by disease, infertile land, and hostile Indians. To this day the road isn't finished, and the only people it has consistently benefitted are logging and mining companies.

Edilson said construction was akin to going to hell and back, that during heavy rains the mud was deep enough to drown a man. He said snakes killed workers, insects killed workers, booze killed workers. He told me a drunken brawl left a machete buried in his friend's arm. He told me he gave up and turned to something more lucrative: poaching. For twelve years he moved cat and otter skins out of Rio Branco, near the Bolivian border. Down there, he said, the jungle got its revenge. That's when he showed me his shins and thighs, lumpy and blackened as if left on a grill. A small crowd gathered to look. We were on the bow of the boat then, and everyone gawked and gasped, then went back to their dominoes. Edilson claimed not to be religious, but every time our boat passed a church, which was surprisingly often, he joined the rest of the passengers in removing his hat and making the sign of the cross.

☐ We arrived early on our fourth day, the river swirling with foam and the trees giving way to steel and concrete, an unlikely urban sprawl called Manaus. I had heard the city's history a dozen times, how in the late 1800s latex turned it from a backwater trading post to a backwater treasure house, from el dumpo to El Dorado, how rubber barons wallowed in their wealth, importing their homes from Europe in prefab blocks, sending their clothes to Paris to be laundered, building an Italian opera house for their entertainment. And how a British botanist named Sir Henry Wickham, the great rubber robber, put an end to the whole charade, smuggling seventy thousand seeds to London's Kew Gardens, where they germinated and then were replanted in the wet and welcoming equatorial soil of British colonies in the Far East. The Brazilian rubber trees flourished in Asia and Manaus fell off the map, at least for a time. In the late 1960s, the Brazilian government declared the city a free-trade zone and made Manaus what it is today, a duty-free shop in the middle of the rain forest.

I wanted out of the city the moment I arrived and hired at random one of the many guides prowling the streets with offerings of caiman hunts and jungle treks. He was a fast-talking, curly-haired caboclo named Assad, and I signed him up for a week-long walk in the woods. Another backpacker would be joining us, a twenty-something New Yorker named Rich. When we picked up my partner the next morning, I got my first indication of his frugality from the name of his digs, "Hotel Cheap!" and the second from his introduction: "How much you paying for this?"

"Twenty bucks a day. Plus boat fare."

"I knew it. So am I, but see that should be the total, not for each person." Uh-oh. Rich started into Assad, demanding to renegotiate. He wanted to pay ten dollars a day, and when Assad wouldn't budge he went up to twelve, then fifteen. To get things moving I told Rich to pay fifteen and I'd cover the rest. He accepted.

We took a boat forty miles north of Manaus, up the Rio Negro to our drop-off point. Though Assad had promised we'd be able to gather all our own food—the only provisions he carried were a bag of rice and a bag of salt—I brought some snacks anyway, as even the most inexperienced hiker might do. Rich thought it more frugal to hold Assad to his precise words, and not two hours into our trek, when his stomach started grumbling and it was apparent we weren't going to stop, he turned to me and said, "Hey, man, got an extra granola bar?" Subsequent requests that afternoon included: "Do you have an extra pair of dry socks . . . Can I bum a roll of 400 . . . Got any Advil?" By the time we made camp I was already eyeing Assad's machete. Way out there who would know?

We walked long and hard most mornings, but in the dense vegetation covered only maybe four miles a day. It was virtually impossible to keep dry. In some areas the forest was submerged, and we waded through shoulder-high water with our packs held over our heads. In other areas the forest seemed to sweat, dampening everything with a sticky white mist. At night we slept in hammocks—the ground too flooded for tents—and I used cords to drape a plastic sheet above me, which blocked the showers that tore through the jungle canopy. It was an unpleasant feeling to be wet all the time, but I was making the pictures I needed for my story and was happy to look at the animals. There were monkeys everywhere, and macaws and toucans. One morning I spotted a greater anteater.

The Cheapskate from the Empire State, as I had taken to calling Rich, was less engaged by our surroundings. His blathering about being wet, about the jungle foot and the crotch rot, and the ineptitude of our guide seemed as much a part of the nightly choir as the moans of howler monkeys. Assad took wild offense at Rich's indictments, getting in his face and threatening to feed him to the piranhas. One night I watched Assad rise from his hammock and take a piss in Rich's water bottle. I needed to ditch these guys.

On the sixth day we reached a small family farm on the banks of the Rio Negro, and the patriarch, Ery, was kind enough to let me stay for a few days. Assad and Rich took off immediately, hitching a ride on a wooden passenger ferry chugging back toward Manaus. Watching them go, I felt as if a malignant tumor had been lasered from my body. Finally some peace. Detachment. My host family didn't speak English, fed me palm hearts and piranha, and put me up in a thatched cabana with an open wall to the river. Let me use their canoe to explore the flooded forests, or *igapos,* where I spent most of my days. That rush of solitude, of being alone in the jungle, finally, inspecting plants and insects and hoping for a glimpse of something greater, an ocelot or anaconda or three-toed sloth. A jaguar. Of being in the middle of the food chain rather than on top; just the rehab I came for.

Ery grew manioc, a stringy, yucca-like starch. He worked maybe twenty acres, though it was hard to tell as his property was noncontiguous. Amazon soil is notoriously infertile; the majority of its nutrients are in the trees and plants. So farmers practice what's called shifting cultivation—working a patch of ground for four years, until the soil is spent, then burning down another patch of jungle nearby. The ash acts as a fertilizer for the thin topsoil, and then the farmer can start again.

Way out there, surrounded by forest as far the eye could see, Ery's methods seemed a lot less harmful than I knew them to be. According to the National Academy of Sciences, for every four-square-mile patch cleared by loggers or farmers, a rain forest loses or relocates 400 species of birds, 125 species of mammals, 100 species of reptiles, and tens of thousands of species of insects. But then what do insects matter to a man struggling to feed his family? Ery had three beautiful children, their faces dark and lovely, and at dusk I went for long swims with them in the brown water. On two evenings we saw river dolphins.

After returning to Manaus, I spent a day doing a little body repair. The bottoms of my feet looked like cottage cheese, and I had botfly bites on the back of my hands. These little red lumps are an injection of larvae, and if you don't lance them you'll wind up with quite the surprise forty days later: inch-long maggots squirming from your skin. As nasty as that sounds, things get far worse in the Amazon. The rivers there are home to a toothpick-sized catfish called the *candirú,* a parasite that is attracted to the smell of urine and has been known to swim into a person's urethra, lodging itself there with retrorse spines.

Only one boat a week was making the six-day trip upriver from Manaus to Leticia, Colombia. Unfortunately for me, the prior week's boat hadn't run and I had to travel with twice as many passengers crammed above twice as much freight. It was a tedious journey with a drunken, surly crew. They fed us tripe and manioc morning, noon, and night, and nobody dared complain. After each meal they collected all the plastic plates, cups, and utensils, as well as their own beer bottles, and pitched them over the side. This was especially distressing to the only other foreigners on board, two Japanese backpackers who were so waste-conscious they flicked the ashes of their cigarettes into plastic baggies stored in their breast pockets.

Then the crew tossed more precious cargo. Three days out of Manaus I heard a scuffle on the lower deck, followed by a large splash. I saw a man struggling to swim to shore. He hadn't paid his fare, someone told me, and the thugs running the boat tossed him into the drink. His best hope now would be to flag down another vessel, if he didn't starve to death first, or get devoured by caimans. I offered to pay the man's fare if they went back to pick him up, but they were busy tearing through his duffel bag and stealing his belongings and would have none of it.

Leticia was yet another soulless backwater, and I promptly boarded a boat called the *Juliana* for the last five hundred miles to Iquitos, Peru. It was a white wooden beauty, and we pushed off with only six other passengers on board. Within a half hour all signs of civilization were behind us. The river was much more narrow here, the Amazon of my dreams. Vegetation swarmed with prehistoric fury: it draped like a curtain over the trees and often over the river itself. In the fierce midday sun, caimans showed no concern for stealth, basking by the hundreds along narrow, bone-white beaches. Occasionally the captain pulled a gun from his belt and pretended to fire at them from the pilot-house window.

For some reason the captain only laughed when I asked his name. He was an unshaven, tattooed mess—the kind of guy who always looks hungover: gut drooping below his shirt, hair flat on one side and sticking out on the other, cheeks pinched to keep from belching. He was friendly though, and at night, over glasses of cachaça, he showed me black-and-white photos of the boat, taken when it was used in Werner Herzog's epic film *Fitzcarraldo*. A bottle and a half later, after the captain donned a clean shirt and proclaimed his entry into the passengers' card game, I climbed the bow ladder and slung my hammock on the roof of the boat. As I swayed there in light, drunken rhythm, watching the jungle pass below the Southern Cross, Iquitos seemed impossibly far away. So did grad school, a photo career, a new life. Yet in two days we were plying along the crest of Iquitos's banks, looking for a place to dock. It's a ramshackle city, notable only for being the end of the line. From there the river winds south, way south to its source on Mount Mismi, high in the Peruvian Andes.

Iquitos depressed me—the crowds, the muddy homes on stilts, the cans of Inca Cola floating in the water. I felt like a patient who had lost his therapist just when he showed signs of improvement. So I caught a flight to southern Peru, hiked the Inca Trail from Cuzco to Machu Picchu, boated across Lake Titicaca, and bussed over the Bolivian Altiplano, all the way to La Paz, then headed due north, by shared car, moped, and my own two legs, until I was back in the Brazilian jungle, in a steaming nowheresville called Porto Velho, and then made a right turn, because that's the only way I could turn, and didn't stop until I saw the arms of Jesus spread above Rio. I traveled nonstop for three months, and when I returned to the States and packed my few possessions into my car and drove west, from Maryland to Missouri, I felt sufficiently exhausted to deal with living in the Midwest for a year. Or maybe two.

six

missouri

The University of Missouri campus is in a picture-perfect small town called Columbia, halfway between the state's urban bookends of St. Louis and Kansas City. They are each two hours away, and that left little motive to flee Columbia on weekends. Not that I needed one at first. The bucolic and progressive air of the town was so charming, an island of cafés, pizza houses, and penny parking meters, all surrounded by a great green sea of farmland, that it made for a welcome transition. And there was a decent amount of class-work to contend with. Missouri's journalism program, the oldest and best known in the country, placed much emphasis on theory. Graduate students were there not just to learn to write or photograph but to become scholars of the profession, required to take classes on philosophy and ethics and history. Or so we were advised during orientation.

At twenty-four I was the median age of my peers, most of whom were in the writing sequence. On the second day of my

Intermediate Photography class all the students were made to project four or five of their best photographs. Staring at their work, I was surprised to find no fellow wanderers, but rather students who were deft at documenting the worlds in which they already lived. Friends, families, neighborhoods; people in their homes and at church; intimate, mostly black-and-white, documentary-style images, encouraging and pretty. The students seemed to have great regard for their own communities, something my images lacked, relying as they did on the foreignness of their subject matter. I was also surprised to learn that few students had produced independent projects, that much of what they showed was assignments from previous photography classes.

Our professor, a photographer named Tab Halbret, required everyone to shoot his assignments in color, on slides, which had long been my format of choice. Back then, slide film was the industry standard for publications with quality reproduction, like *National Geographic, Sports Illustrated,* and the three newsmagazines. The tradeoff is that slides are unforgiving, demand perfect exposures, in other words require that you be a photographer. Halbret's first assignments focused on practical applications, things such as lighting and color balance, having us photograph the same outdoor scene once an hour for twelve hours, say, so we could realize what light does to a scene's colors and mood. Light has an infinite variety of characteristics, most invisible to the human eye. And learning how it will look is like learning a hidden language. Its appearance changes with the time of day, the humidity, the barometric pressure, the season, the setting. The only way to learn the variances was to burn a serious amount of film. And that's what I did.

Learning how to frame an affecting photo was a little more tricky, coming from the right side of the brain. The industry cliché that it can't be taught—as in, you either have an "eye" or you don't—is not entirely true. Learning photography is a lot like learning how to write: the more you read, the better you do it. And in the same way that a writer's command of language, of word choice and sentence structure, allows him to unify the ingredients of a scene, so too does a photographer's visual acuity: to show a reader those elements that matter most. To convey information in a new and interesting way. To "make" instead of "take" pictures because these images are our own creations. Not a robotic, Web-cam depiction of reality but a concise and humanistic conveyance of it.

In my grad school days, before I was better skilled at discerning a scene's visual structure—all those elements, hidden in plain sight, that can provide the architecture of an interesting picture—I would blur my eyes while looking through the viewfinder. All the distracting details would disappear—the clutter on someone's desk, say, or the traffic on a distant road, and in its place would appear a palette of colors, of shadow and light, of lines, some parallel and some conflicting. From this simplified perspective it was more easy to orchestrate an aesthetic, a pattern from the chaos, to move myself or my camera this way and that, until symmetries emerged. Pulling designs from the most mundane environment was for me an issue of learning how to process visual information. Like pulling words from a jumble—you have to train your eyes to find that hidden nugget. It also didn't hurt to study how the masters did it.

The shooters I admired as a student, whose work I reviewed religiously and tried to emulate, were still of the *National*

Geographic variety—the ones venturing to the far corners of the map—not just for their aesthetic accomplishments but because those were the places I longed to visit. My regard for the yellow magazine would continue throughout my career, though the same can't be said for all photojournalists. In the eighties and nineties the industry beef against the *Geographic* was that the pictures on their pages were beautiful things, too beautiful, without a dark side, swept clean of gritty realities that might scuff the magazine's polish. Though they have since come around, covering unpleasant issues with true tenacity, their sanitized perspective served me well, arousing my wanderlust when I was still a child. In return for that gift, I maintained a stubborn allegiance. The yellow magazine was the boyhood crush I couldn't abandon.

For a fix of hardcore journalism I learned to direct my vision elsewhere, to those depicting a less glorious view of the world. Three whose work that influenced me the most: Eugene Richards, the great social documentarian, and his images of wild-eyed crack users in *Cocaine True, Cocaine Blue,* his camera tight on all those guns and needles, on that woman about to blow some dude, unzipping his pants, her baby clinging to her back like an afterthought; Luc Delahaye, a young and prickly Frenchman whose album of a winter journey across Russia, *Winterreise,* depicts a place without light, both literally and metaphorically, a place of Depression-era housing and men in various stages of drunkenness, of women with black eyes and of scabby, unsmiling children sleeping in the bowels of some building, or visiting a male stranger in one of the apartments, the resignation on the children's faces hinting at sexual abuse. It is the most morose, unbearable, and accomplished photo book of my lifetime.

And of course Jim Nachtwey, a name synonymous with sorrow. His epic *Inferno*. It's almost a cliché for a photographer to proclaim admiration for Nachtwey's work, so industry-wide is his influence, so moralizing his imagery. But *Inferno* is impossible to ignore—AIDS, war, famine, ethnic cleansing, all those dead or dying bodies, too many for one man to experience. And yet it seems he is always there, at every conflict, every disaster, revealing for the rest of us the worst the world has to offer, reminding us that sorrow has significance, for without it there would be no empathy, and without empathy there is no humanity.

There are dozens more I admire, and they are at once journalists and humanitarians, the subjects of their creations—class, poverty, war—liberating the medium from the snobbish trappings of other art forms. Photojournalism is accessible; it is about the world, for the world. And its players take more risks, endure more hardships, witness more misery in order to practice their craft than any other artisans I can think of. When they make a picture, they are not imaging a scene but standing right before it. The crackheads and Russian whores and people dead or dying all an arm's reach away.

▢ In addition to our weekly assignments, Halbret required us to produce an extended documentary project: a story told through a series of pictures. I decided to photograph the nearby Mennonite settlement of Excelsior. I jotted up a proposal without bothering to visit the place, and once it was accepted, figured I had better go down there to check it out.

Driving south on Missouri's Route 5 felt a bit like time-traveling. The two-lane road wound through rolling Ozark prairie and lime-green alfalfa fields. At an exit just past mile marker 118, near the town of Excelsior, the blacktop turned to dirt and the cars were replaced with carriages, the horses and buggies of eighteenth-century Europe. One-room schoolhouses appeared, and homesteads with grain silos in their backyards. And clotheslines draped with overalls and gingham dresses. Road signs were homemade and proclaimed such messages as "Worldly amusement and spiritual death go together." Phone lines were sparse.

I drifted down this road and that, looking for Mennonites to approach. This search is the worst part of any photo project, having to approach total strangers and make an appeal to enter their homes, their lives. Photographers are beggars, subsisting on the welfare of their subjects. Our very existence is sustained by those few open-minded souls, the ones who sympathize with our projects, the ones who see value in disseminating information about whatever community, culture, or lifestyle it is that we are photographing. There are some in every community, even ones like this. But finding them is the most difficult and unpleasant task of any assignment. Making pictures is the easy part.

Excelsior was home to three hundred Mennonite families from seven different congregational orders, ranging from the Old Order, the most conservative in the faith, to the Bethel Order, one of the most progressive. They migrated there from Pennsylvania a century before, looking for cheap land, fertile soil, and geographic isolation, isolation from guys like me, it seemed. Those I approached returned my introduction with a nod, then kept right on walking, driving, plowing their fields. In town I located one of the community's Old Order ministers at a woodworking shop, cornered him with my pitch—MU student working on a school project, eager to learn about your community, to document it on film. He was the first to volunteer a response, which was not a response in the literal sense of the word, touching as it did on everything but my request, from his morning constitutional to the moral cleansing of AIDS. Because there *are* lots of fags out there, and they could soon come to Excelsior and I wasn't a fag, was I?

Though the Old Orders were the obvious visual catch, with their buggies and beards and straw sombreros, I figured I had better start with one of the less conservative orders. The following Sunday I showed up uninvited at the church service of a group of Eastern Mennonites. Named for its original location in eastern Pennsylvania, the order was more commonly referred to as Black-Bumper Mennonites for its members' proclivity to paint the flashy chrome bumpers on their vehicles a sedate black.

They arrived just before nine in a convoy that could have been mistaken for a funeral procession: a dozen all-black sedans with their headlights on. Watching them watch me from their cars as they parked, their white faces staring at the stranger before them, I had a flash of self-consciousness, realized I should have dressed better, gotten up earlier and had a shower. A shave. I should have shaved. And swapped my ride with a friend's. That damn Jeep. It must have seemed the very embodiment of sin—fire-red with a soft convertible top, wheels muddy and oversized, bumper sticker that read, "I'm pro-choice and I vote!"

When they emerged from their vehicles, they congregated in a circle, peeking but no longer staring, gathering to chat. I hopped out and was relieved to see some of them approaching me. They listened to my request intently, patiently, then invited me to attend their service. I didn't go back for my camera, not wanting to come on too strong. A novice mistake. After the service one of the Mennonites invited me to his home to discuss the sermon with the other men. I participated as best I could. They seemed to like me, and why shouldn't they—a young student unaffiliated in matters of faith, exhibiting interest in their beliefs, their lives. Once again, I left my camera in the car, thinking it only polite to get to know them first.

It was silly, of course, to feel the need to display a personal interest before a professional one. I had come there to report and photograph, and that was nothing to be ashamed of. That's what journalists do. But now that I had demonstrated photojournalism as a secondary motive, sugarcoated my interactions with a feigned, wide-eyed affinity for their nonconformity, to suddenly whip out a camera would seem duplicitous. Indeed, when they invited me to the following week's service and I presented myself outside the church with my Nikon F3 hanging from one shoulder and a notepad in my back pocket, they looked perplexed. And when one of them politely asked me to leave the camera behind, I obliged, sat through yet another two-hour service, this time wondering just how to reprioritize in their minds the reason for my visits.

At their postservice rendezvous I made another public appeal to start photographing. The host, a large, gentle man named Jonathan, surveyed his fellow male parishioners. "We'll have to think about it," he answered.

"Well, it's what I'm here for. I mean it's nice to learn about all this but I also need to make pictures." They looked at each other again, nobody wanting to give the go-ahead. Their reservations

were not entirely religious. Unlike the Old Orders, whose doc-
trine was strictly against graven images, the Black Bumpers made
photographs of themselves. They even had some happy snaps up on
their refrigerators. The real issue, perhaps, was that they thought
of me as a challenge, as someone shopping for faith instead of
photographs.

"We'll have to think about it," Jonathan said again. I sat
through their discussion anyway. Through the window behind the
men I could see their children, the girls with their hair veils and
Laura Ingalls dresses, the boys wearing oversized black suits and
black hats. They were playing ring-around-the-rosy, and not one
of them was laughing. It was a great picture, and instead of making it I was stuck inside, listening to these proud, godly men ask
each other questions about the book of Luke.

Driving back to Columbia, I worked myself into a lather, having shot less than three rolls in two and a half weeks. This had to
change, would change. The next weekend I would revisit the Old
Orders and photograph them without photographing them, shoot
the homemade signs and the dresses on the clotheslines and the
buggies parked outside their church, images that wouldn't rattle
their religious concerns but that would still advance my story.
And when I ran out of those peripherals, those scene setters, I
would search out willing subjects, would not leave town without
securing at least one family to photograph.

The following Sunday dawned cool and bright, and I spent
much of the morning standing by the side of a quiet country road,
photographing Old Order buggies rolling to and from service.
Those traveling inside the buggies were invisible, their black wares
camouflaged in dark shade. "That your car there? You'd better

move it," came a voice from one buggy as it passed. An arm extended out the window, pointing to my right. One hundred yards away a group of Mennonite men had surrounded my Jeep, which was parked in the grass on the side of the road. Their coats were off and they seemed a single, many-limbed entity, black on bottom, blue on top. Were they rocking my car from side to side? Pounding on the hood with their fists? I ran toward the crowd, and as I got closer they spread out a bit, their expressions seething. In a ditch next to my car was another alarming site: an overturned buggy, an overturned horse, and a very bloody Old Order Mennonite.

"Your car done this!" screamed an old man with a Fu Manchu beard.

"Done what? How?"

He brought his face inches from mine. "Spooked his horse!" His eyes were fierce and his breath was nasty and I had a sudden urge to yank his beard, to force him to the ground by those mangy hairs and yell into *his* face, "Just how does a parked car spook a horse?" Just then a second man approached me, leaned forward, and spat in my face. Others followed, bringing up mouthfuls of goop and letting them fly. Someone grabbed my shirt to keep me from fleeing.

"You're pacifists!" I remember screaming before pushing my way out. This wasn't the breakthrough I had envisioned.

I jumped in my car and drove it into the church parking lot, then jogged back to see about the injured man. By then his horse and buggy were righted. The blood on his face and shirt came from a single, nasty gash on his forehead, a gash that needed stitches. The windshield on his buggy was broken and one of the wheels no longer spun. His horse pulled the buggy anyway, the broken wheel drawing a long, jagged line in the dirt road. The injured Mennonite walked behind his carriage, supported by his wife and in the company of his community.

This was bad. Insurmountable. Inexplicable. Cars zipping by at fifty mph don't spook these horses, let alone cars parked just off road. It was having my top down, I surmised, a move that caused carriage drivers to slow down as they passed, looking inside. The man must have veered off road trying to get a peek, then failed to right his horse in time, slid into the ditch that was just past my car. It was not my fault, I tried telling myself on the ride home, but the thought wouldn't stick. Had I not been there it would never have happened. Yes, I had done this to him, and I was so mortified. That poor man. His face. The rivers of blood flowing downward, like zombie makeup. His mouth open though making no sound. Would he get medical treatment? Would he be out of work? They just wanted to be left alone. Was it worth disrupting their lives for a few photographs?

"Hell, yes," said my professor, Tab Halbret, "so go back there and make it work." I was taken by surprise, having already surrendered the idea in my mind, though eventually realized he was right. I justified his opinion—and mine—by considering the approach a writer might take. If there was a significant news event in the Mennonite community—a suspicious fire, say, that claimed innocent lives—a writer wouldn't avoid investigating it because the Mennonites are a xenophobic community. To treat Mennonites without the same journalistic scrutiny as other citizens would show bias. Likewise, picture essays are not made exclusively of open communities. In fact, the most informative picture essays are those made of closed communities, ones the journalist has been able to enter and reveal to the public. While each of these groups brings to the table its own sensitivities, these issues are detours, not stop signs. If someone doesn't want his picture made, you don't just give up—you say thanks and move on to somebody else. And it was not like my coverage of the Mennonites was so intrusive, standing alongside the road or approaching people with my pitch.

A few days later I found myself back in Excelsior, my nerve newly hardened, walking up the front steps of Old Order homes, knocking on front doors like a salesman. After a few polite rejections I stood before a farmer named Ivan Zimmerman. Yes, I could photograph him and his son Zach if I wanted. They were having lunch now: peanut-butter-and-jelly sandwiches with chunks of sausage on the side. The two went back to their meal, their conversation, paying no mind to me in the background, making frames. They spent the rest of the day combining their fields of corn, then hominy. Near dusk they poured the grain into a massive old carriage, the kind you see in hay rides, and towed it toward their barn. I shot from atop the carriage, my legs knee-deep in grain, looking down on these two driving their tractor. The sun was low and the fields were auburn and the dirt road stretched long and inviting in front of them. My first decent picture.

Before I left, Ivan told me that his neighbor, Abraham Zimmerman, ran a buggy-repair shop and might be willing to be photographed. I headed straight there and made my pitch, the camera dangling from one shoulder. He nodded yes and told me to come back Monday morning. It was a fine situation, with his sons sanding and painting the spokes of a giant carriage inside their garage. Abraham knew another Old Order who might help out, this one a pig farmer. He, too, agreed and soon enough the project was rolling. At the same time, the Eastern Order had gotten over my initial approach, poorly conceived as it was, now letting me photograph various aspects of their lives: their pre- and postchurch gatherings, their jobs during the week, and a limited amount of home life. On weekends I brought down a little slide viewer to show them some of the images I had made. As most of my subjects had never subscribed to a magazine or newspaper, it helped to illustrate the role of a photojournalist, a documentarian: to show that those quiet moments I sought to picture, the ones that often made them giggle, were not silly at all. And it did help, encouraged them to act natural, as if I wasn't there. Just after Thanksgiving, when my subjects had had about all of me they could take, I called it a wrap.

☐ With my first project completed, I was freed up enough to socialize with my fellow grad school students, joined a small clique made up mostly of writers. And of Deirdre, unaffected and with a breezy air. A fine listener, writer, reporter. Born in Ireland and raised in Chicago, she was a different species than I—controlled and urbane, never had a critical word to say about anyone. She was also lovely to look at. The lush green in her eyes and the red highlights in her hair; a presence I felt physically, those colors of her.

I first noticed her in a grad school elective called Philosophy of Journalism. The class was a two-hour-long snore-a-thon, with some gray and humorless academic droning on about arcane ethical dilemmas. I wasn't sure why I chose it as my elective, my history with philosophy classes being quite sordid—and my interest, apparently, no more evolved—yet instead of dropping the class I hid like a degenerate in the last row, a baseball cap pulled low over my head. Deirdre sat in the front, and I thought it odd that this woman would eat her lunch during class; always a homemade sandwich pulled from a brown paper bag. She also kept her feet tucked primly beneath her chair, though whenever the professor offered an insight that she found interesting she wagged them both from side to side.

Months later, after we became an item, she'd wait for me in the doorway after class, then latch her arm in mine when we exited, as if departing a formal gathering. It seemed to me a proclamation: "He's mine." A little act that made me feel bulletproof.

She fled when I first tried to kiss her, having been lured to my apartment to watch a movie with a group of our friends. Only I didn't invite anyone else—Deirdre was kind enough not to act suspicious—and when I made a go of it she mumbled something about having a boyfriend back in Chicago, then walked out my door and into a driving October rain. There were next-day apologies from both of us, and she didn't betray my indiscretion at future fellowships.

Deirdre came into journalism as an aficionada of alternative weeklies. Which is to say we shared the same progressive political views. All of us did. Our troupe would gather for weekly dinner parties and pilgrimages to the nearby Les Bourgeois Winery, with its cliff-top café overlooking the Missouri River: the afternoon wine buzz, the leftist chatter, the crisp, autumn cool. I loved this company, our liberal band of scribes—everyone bright and ambitious and ready to right the world.

The novelty of living in small-town America was by then behind us, and dissing our surrogate state, which the snarkiest of us referred to as "misery," became a favorite sport of our social gatherings. In truth, none of us disliked middle Missouri, were perhaps secretly grateful for such an easy target. It was the lack of nonacademic escapes, of restaurants or clubs or art-house movie theaters. And the closest thing Missouri had to a national park was the Ozark Mountains, which were not actually mountains, as the name promised, but wimpy hills sprinkled with double-wides, cookie-cutter craft shops, and a run of eateries advertising a peculiar combination: barbecue and ice cream. Then there were St. Louis and Kansas City, not exactly cultural oases. Both cities' downtowns were nearly deserted on weekend nights, we soon learned, sad Midwestern beacons of white flight. Strolling through their dark and empty urban centers, it was as if a neutron bomb had gone off, as if we were the last people alive, the stoplights still changing though there were no cars on the road.

Sometime after Thanksgiving, Deirdre's other paramour gone or forgotten—I can't remember which—I made another move, asked her to go on a trip alone. It was an opportunistic proposal, drawing as it did on our group outings. And yet she smiled and didn't bother to ask where. It was a mistake on her part. We ended up in southern Missouri, in Branson, "the Live Music Show Capital of the World," where country singers long dead to that industry are resurrected as icons; the wheezing pantheon of equally aged pilgrims who, like Catholics to Medjugorje, come from all over America to see this small-town miracle, and who were jamming the parking lots of the many concert halls, barbecue-and-ice cream joints, and putt-putt golf courses with their oversized

RVs. We joined the big-haired, God-fearing, flag-waving retirees for some family fun—the show we saw ended with everyone standing, hands on their hearts, singing "God Bless America." Then we fled town for a cabin on a lake, one we saw advertised in a local paper, one that didn't prove as romantic as I'd hoped.

The "cabin" was really a refurbished garage and was in the backyard of an Arkansas man who twice asked if we were married. It had an orange velour bedspread with matching drapes and a view of the owner's unmowed backyard. The entire evening I didn't dare canoodle for fear the guy was watching through a peephole, ready to come charging in with a shotgun. We drank until the setting seemed a little less depressing.

Those early days of our relationship, venturing here and there but never quite committing: jobs, careers, distances, everything uncertain. Then came Texas, Big Bend, the two of us alone in the desert, our surroundings stripped bare, the clutter gone, the lens focused, not a single sensory trace of our species, no sign that it existed beyond us. That blue sky and orange rock. I was bound to her, to our environment, the clarity it offered, like seeing everything in nothing. And with that clairvoyance a simple truth: this love existed, yes. It was she and I and how foolish we had been to fret about the future, those things we can't control. We dove in and the rewards were immediate. We were happy.

❏ Photojournalism students are expected to spend their summers interning at a newspaper, the bigger the better. Most students send off a blizzard of query letters: the *St. Louis Post-Dispatch*, the *Albuquerque Journal*, the *Spokesman Review*, the *Des Moines Register*, the *New Orleans Times-Picayune*, and so on. Great papers, all. Though newspaper photography was not my bailiwick. I had no interest in covering community journalism—largely because I wasn't skilled enough to produce pictures in run-of-the-mill settings, which I presumed an intern would have to make. I wanted to work on stories of national significance, and with graduation nearing I sent my lone internship request to *U.S. News & World Report*.

I had long admired *U.S. News* for running their own photographers' work, at least more so than *Time* and *Newsweek*. Photojournalism is not just about shooting, after all, but about getting published. What's the point of busting your ass for an image nobody will see? *U.S. News* was also the only major news mag based in Washington, which would offer a cheaper lifestyle than New York City.

Months earlier, *U.S. News'* director of photography, Finnegan Grove, came to Mizzou to help judge the Pictures of the Year (POY) competition. Hosted by Missouri's J-school and now called Pictures of the Year International, the competition is photojournalism's premier spectator sport. It is the country's largest and most influential photo contest, where a panel of judges make lightning-quick decisions to winnow the year's best photographs from thousands of entries. Every picture is projected on a large screen and stays up for as little as a second before each judge shouts his or her verdict: "Out," "Out," "Out." On the occasion of an "In!" the image is moved to the second round. Eventually each category is reduced to twelve or so images, whereupon one of the J-school's student volunteers will read aloud the captions to give the judges more information. Then the winners are chosen.

Between rounds, I showed Grove my portfolio and made a spirited pitch: my goal was to be a mag photographer, I could shoot chrome, was from D.C. and knew the place well. He dragged his loop quickly across my slide sheet. There were other photographers waiting. Other portfolios. I asked him about internship possibilities. He threw me a vague compliment, told me to drop him a letter. He moved on to the next student's portfolio. I sent the letter two weeks later, and long after I had written off my prospects, Grove wrote me back. Would I be willing to start in June? I read his letter a dozen times, then folded it in my pocket and went for a hike at a nearby state park. I read the letter there too, on a wooden bench overlooking the Missouri River. I felt lucky and proud and happy and terrified. Breaks didn't come any bigger than this. And they didn't come twice. *Don't. Fucking. Blow it.*

The only thing standing between me and my gig with *U.S. News* was the dreaded "professional project," Missouri's signature assignment, a full semester dedicated to the production of a single body of work. Having already hit the internship jackpot, I was less than enthusiastic about the task. Just a few days before presenting what was supposed to be a thoroughly researched proposal to my "project committee," a board of three professors who "yea" or "nay" your proposal, I scrambled to come up with an idea. I would do a piece on . . . Native America. On the Navajo Nation. Yes, in northeastern Arizona. The warm sun and endless sandstone. Me with the top down, cruising the long and dusty roads. Pictures everywhere. I'd make some Indian friends and learn about their culture. But it was the topography, the hoodoos and spires and empty canyons, empty except for me, that's what whetted my appetite. To be alone in all that space.

Deirdre's project was taking her to an alternative weekly in Durham, North Carolina, and before we parted, there was time for one last road trip, this one from Mizzou to Key West with her aunt and father, the four of us crammed into his car, though happy to have the windows rolled down and to feel the warm air on our faces. As was the case with our maiden voyage, the going outshone the getting there. I hate Florida, I suddenly remembered when we arrived: the trailer homes, the family parks, the far-right lunacy, where they blow up abortion clinics. It is America's whang, to borrow a *Simpsons* observation. And to borrow one from literature, the final chapter of too many Rabbit Angstroms, slowing traffic with their land yachts, with their northeastern air of autonomy. All those settlers, the weight of their collective demise palpable, dispiriting.

I had convinced our road-weary crew that Key West would prove the state's savior. That stopping in Tampa or Miami or even Key Largo would not cut it. That we must forge ahead, by God, due south until we could drive south no more. And when we did just that there was near mutiny, three Fletcher Christians to my Captain Bligh. All the island's hotels were booked, presumably with the herds of frat boys we saw prowling the streets. I knew nothing of this migration—spring break, yes, but Christmas?—and stared from the car at all the like-minded males: white, buff, and shirtless, sporting backward baseball caps and red plastic beer cups. We found the one hotel room on the island they had yet to invade, which was tight for two people, let alone four, and was where Deirdre's father, his tolerance worn thin—

the close quarters, the crappy weather, and all those miles that lay ahead—made a now-famous threat to boot me onto the street if he had to "watch another fucking bird documentary." What a disaster. They retreated north, me west.

seven

arizona

At a gas station just outside Tucumcari, New Mexico, I pushed a pair of Vivarin through their foil seal. An attendant handed me my cup of coffee to help wash them down. He had chunks of turquoise in his hat and belt, around both wrists, and dangling from his neck. I'd driven just twenty hours from Missouri, which in that damn Jeep felt like twenty days. I couldn't go much over sixty mph, and the canvas top was whipping wildly in the frigid wind, like a tent atop Everest. In the night I tried to tune into President Clinton's first State of the Union address, but had to turn the radio up so loud I worried the speakers might blow. Or my eardrums. And at 2 a.m., somewhere in western Oklahoma, I pulled over for a snooze, moving into the passenger seat, reclining it as far back as it would go, and zipping myself into my sleeping bag. I was out for maybe fifteen minutes when it started hailing golfballs. I watched them bounce off my hood and kept myself awake worrying they would tear through the roof.

Now I was fighting the first signs of overnight drive syn-
drome, the highway blending into the surrounding desert, the
mountains in the distance not seeming to get any closer but farther away. I washed my face, refilled my coffee, and hit the road
renewed, knocking out 250 more miles on an extended caffeine
buzz. When I finally passed the sign welcoming me to Gallup,
New Mexico, the eastern gateway to the Navajo Nation and self-
proclaimed Indian Capital of the World, I wondered what all the
rushing was for.

On either side of Route 66 rose a forest of neon signs, blaz-
ing like Vegas. But instead of casinos, they trumpeted cheap booze,
fleabag motels, Indian pawnshops. The last crammed obscene
amounts of turquoise in their display windows, a tropical blue
sea of other people's jewelry. I checked into a Motel 6, showered, washed my dirty clothes in the sink, then ate dinner at a
McDonald's. An Indian man staggered in without shoes, his socks
wet and floppy, his voice aggressive. He tried to order something
and everyone went about their business, eating French fries,
pumping ketchup, giving back change, with veteran disregard.

I went to a Shop 'n Save to stock up on supplies and sat in
my car in the parking lot, staring at all the shoppers, dark and
overweight, the men wearing tight Wranglers and black cowboy
hats, the women in sweat pants and puffy coats. They loaded bag
after bag into their rusty pickups to bring back to the reservation. It started snowing. What on earth had I been thinking? I
didn't want this, not more of this, to pester people while they
went about their lives. "Excuse me, I'm some asshole working
on a graduate project. I've never actually met a Native American
and the truth is I don't know a damn thing about your culture.

But since I was a kid I've had this need to venture into the yonder and hey . . . you guys were wanderers too, right? So can you help a brother out? Let me make some pictures while you grocery shop? Drive your kids to school? Sit at home in front of the TV?" I mean, what did I think I was going to photograph? A drum circle in Monument Valley?

The plan sounded far more studious as presented to my project committee. I would encircle the Navajo Nation in my car—finding families to live with along the way—and photograph and report on their attempts to balance tradition and modernization, ancient Navajo culture and encroaching Anglo society. It was a legitimate conceit, *hozho,* or balance, even if I didn't realize this until after writing my proposal, in a crash course over Christmas break on the Navajo worldview. In the beginning, when First Man and First Woman emerged from their underground world, they saw the Earth as living in a state of order—animals living in proper relationship with one another, all elements functioning symbiotically. They thought this land the very essence of harmony, beauty, happiness, and gave flesh to the *Dine,* the People. Their world had hozho, a physical and spiritual symmetry, not unlike the Chinese Tao, and the People were responsible for maintaining it.

The Navajos' love for their land is easy to understand: in scope and drama it is unrivaled. *Dinetah,* the Land of the People, is the largest Indian reservation in the country: it's the size of West Virginia. Stretching twenty-six thousand square miles across northeastern Arizona and into Utah and New Mexico, it serves as a cultural buffer, a half-hidden country within our own. And it is beautiful, otherworldly: a place of Martian red monoliths and indigo canyons, of jagged mountains, juniper forests, and unrivaled openness. On the morning of my arrival, however, these topographic marvels were hidden behind blowing snow. I had fled Gallup at first light, and I pulled into Window Rock, Arizona, the capital of the Navajo Nation, under a barrage of fat, wet flakes.

☐ Precisely one minute after watching two elderly women waddle across a parking lot and unlock the office doors of the Navajo Tourist Board, I went in myself. They responded to my request for a host family with blank stares. And then one proposed a name: Alvin Phillips. I rang him from a pay phone outside a strip mall and he offered me a vacant trailer on his lot, said to come look at it in the evening. I walked back to my car and sat in the driver's seat, not sure what to do with myself. The parking lot was wet and the tires of a pickup truck sizzled as it passed, then nothing. No sounds. No people. Nothing worth photographing. This sucked. My watch read 10:30 a.m. Two-and-a-half months? I imagined bailing on the whole project, heading east on the road before me and not stopping until I got to Durham, where Deirdre was writing for the alternative weekly, the *Independent*. I'd go to her office, sneak up behind her as she headed to her car. That moment of excitement before I revealed my presence, that surge in my heart as I got closer and closer, then reached out and touched her on the shoulder. She'd turn around quickly, her hair airborne, her eyes startled. She'd squeal with delight and lock her arms around my body. The vision made me more depressed. Careers first, our early mantra. And I suppose it was the right one.

When I met Alvin at his compound west of Window Rock, I re-recited for him my two-minute project pitch, not because I needed to but because he wasn't speaking and the silence was killing me. He suggested I photograph his grandparents; that is, if they let me. They lived in a hogan—a traditional dwelling made of mud and corbelled juniper logs—a few miles south. Then he pointed to the trailer-for-rent, which lay well behind his house in a small clearing of Ponderosa pine, glowing white in the deep, underwater darkness of the surrounding woods.

"How much do you want for it?"

"That depends. How long you staying?"

"Maybe three days. Maybe a week."

"For three days I think three hundred dollars. In advance."

Now I was the one who stared. The three-word response blinking on my mental teleprompter—go fuck yourself—seemed a tad unwise, given my predicament. I summoned a more mannerly reply. "I can get a hotel room in Gallup for fifteen dollars." No response. That silence. "I'll give you ten bucks a night . . . and help with chores." The latter was not a selfless gesture, but a way to integrate myself into his daily routine.

"Okay," he said. As he walked away he added: "If you hear the dogs barking, don't open the trailer. Stay inside."

"Any reason?"

"I seen a skinwalker there. In those woods. In the night." A skinwalker is Navajoland's answer to the bogeyman—a witch that can turn itself into animals. At first I thought he was idling for a laugh, playing on Navajo stereotypes, like a Romanian saying that he saw vampires, but he didn't return my smile.

The trailer had seen better days, and not in a long while. It was wet and cold, the same temperature as outside. There was no water, no bathroom, no bed. There was spilled food on the floor and mouse crap on most surfaces, little black rice poops. And in the hallway the scat of something larger, something that had been chomping on the mice, judging from the digested hair and bones. There was an AK-47 on the couch. With a full magazine. I picked it up and aimed it out a window. Can you shoot a skinwalker, or do the bullets just go through it?

I split some wood from a stack outside, made the pieces small enough to fit into the iron stove, and got a fire going. Then I stuffed the stove full of coal, a pile of which lay beneath a plastic tarp next to the wood. Ten degrees tonight, the car radio had said. The stove clanked as it warmed, blue smoke flowing from its metal door. The smell was sharp and acrid and reminded me of the leper colony in India, which was surrounded by coal mines. Funny that I felt just as out of place here, in the States. My sleeping bag fit snugly on the couch, and I sat on it and opened a can of Del Monte fruit cocktail. There was the crunch of footsteps in the snow, a knock at the door. Alvin said he needed his gun, and when I handed it to him, he slung the weapon over his shoulder like a mercenary and walked off.

For the next four days I couldn't find a picture to save my life, or to start my career. Alvin allowed me to photograph inside his house only once, during his Super Bowl party. People sat before the TV not saying much, and at halftime they cut into a white cake with the words "Go Cowboys" written in blue icing. I visited his grandparents often, a short, haggard, smiling duo who lived in a one-room log cabin in the forest, high up in the Chuska mountains. They were the picture-perfect couple in the picture-perfect setting. Only they had no picture-patience, allowing me to make a few frames the first day I arrived and then promptly declaring my photo job completed—and my chauffeuring job begun. They asked me to drive them back and forth to Window Rock, to Albert's house, to their singer's, or medicine man's, hogan, and in a blatant display of suck-up I fulfilled each request. My groveling failed to generate the photographic rewards I'd hoped for, however, and eventually I stopped coming around.

In Window Rock, when it wasn't snowing, I worked on landscapes and street scenes, though even while I was taking these pictures I knew they didn't work. And I popped into the KFC once a day, not to eat—for that I was frequenting a gas station that sold premade sandwiches in plastic triangles, the only non-fried meal I could find—but to lock myself in the bathroom and wash the coal dust off of my face and out of my nose. It was depressing, this existence, my failure to connect, the dreary weather, my daily visits to a fast-food joint with a white towel in my hand and a blue plastic soap dish in my pocket, so I decided to push on to a different town and search for a different family.

☐ At first glance, the home of Herman and Harolyn Tazzie looked as if it belonged in rural Appalachia. Their three-room trailer sagged between cinderblocks atop a muddy plot littered with empty food cans, soiled diapers, and used car parts. Chickens and sheep rummaged through the mess, risking attacks from barefoot children or one of the two dogs of indistinguishable breed that lived under the trailer. Most of the windows inside had been broken and pieced back together with duct tape. There was no telephone, no running water, and often no electricity. A single wood-burning stove warmed the trailer.

Upon further examination, however, distinctive characteristics appeared—a clothesline draped with home-dyed yarn, a rusty pickup with a faded bumper sticker proclaiming "Red Power," and in the backyard, camouflaged among the piñon trees, the family hogan. Herman and Harolyn were in their mid-thirties, had seven children (six boys and one girl), and had not seen steady work in seven years. Though Harolyn spent much of her time weaving traditional Navajo rugs to sell at a trading post, they got by on federal welfare and state food stamps.

A friendly man named Levi Tso, a community service worker from the local tribal government chapter, led me to this family. After fleeing Window Rock, I had driven northwest to a town named Chinle, on the rim of the rugged and beautiful Canyon de Chelly (pronounced de Shay). The canyon is three gorges in one, slicing through the heart of Dinetah like an inverted mountain chain. From an overlook you can stare a thousand feet straight down, the canyon wall perfectly sheer, as if someone had removed part of the earth with a ruler and scalpel. Unlike its geologic cousin, the Grand Canyon, three hundred miles west, Canyon de Chelly has a long history of supporting life. About 450 families were still living in its interior, farming the same land the Anasazi Indians did two thousand years earlier. It was with one of these families that I had hoped to hook up, though Levi told me that during winter they left their canyon hogans for trailers up on the rim.

Levi was the kind of contact every photojournalist dreams of encountering. He was smart, well connected, and cooperative. He knew one of the said families and was sure they'd let me stay with them, picture them; and within three hours of our first meeting I was driving behind his car onto the Tazzies' lot. It was about fifteen miles east of Chinle and a few hundred yards off the canyon rim, a broad, brown clearing of brush and piñon. A dozen trailers shared the space—the homes of the Tazzies' extended family— scattered at odd angles. Dogs charged at our cars as we entered, their maws a blur of pink and white, their eyes wild. When Levi hopped out of his car, he made like he was picking up a rock, and the pack dispersed.

Levi walked off to chat with a man working beneath the engine of a blue Camaro, and I followed. "They're in that one," Levi said to me, pointing to Herman and Harolyn's trailer. When I didn't move, he shouted, "Go. Tell them I sent you." I climbed a set of homemade wooden steps and rapped lightly on the trailer's front door. I could hear voices inside, a TV blaring. I knocked louder and two children answered, one naked except for a diaper and the other sucking a Popsicle stick. They left the door open and sat back down in front of the TV, which was showing *Home Alone 2* before an audience of nine, maybe ten kids. One was lying on the floor beneath the TV, his heels up against the screen. Another was wearing bright red boxing gloves. None of them looked at me. And they were silent now. There was a giant loom in the corner of the room, made of yellow piping, and on the wall behind it a small shelf displaying some trophies.

"Are your parents home?" A boy on the couch pointed down a dark, wood-paneled hallway to a closed door. "Can you get them for me?" I asked. Nobody moved.

"They're down therrrrre," the boy on the couch whined.

I walked down the hallway, passing two open doors: the first of a small room with a bed of blankets on the floor and with posters of basketball players pinned to the wall, the second of a bathroom that had been turned into a storage room, with boxes and stuffed, plastic lawn bags piled eye-high. I knocked on what I presumed was the parent's bedroom door. There was whispering, giggling, then a woman's voice, loud and shrill. "Ty?"

"No." There was the sound of covers moving, of bare feet on linoleum. Waves of darkness moved across the light that seeped beneath the door. A man answered. He was shirtless, his short black hair oily and erect. He had a pencil-thin mustache. He looked both Mexican and Korean. His eyes were puffy. I told him who I was, what I was doing. Behind him the quiet was pronounced, the non-sound of someone trying to listen. I asked him if I could stay with his family, photograph them. I could pay him for board—ten bucks a night plus help with chores—but not for making their picture. He said okay and closed the door.

The pair emerged near dusk. Harolyn greeted me with the feather-light handshake popular in those parts, then placed two large plates on the dinner table, one piled high with slices of Wonder Bread, the other holding two hunks of Spam. Children sliced them into sandwiches and went back to the TV while the three of us chatted at the table. They were remarkably open, complaining about their employment troubles. There was simply nowhere to work, Herman said. Chinle was small, an intersection really, home to a Basha's Grocery Store, a hospital, a Burger King, a laundromat, a handful of jobs for hundreds of square miles. During the summer months he herded his sheep into the canyon, and later butchered them for their meat and skins. During winter he chopped piñon trees into logs, loaded them into his brother-in-law's pickup, and sold them as firewood by the side of the road.

Harolyn sold her rugs in Shiprock, New Mexico, and at the Hubbell Trading Post south of Chinle.

Established in 1878, Hubbell was now a National Historic Site, and I had visited it on my way to Chinle. Its walls were lined with hundreds of rugs, stacked thigh-high, and attached to each a Polaroid of the creator, the artist, the weaver, staring expressionless into a white burst of light. They made quite a photo-essay, these instant portraits. The uniformity of background, stance, and mood; images meant to convey individuality but that instead revealed something closer to sorrow. Or so it seemed to me.

Herman and Harolyn put me in a room with the two oldest boys, though I'm not sure where or when they slept as they were never there. The other five children slept on the floor and couch of the living room, near the wood-burning stove and in front of the TV, which stayed on through the night. I unrolled my sleeping bag on the floor, climbed in fully clothed, and closed my eyes. It was past midnight. The room was already cold, and I was lonely, depressed. On the other side of the wall the TV was blaring, then went silent for a few moments. I heard one of the kids sticking a tape in the VCR and the sound of *Home Alone 2* beginning again.

◻ The Tazzies' poverty was typical of families on Dinetah. As with every other Native tribe, the aftershocks of acculturation—of two centuries of genocidal treatment, of forced assimilation and cultural abuse—have strained the Navajo inheritance. At the time of my visit, unemployment hovered around 50 percent, and 40 percent of Navajo homes were relying on federal welfare assistance. Education levels were low—a majority of Navajo over twenty-five years old had not gone beyond the ninth grade, and alcohol consumption was on the rise. The Navajo Nation Council estimated that more than half of adult Navajos were drinking *toh lizhin,* or dark water. Though that was well below the national average, alcohol was banned on the Rez.

Life with the Tazzies was neither exciting nor boring—a photographic purgatory from which it was difficult to escape. In the mornings I'd help Herman haul wood for a few hours, stopping at opportune moments to make a few frames. He'd chainsaw piñon trees into little logs for his trailer's stove, then store the rest to sell. In the afternoons I photographed whatever I could find: Harolyn weaving, cleaning, giving haircuts, the younger kids wrestling, boxing, watching TV. On those days when I foresaw no pictures on the horizon, I'd hike to the base of Canyon de Chelly, sit and stare at White House ruins, the canyon's famed centuries-old Anasazi dwellings. As Levi had said, there was no activity on the base in winter, which meant no pictures to advance my project. But being alone down there was its own reward.

Herman's father, Mark, was a medicine man, and on the occasion he had a ceremonial to perform, he allowed me to photograph his preparations, though not the actual rite. This brought me terrific anxiety, to watch a Blackening Way, the sick patient nude, smeared with mutton lard and charcoal, Mark prancing around him with his rattle, all this happening right in front of me, the pictures found, the hard part done, and not be able to lift my camera. One evening Mark gave me permission to make one frame, one goddamn frame, which was worse than none, I learned—to stare through the viewfinder the entire night, one finger on the shutter, wondering when it was going to happen, the best opportunity. Was that it? Should I wait? Did I just miss it? Should I go outside and hang myself?

In the midst of one of his father's performances, Herman leaned over and asked if I would drive him and Harolyn to Gallup the following morning. They wanted to do some shopping. It caught me off guard, Gallup being 120 miles away, but I agreed. We left at 10 a.m., and when we reached Chinle they told me to stop at the Chapter House (the local governing body), that they had a meeting they needed to attend. They stayed inside for two hours, then directed me to the post office, then to one of Herman's relatives' homes, then to some place to try and get their phone turned back on, then toward Gallup again. It was snowing now—sideways—and I was already miffed.

We reached the town in midafternoon, stopped at a strip mall (where Herman said he needed to visit a tax return office, though he returned to the car clutching a brown paper bag), an electronics repair shop (to see if Herman's microwave was fixed), the laundromat (they had two black lawn bags full of clothes. But wasn't there a laundromat in Chinle?), an aimless search of Gallup for Harolyn's aunt (who allegedly was shopping here as well), back to the laundromat (to put the clothes in the dryer), another strip mall (where Herman had a coat on layaway), the grocery store (after which we struggled to fit ten bags of food in the back of the Jeep), back to the laundromat (where we folded the clothes and put them back in the bags and onto Herman's and Harolyn's laps in the car), the Wal-Mart (where they bumped into Harolyn's aunt, who, I was surprised to realize, was the woman who lived next door and who was driving an empty pickup), another grocery store (because now they had room to put things in the bed of her pickup), and then at 8:30, finally, back toward home. It had now been snowing for eight hours. The roads were skating rinks, I couldn't see twenty feet in front of me, and could hear an empty bottle kicking around the feet of my passengers. When we pulled up to their trailer, Herman's eyes were glazed, his expression loose. He said he needed to go to Shiprock on Sunday. I told him to find another driver, then left the two of them to carry in their own groceries.

I did concede to local errands, which included frequent visits to a shuttered house outside Chinle that Herman said belonged to his uncle, though Herman always entered around back and returned to the car concealing something beneath his coat. He and Harolyn started staying in their bedroom for days at a time. One night in the woods behind the trailer, where I had gone to piss as there was no indoor bathroom, there was the sound of approaching footsteps, then of someone retching. Herman was twenty feet away, hadn't seen me in the dark, and was puking standing up. I waited until he walked back into the trailer before moving a muscle. Journalistically it was becoming more difficult to ignore, their drinking, getting as it did right to this issue of balance. My stomach wrenched at the prospect: asking this couple if I could photograph that part of their lives. Then again, perhaps they had been trying to tell me about it, buying the booze in front of me.

One afternoon I found myself alone with Harolyn outside her sister's house, where I had driven the two of them for another errand. We were sitting on a bench in the front yard. I came out with it. "So about these alcohol runs." She looked surprised. Angry. I knew immediately I had screwed up, been too indelicate, accusatory; an amateurish mistake.

"I'm sorry we lied to you, Jim. We have seven kids."

"I'm not mad or anything. I just want to know more about it." Harolyn walked into her sister's house, and when she returned with Herman, they walked right past me, climbed into her sister's pickup, and drove away. They didn't ask for any more rides, and apparently took their drinking elsewhere, as it was the last I saw of it—or them, for the most part. They'd go into town for an errand and not return until dusk. Car trouble, they'd say. When they were home, they spent most of their time in the bedroom. Soon all the wood Herman had piled outside the house was gone and their kids were making after-school runs into the forest to gather more. Their oldest, Ty, was unconcerned. This behavior was normal, he confessed one night in his bedroom, more normal than what they had displayed earlier. That was them acting for my sake.

I figured it would be better if I moved on, and the same night showed the first signs of hepatitis. My body felt wrenched, as if a group of thugs had beaten me with Louisville Sluggers. There was a fever, chills, stuff coming out of my nose that made me stare at the Kleenex. I had trouble hearing out of my right ear. At five in the morning I drove to the Chinle Hospital, where I was told that the facility was only for Indians. "Even my husband can't get treated here," a white doctor said. I drifted back to my Jeep and drove fifty miles south to the town of Ganado, which had the next-closest hospital.

"Hepatitis A," the doctor there said. "All that sheepshit in the water." He gave me a gamma globulin shot and sent me back to Chinle, where I checked into a motel and slept for three days. I would have stayed longer if I could have afforded it. When I popped by Herman and Harolyn's home to tell them I was feeling better, was leaving Chinle, I nearly ran over two of the dogs. They were lying dead on their sides near the entrance to the compound, their mouths humming with flies. Herman Junior answered the trailer door, said his parents had gone to Chinle in the morning and hadn't come back. I left him a good-bye note to give to them.

"What happened to the dogs?

"They shot them," he said, pointing to one of the neighbor's trailers.

"Why?"

"I don't knooowwww." He slammed the door.

The hide of a goat that Herman had butchered a few weeks earlier was still draped over the porch railing. We had all gathered outside to watch. Herman dragged the animal by the scruff of its neck, its legs tied together. "A decent meal," he offered as the occasion, and that was as a good a reason as any. Harolyn slit its throat, then sawed off its head. Herman had gutted and skinned the animal. Blood covered his arms like wet paint, and he smiled at the absurdity of it. The sky was blue and everyone watched. It had been a nice moment.

☐ As I headed north to Monument Valley on the Arizona-Utah border, pickup trucks raced by me with cargo beds full of children. They were wrapped in red blankets and waved ecstatically as they passed, hair flapping in the wind, skin the color of wheat. I drove past road signs for places called Many Farms, Sweetwater, and Two Grey Hills; past young girls setting up roadside jewelry stands and men on horseback guiding herds of sheep; past purple valleys, smoldering red mesas, and an eighty-mile stretch of desert, notable only for occupying what Edward Abbey, the agrarian anarchist, called "a beautiful blank space on my map."

Another trailer experience was out of the question. I had enough poverty pictures, decided to choose a family rather than have one chosen for me, to drive around until coming upon a photogenic homestead, then ask to stay. That homestead appeared a dozen miles southwest of Monument Valley, after a series of random turns along unmarked dirt roads; a lovely mud hogan that sat between a large, circular sheep pen and what looked like a chicken coop. There was a trailer on the lot, but it was small and well kept. I knocked on the hogan's wooden door. No answer.

When I turned to leave, a blue pickup truck pulled behind my Jeep. Two men stared from the cab. I waved. When they emerged, they headed towards the sheep pen, prepared to ignore me. The older of the two was tall and bulky, with black hair that hung straight and silky from a center part. "Excuse me. Sorry to intrude." They slowed enough for me to catch up, for me to blurt out my request. They stared through black sunglasses. I was the person nobody wanted on their property. The desperate-looking man asking if there are any gutters he can clean. The smiling, snow-white pair clutching the Book of Mormon. Worse. I had come to live with them.

There was whispering in *Dine,* their native language. More staring. "You can stay on the couch in the trailer," the tall one said, "if that's okay with my other son. He'll be back later." They walked off. I sat in my car, waiting. The sandstone turned orange, rouge, dark. There were crickets and so many stars. I read by flashlight, made a peanut-butter-and-jelly sandwich on the hood of my car, listened to the radio. A pair of headlights jiggled up the road, paused at the sight of a strange car, a strange person. A man hopped out of the passenger seat, and when he entered the hogan, there was a brief leak of warm light, soft and flickering, like that of a campfire. The car drove off. I was reclined in the passenger seat when the tall man with the long black hair knocked on the door and told me I could stay.

His name was Clayton Wallace, he was in his early fifties, and he worked as a councilman for the Oljeto, Utah, Chapter House. He also herded sheep, a task that didn't prove photographically rewarding, as the sheep spread themselves too thin for the camera. Clayton's wife, Vanessa, did a fair share of shepherding as well. She was weathered and diminutive, the red velveteen blouse she wore most days draping off her shoulders, as if from a hanger. She didn't speak English, though she smiled and nodded a lot. And she was kind enough to let me picture her brushing Clayton's hair, which she did twice a week, outside, on those mornings he washed it. They were uninhibited before the camera; no deer-in-the-headlights stares or embarrassed guffaws.

For the first few days my inability to take full advantage of their unaffected behavior, of this pristine environment, to record something more than a mundane act in a beautiful setting, resurrected familiar pangs of self-loathing. We are neurotic children, photographers, our emotions never straying far from illusions of total defeat. Of a career lost, a life in ruins. Particularly during those projects we have yet to get our arms around. Perhaps it is a perverse stimulus, this cloud of dissatisfaction that hovers above our heads: an incentive to keep looking, trying, creating. There are better pictures out there, always. We know this because we see them in our minds, an omnipresent, cerebral slide show of impossible images and unachieved scenarios. Though six weeks into this project I no longer felt inspired. I felt drained. Impotent. Unable to produce.

The clouds lifted by chance on a Sunday morning, just moments before I was to drive to Monument Valley. Through my windshield I noticed Clayton's sons carrying armfuls of wood behind their hogan. They were heating a pile of smooth river rocks, draping a thick blanket over the entrance to a sweat lodge. Some of Clayton's fellow council members were there, chatting, poking at the fire, undressing. They do a sweat here every week, one told me, and I rushed back to the Jeep for my gear. It was not purposeful, Clayton's neglecting to tell me of this practice, despite my many requests to photograph something, anything, halfway visual. Like my other host families, the Wallaces didn't seem to recognize those parts of their lives that an outside observer might find interesting.

"Don't take a picture of my asshole," Clayton joked as he stripped, which I guessed meant the rest would be okay. He cinched his hair into a ponytail, tied his foreskin closed around the head of his penis with a strand of yarn, then crawled on hands and knees into the sweat lodge. The others joined him for the first of three rounds. From their earthen sanctum there came songs, deep and guttural, like those of Tibetan monks, and after fifteen minutes the men reemerged damp and dazed. They rolled themselves in the sand, which stuck to their bodies like flour, then lay face-up in the noon sun. One of the men asked me to join them, and though I was eager to photograph, saying no seemed an unwise option. I stripped naked and tried with much resolve, and little success, to tie the ceremonial yarn around my foreskin. This ritual was written for the uncircumcised and that little boyhood snip had left me short-skinned.

"Muslim?" one of the Indians asked.

"Me? No. Why?

"'Cause you look it. And you're circumcised."

"They do this to everybody." I made a snipping motion with my fingers.

"What for?"

"Well . . . they used to think it prevented disease. And stopped kids from beating off."

"Does it work?

"Nope." There was laughter, the first I'd heard in two months. I pushed in hard with my thumb, got the lasso of yarn in position and yanked it shut.

The inside of the sweat was tight, black, suffocating. The air seared my nostrils and dried my lungs. There was no light. Wet skin pressed against mine, twitching with the inflections of songs and emitting a sour odor. Sweat dribbled into my eyes. Voices raised and lowered. Bodies shifted positions, struggled to find space, as if the slick, naked lot of us were balled in a womb. I covered my face. Eventually the carpet lifted and there was brightness, a nuclear blast of white light, and we emerged in a world with air so cool, abundant, perfumed with cedar and piñon. We rolled like kids in the dirt, and the desert clung like a garment.

While the others continued their ritual, I thought it time to began mine, and though my history in photojournalism was by then still short, I was quite sure I had never, nor would ever, look so certifiable while holding a camera. Sugarcoated in orange sand, wearing only knee-high cowboy boots, I felt like a deranged stripper—one with a strand of yarn holding back the goods.

But the pictures! There the men were, sprawled on the ground before me, a quarry immodest enough to excuse my own appearance. As landscapes go, it had great personal value, this desert of naked Indians, waking me from my malaise like a defibrillator to the chest. This is what photographers desire. Always this moment, when time and money and labor are suddenly rewarded. When that dark and demoralizing gap between bumbling intruder and privileged witness is finally bridged. When the images lie before you, *right there,* and for five, maybe ten seconds, while hurriedly setting the correct exposure, while assessing the angle and lifting the camera and preparing to fire that first burst of frames, you hear a song of success in your mind: *Oh yes, oh yes, oh yes.* There is no more indelible experience for the photojournalist, this brief and elusive rapture, this conquest before the long-sought lay, this open-field dash just as the end zone emerges, all pretty and green—yours for the taking.

The project fell into place from there, as these things have a way of doing. Long-sought situations arose as if on cue—a wedding, a song and dance (or Navajo pow-wow), a Christian revival, a tribal police ride-along, even a group of men building a hogan in Monument Valley. Then one morning I awoke with the most liberating realization: I had enough goddamn pictures. Within moments I was on the road, then calling Deirdre from a payphone outside a Burger King, telling her I was finished, was coming to see her, would make it there by Easter Sunday.

I rambled east the rest of the day, following four-wheel-drive trails over the Chuska Mountains, then descending into the San Juan Basin. This was the far northeast corner of the Rez, the land so flat I could see Shiprock, the eroded remains of a giant volcano, some twenty miles out. The Navajo believe Shiprock is the petrified remains of a flying monster, rising phoenix-like from the New Mexican desert. They call it *Tse Bit Ai,* "rock with wings." I drove to its foundation, stared straight up and watched clouds sail in fast motion past its pinnacle. It looked gothic and hideous, as if warning the curious not to continue. That gave me satisfaction, that I was returning from the opposite direction. I climbed a small buttress and ate dinner—red beans and fry bread—while Shiprock threw its shadow east like an arrow.

eight

burma

The first time I saw Bagan, the deserted, thousand-year-old remains of what was once the grandest religious city in Asia, I was flat on my back in an oxcart. Which meant I couldn't actually *see* Bagan, all the Buddhist monoliths rising from fields of millet. I only saw the spires passing above me, all dreamlike and pretty. Some were white and steepled, like the Mormon Tabernacle; some silver and shiny, like a giant Hershey's Kiss; some red-brick and crumbled, like a Civil War bastion in the Deep South.

There was no sound but the clop of hoofs and the twitter of birds, and I was mad at myself for ignoring the warning signs. I had felt this rising in my body for months but didn't slow down, and the repressed sicknesses and fatigue of a year's worth of traveling now manifested themselves all at once in a kind of corporal crash. And literal one. When I lumbered off an all-night bus from Mandalay, I missed the last step, fell flat on my face, then threw up. I'd never felt worse in my life. I was cold though it was already hot and my clothes were damp with sweat. My head felt swollen, dizzy, ready to split, my stomach gaseous, my throat burning. I thought I had malaria. Nasty stuff, that Larium, but I should have been taking it. When two nice young men helped me into the oxcart and sent me off to the hospital, I fell right asleep. Only maybe I didn't, as I remember those spires.

☐ For the first six weeks of my internship at *U.S. News & World Report,* I had sat behind a desk that someone had placed rather thoughtlessly at the far end of a sixth-floor hallway, praying for an assignment yet fearful to complain I hadn't gotten any, and pretending to read the latest issue of the magazine whenever I heard someone approaching. I had made the rounds of the picture editors, all eleven of them, showing my portfolio and asking for assignments. Any assignments. The editors were chatty and encouraging, as friendly a bunch as a photographer could hope for, though none of them picked up the phone and dialed my extension. Back then, there were no office computers for Web surfing, and the hallway in which I was relegated had no TVs to watch the news. So I sat there much as I had in my parents' basement, tucked away from the world while everyone else went to work.

U.S. News had six staff photographers in D.C. at the time, plus a half dozen contractors (photographers guaranteed a certain amount of shooting days each year) spread about the country. The D.C. crew seemed to have paired off by age and character. There were Dustin and Poss, the young'uns: handsome, whip-smart, and motivated, as likely to jest about their assignments as they were to diss Washington (nowhere to eat, nothing to do, everything is better in New York); Ted and Gilles, the fortysomethings: breezy, sweet-souled, and absorbed with family, or so their Monday-morning weekend roundups implied (took the kids camping, skiing, wind surfing); and Lloyd and Mack, the old-timers: white-haired, tough-tongued, and eager to mentor, as well as to spin yarns from yesteryear (so there I was in the Oval with Dick Nixon, outside the Dallas jail that held Lee Harvey Oswald, at the Munich Olympics with the Black September kidnappers).

The boys, as they were collectively known, were chatty and talented, team players all, which is something of a rarity in the profession. I desperately wanted to be part of the club. But while they ran back and forth to assignments, reappearing periodically with their catch—rolls of exposed chrome sealed in a white *U.S. News* film envelope—their brows sweaty, their movements rushed, their expressions surprised to find me still sitting behind my hallway desk, in my editor-imposed exile, I figured I wasn't long for lasting.

On my first day, Lloyd, one of the old-timers, had an assignment on Capitol Hill and was kind enough to let me tag along. He'd help me get a temporary Hill credential, he said, and show me how to get around the place. I wondered if I would survive the drive there: when someone cut off his car on Constitution Avenue, Lloyd morphed into a geriatric version of Freddie Krueger, first trying to change lanes to catch up with the offender—an attempt that heavy traffic thwarted—and then putting as little space as possible between his front bumper and the offender's rear one. "Bite my ass!" he screamed out the window. I liked him instantly.

After we parked, Lloyd pulled his cameras from the trunk and threw the gear around his shoulders and neck. His cameras had elastic straps, which were not unlike mini-bungee cords, and when we ran across an intersection to beat the light, Lloyd's gear took flight, bouncing this way and that, clanking, nay, slamming together, metal against metal, metal against glass, glass against glass. And Lloyd didn't seem the least concerned. I later learned that the local Nikon reps, the ones with the Sisyphean task of repairing his gear, had nicknamed him Captain Impact. "We're having fun now!" Lloyd shouted while we ran.

Lloyd talked fast, too fast, with each sentence cutting off the one that preceded it. "Okay," he began, "this is Dirksen and that building's Russell and the Hill has its own subway, did you know that? You grew up here and you didn't know that? Well, you catch it in the basement of the Capitol by the ah . . . from ah . . . well, fuck, I don't know where you catch it, but you can take it from the Capitol to Dirksen or to Russell. Though for Hart it's easier just to walk from Dirksen 'cause Hart and Dirksen are connected. Got it? Oh and if you're going to Hart bring lots of 64T (tungsten-balanced slide film). Same for the shithouse (the White House) and man is it a goat fuck (crowded) over there. But at least it's well lit. Good times. Good times! Anyway not so much here. Darker than a monkey's ass if you ask me so always bring your sticks (tripod). I plant the long glass (300 mm lens) on the sticks, but you can do whatever you want. Hell, I don't care. Put your 20 on it for all I care. Do what you want. Got it? That's the idea and where's your camera? You're a photographer and you don't have your camera? What if somebody jumps out a building?"

I pretended to absorb everything while praying to God I didn't get an assignment on Capitol Hill before the weekend, when I could figure out the place for myself. The next day I went to the White House, where fortysomething Gilles was on duty and needed a second man to cover a state visit from Boris Yeltsin. Gilles handed me a ladder in the press briefing room and told me to wait by a set of white double doors. When they opened, he said, carry the ladder to the South Lawn and set it up to secure a photo position for myself to shoot President Clinton and President Yeltsin together. I stood there for half an hour when a call came over the intercom, telling those who wanted to preset for the event to gather at the said double doors. Photographers came from nowhere, swarming the doors and butting in front of me, and suddenly I was last in line. When the doors opened, they speed-walked past the Rose Garden, jousting each other with their ladders, then one started to run and several acted in kind, sprinting across the South Lawn, their ladders clanking into one another's, their credentials swinging from their necks.

Approaching a chain-link stanchion, they lifted their ladders waist-high and slammed them down on the opposite side. I was so surprised by this dash, so predetermined to make a professional first impression on my new colleagues, that I walked the whole route and was left with the worst position, one that would offer a profile of President Clinton and no view of his Russian counterpart.

"So is this how it works at the White House?" I asked the photographer who'd started the stampede.

"What?" he said, not so much as a question but a statement, as in "Got a problem with it?" Since this was just a preset everyone drifted back inside, everyone except me, as I was now trying to figure out how to rectify the situation. Gilles came to check on me and I pointed to my ladder.

"I got the worst position." Gilles picked up my ladder and squeezed it just to the side of the photographer who had started the mad dash.

"Now you got the best."

The internship slid downhill from there, at least until mid-July. I poked around the Hill, the White House, our in-house studio, though these beats were already occupied and nobody needed my help. I read the Associated Press daybook, which gave a daily rundown of news events in the city, and photographed those that looked interesting, though the editors didn't have much use for them. And I sat at my desk, sat there until 6 p.m., generally, then drifted back home to Deirdre. We were sharing a dreary studio apartment across the Potomac in Rosslyn, one with a twin bed inside a walk-in closet. For an entire summer we slept in a closet. Then she got a gig with the *Baltimore City Paper* and moved up to Charm City. I wasn't worried at first, figured we would do the weekend thing. But then the editors started calling.

My first official assignment for *U.S. News* was an exterior of a Kentucky Fried Chicken, and I brought back enough pictures to make a mini–photo essay. Next came a military story in New York, then a Civil War reenactment in Virginia, then a congressional race in South Carolina, and just like that the barriers were broken, and I was working every day. When the internship was almost up and I was sending cover letters to every major newspaper in the country, I happened by Finnegan Grove in the hallway. "Don't go anywhere, okay?" That was it. Four words and I had one of the most coveted positions in photojournalism: a staff job with *U.S. News & World Report*.

☐ The magazine's headquarters was an eight-story building of red brick and green glass, more suburban-looking than city, positioned between Foggy Bottom and Georgetown and fronting a park known as P Street Beach, whose more wooded parts were popular as a conjugal hideaway with the local gay community. The building was large enough to have its own parking garage, cafeteria, and photo lab, yet the offices never seemed very busy, or even fully occupied. My image of a major newsroom was still that of *All the President's Men*—a giant field of messy desks and cubicles with reporters typing madly, a phone to each ear, while editors groundhogged above their partitions, impatient and red-faced, wondering where in God's name was the copy. Maybe that's how it was at a newspaper. But at *U.S. News,* the offices had all the nervous energy of a public library.

The magazine was in third place in the newsweekly wars, with fewer subscribers than both *Time* and *Newsweek.* But nobody seemed overly concerned. On the contrary, the theory was to let those two duke it out while we followed our own path, filled our own niche. The magazine had made a name for itself with its annual college and hospital rankings, its inside-the-Beltway coverage (*Time* and *Newsweek* are based in New York), and its putting itself above placing Hollywood glitterati on the cover. Though it didn't have near the resources of *Time* and *Newsweek,* the sass of the *Economist,* the pop stardom of the *New Republic,* it did have brains. A future ad for the magazine read, "Smart News for Smart Readers," and I thought that was an accurate description.

Grove wasted no time throwing me into the mix, sending me to Haiti my second month, then around the country with President Clinton, then around the country on my own. The last was an assignment that would have made Jack Kerouac grimace—a series of portraits in forty-two different states. And there was no budget for the project, so I'd have to drive the whole thing. I made the trip in two giant, asymmetrical loops, one east of the Mississippi and one west. It took me two-and-a-half months, pausing for additional assignments here and there, as well as to get some private time with all those obscure national monuments I'd never get to see otherwise, like White Sands and Devil's Tower and Craters of the Moon.

When I finally made it to Baltimore to see Deirdre, I shouldn't have been surprised to feel a chill wind in the air. She was there by herself, not a needy person but in want of companionship, having come to the East Coast so we could be a couple. Yet in the past year we had spent just a handful of weekends together. We were hanging on by a thread, I suddenly realized, and things were only going to get worse.

"So what are you gonna do with all your comp time?" It was a gray and windy Sunday in October, and we were sitting idle on a Druid Hill Park swingset. I was about to head back to D.C. I knew what she wanted me to say, that I was thinking we could use the time to get away. Just the two of us. Go to the Outer Banks, maybe. Or just stay here; lie around like lovers do, in bed until late morning, drinking coffee from oversized mugs and reading the *New York Times*. But I was too afraid to slow down, too eager to prove myself.

"I'm thinking of Burma." I looked at her, but she didn't look back.

"Burma," she said, nodding her head and staring at the ground. A lock of curls blew into her face, and she let it hang there, her hands clutching the cold metal chains. She had on a black coat, black pants, black shoes. It felt like a funeral.

"They're offering four-week tourist visas for like the first time ever, and it's enough time to photograph the whole country. I was thinking maybe I could do a travel piece and sell it back to the magazine." She nodded more, poked at some fallen leaves with her feet.

"So when are you doing this?"

"I was thinking over the holidays. When it's quiet at the office."

She glanced at the gray sky, then back to her feet. "Then straight back to work, I suppose."

"This is how it is with photojournalism, you know."

"This isn't how it is. This is how you make it."

"I want to keep my job, yes. Then slow down later. I will slow down."

"I hate this."

"Think of it as a residency."

"I don't want to do this."

"And what do you do when the two loves of your life appear at once?"

"I don't know, Jim."

"I promise I have it in me, to make you happy."

"I don't want to do this!"

"I promise things will get better."

"Jim, really." Finally she lifted her eyes to mine. "I don't see us lasting until then."

☐ Though the country's much-touted "Visit Myanmar Year 1996" (Myanmar being what that ruling junta call Burma) was just a month away, the soldiers in Rangoon's Mingaladon Airport had yet to receive their civility lesson. On discovering my film and camera gear, a customs agent had doubts about the "tourist" part of my tourist visa and ordered a soldier to squire me into a private room. He used the barrel of his rifle to rummage through my bags, which didn't prove a very effective method. Then he stared at me for the length of time it took him to smoke a cigarette, which felt like a long time indeed. "Whiskey," he said finally. I had whiskey, that being the international currency of payoffs and bribes, and relinquished one of my duty-free bottles of Red Label. Then he relinquished me.

As encounters with Burmese soldiers go, mine was better than most. For much of the previous four decades they'd terrified millions of Burmese, enforced the orders of a repressive military regime, and kept foreign tourists, journalists, and businessmen at bay. Not that these soldiers could take all the credit for Burma's staunch xenophobia. Dictators, drug lords, and antigovernment insurgents had done their fair share as well. In the nine years since Burmese soldiers had massacred three thousand prodemocracy demonstrators in Rangoon, civil strife had been squashed and the hermetic nation was cautiously opening its doors. Like its neighbors Laos and Vietnam, Burma was banking on tourism to jump-start its economy. The country had an annual per capita income of $230, one of the lowest in Southeast Asia. And human rights–inspired boycotts on Burmese goods had crippled its exports—legal exports, that is. At the time, American Drug Enforcement Administration officials believed that as much as 50 percent of the heroin on U.S. streets came from Burma.

The idea that a rogue, repressive nation was hoping an influx of foreign travelers would help alleviate its economic woes seemed an interesting story, and a controversial one. In preparation for Visit Myanmar Year 1996, the country's military leaders reportedly forced much of the citizenry to repair, and pay for, infrastructure improvements themselves. Western human rights groups wanted visitors to boycott the country as a form of economic sanction. As a traveler—and a journalist—I didn't believe in blacklisting such a place, any place, no matter how politically incorrect to visit. How did isolating countries like Burma—or Cuba or Iran—help them to democratize? Exposure to foreign travelers means exposure to foreign ideals, foreign scrutiny. And anyway, the majority of visitors to Burma are backpackers— the light of foot and tight of wallet. The likelihood of these ragamuffins financing Burma's military junta was zero to none.

Though I was feeling a bit rundown, I arose before dawn each morning, hired a three-wheeled motor scooter, and tooled around town, looking for photographs. From a purely photographic standpoint, Burma was a wonderland. A treasure trove. An ethereal, old-Asian mix of agrarian landscapes, untouristed temples, and wildly handsome people. For weeks I didn't have a bad shooting day, not one. Each night I returned to my hotel well after dark, weary and famished, exposed rolls of Fujichrome stuffed in every pocket. Though I felt ever worse, was getting the kind of hot flashes I've since learned only come when I've reached an extreme state of exhaustion, the pictures were so plentiful that I didn't want to stop. I'd rest when I got back to Bangkok, maybe splurge for a stay at the Oriental. Then, on the all-night bus to Bagan, my body gave out.

The doctor spoke English, which surprised me. She stayed with me for two hours, doing tests, giving me fluids. She told me I didn't have malaria but I did have just about everything else—giardia, strep throat, influenza. She gave me an injection of something, and a little bag made of newspaper that was full of pills. On the outside she wrote "white = aspirin, yellow = Fasigyn, pink = penicillin." She wouldn't take any money. She had a horse cart take me to a hotel, where I got a room with a ceiling fan and a private bathroom and slept for the better part of four days. The hotel staff knocked and opened my door periodically, delivering unordered trays of fried noodles, 7-Up, and egg-drop soup.

When I emerged from my hotel room, my body felt as light as a balloon, as if my growing sicknesses had been weight belts and now that they were off I was less bound by gravity. Or maybe it was just the pills. In a predawn fog I pedaled one of the hotel's one-speed bikes into the quiet, dusty plain of Bagan. It was a dream world, an alternate reality where modern life didn't exist: no cars or touts or souvenir stalls; no ticket booths to pass through; no signs saying do not enter, touch, climb, explore, or have any fun whatsoever. Just brown paths winding through green fields, themselves laid out between the remains of a Buddhist kingdom, abandoned and overgrown.

I walked inside the biggest temple I could find, a Mayan-like red-brick pyramid that my *Lonely Planet* guide said was called Dhammayangyi. I used a flashlight to follow a narrow tunnel to a set of stairs, then climbed up and up, reemerging on the outside of the structure for the last half to the top. There I hung my legs over the edge and stared at the crowns of temple after temple, the palm fronds, the morning mist rising. It was perplexing,

a site on par with the Taj Mahal, the Great Wall, the pyramids—
yet without any of the fame, or apparently the popularity. There
were 2,217 temples in front of me and virtually no other people. What more could any photographer ask?

☐ The magazine bought my story. They had passed on my initial proposal, but now that the project was complete, now that I
had made the trip, written the story, taken the photographs, they
agreed to publish it. Though I was on staff, they had to pay me
space rates, since I went on my own time and dime, and I reinvested the money on a project in Cuba. And when they bought
that one, I reinvested the money on a project in India, and when
they bought that one, I decided not to push my luck any further,
confident I had proven myself a hard worker. And just in the nick
of time, as there was a new sheriff in town. Madison West, a picture editor from *Time,* replaced Finnegan Grove as the director
of photography. I liked her immediately, even though she cut one
of the photographers (another shooter retired, while yet another
moved to the word side, leaving us with just four staffers). The
way I saw it, cost-cutting was a new reality of the business. *Time*
and *Newsweek* had just whacked all their staff photographers but
one. Trimming our staff, while regrettable, seemed wiser than
risking all our jobs. Which is to say I thought West was smart—
and tough, didn't take shit from anybody. She had a highly com-
petitive vision for the department, and a defined vision is just what
every photo staff needs to ward off the more powerful, though less
visually appreciative, in the building.

   And she kept me just as busy with assignments, which is all
any photographer can ask. Campaigns and impeachments, the

pope in Cuba and the president in China, unification in Hong Kong and Princess Di's funeral in London; some of it was august and some of it was unnerving. I loathed the crush of other photographers, the media frenzies that brought every jackoff with a camera from here to Timbuktu into the same grandstand, the same space of twenty feet. Thankfully West gave me plenty of assignments on the opposite end of the scale—the ones where I could indulge my aloneness and head off in a rental car across Alaska or Utah or Montana—to give my job ballast.

All in all, it was a wonderful time. I had momentum, velocity, force; I was earning accolades from my editors and respect from my peers. I was buzzing around the world, and through the blur of airports and crowds and foreign countries I could see the career I had always wanted, feel the simple and meditative pleasure of a life so singularly focused. I was traveling for a living, being paid to make pictures. I was a photojournalist.

Things turned around for Deirdre and me as well. When I returned from Burma, I handed her a *Lonely Planet* guide for Hawaii, a thank-you trip for not giving up on me, and could feel the doubt in her heart give way to longing. Not because of this tropical carrot, I did realize, but because she had been struggling to reconcile her vision of companionship with the one I had to offer, flawed as it was. And now her eyes, her smile, her hand clutching mine all demonstrated the most coveted ability in any relationship: a willingness to compromise.

Some weeks later, along the long and windy road to Hana— the warm sun flickering through the forest of palm trees like light from a movie projector, Deirdre tanned and tired and dozing off next to me—I realized my skills of compromise were perhaps not as well honed. The excursion had been a way for me to be with her while still feeding my habit after all. And shame be damned—if foreign places were the parameters in which our relationship thrived, then why not?

I was flush with frequent-flier miles, and when I wasn't traveling for work, I was now traveling with her, and no matter what national park we fled to—Denali, Yellowstone, Banff, Olympic, Canyonlands, Rocky Mountain, the Smokies—it was never enough. Packing up our tent and getting on our return flight felt as premature and unnatural as stopping a piss midstream, as pulling yourself from one of those dead-to-the-world afternoon naps. It was wholly against my biology, and the moment I got home, the very afternoon I got back to Washington, I walked to Borders bookstore, bought a travel guide for the next destination, and started planning.

Soon enough Deirdre was back with me in D.C., had landed her gig with the *St. Louis Post-Dispatch,* and was off and running herself: Senate races and presidential campaigns, economic change in Cuba and political upheaval in the Middle East. Her travels made mine less taxing, lifted the veil of guilt that hung over each departure. All at once our love was portable, capable of greater and greater distances, of longer separations. She was happy, I was happy; it worked. For a time anyway. We had infinite energy and were bursting with life and love and tales from our ventures, and it felt so exhilarating, to keep my foot off the brake, to keep gathering speed, moving and shooting, moving and shooting. Then rendezvousing with Deirdre in D.C. and feeling that divine togetherness, the worth enhanced from its rarity. Then running off with her to some exotic locale.

Slowing down and having kids was something other people did. Older people. Office people. The well-shaven ones commuting in their SUVs, with country-club dues to cover and great green lawns to maintain. The ones who went on cruises with other couples. Or on wild Vegas weekends with their buddies, trying to convince themselves, and each other, that they weren't really leading staid suburban lives. Screw that. I'd have rather been shot in the head. Had my nuts chopped off. America's myopic masses, the elements of their safe and insulated existence passing before their eyes like Plato's shadows. There was a great big world out there, and I wanted to see every last part of it.

Even proposing to Deirdre was a travel opportunity, one driven by love, I later assured her, because with so many places yet to see, how silly to propose in Washington. So off to Ko Samui, to the porch of a teak beach house, the moon glittering off the Gulf of Siam, the whole of our journey still before us. And after she accepted and we ventured farther south, down the lush and sultry tail of Thailand, the limestone cliffs, the long-tail boats, the emerald lagoons, I flew off to India, to Kashmir, another assignment. She flew home alone.

nine

california

The most distinguishing visual characteristic of Van Nuys, California, is that it doesn't have one. This valley town, the first you reach when taking the 405 from L.A. over the Santa Monica Mountains, is a featureless, quasi-urban mishmash of strip malls, office parks, and windowless warehouses, stretching for miles without the slightest aesthetic relief—a tall building, say, or a sizable swath of green space. There is little for the eye to grab hold of, or for the brain to use as a base for establishing a sense of direction, so it's as if the town is saying, "Nothing to see here. Now move along." Which of course means there is something to see.

Indeed, the true heart of Van Nuys, and its claim to fame, beats, screams, throbs behind closed doors. And after another failed attempt to peek inside some of these buildings and photograph the goings on, I was less concerned with the town's commercial camouflage than with how to break the bad news to my boss. The project had been my idea.

In the spring of 1999, much of the world's attention was focused on the tiny Yugoslavian province of Kosovo. NATO forces were bombing Serb targets inside the province, and the Serbs, in turn, were driving Kosovars out of their homes. By mid-April a half million refugees had fled Kosovo for neighboring Montenegro, Macedonia, and Albania. It was the year's most dramatic photo story, and the assignment went to a Washington freelancer named Danielle Lee. At the same time I got assigned to the Tidal Basin to photograph a rogue beaver that was devouring some of Washington's famed cherry trees.

I spent five minutes on a Thursday afternoon shooting a courtesy roll of a half-devoured tree trunk, then lay down on the white and sun-warmed marble steps of the Jefferson Memorial, bitter and depressed. Like most Washingtonians I don't make an effort to visit the Jefferson Memorial, yet when I find myself there, I have trouble leaving. Its waterfront perch makes for a pacific retreat, especially on April afternoons like that one, when the first blossoms have fallen from the cherry trees and are drifting across the footpaths in fragrant swirls. The tourists were out en masse, but confined themselves to picnic blankets beneath the blossom canopy. I watched a Japanese shutterbug in the distance convince his young partner to climb one of the trees. She put her foot in his hands and pulled herself atop a heavy branch, then squatted to keep her head beneath the petals, her right hand holding the trunk for balance, her left clutching shut the bottom of her dress. He lay in the grass beneath her and angled his camera upwards. Everyone's a fucking photographer.

Why hadn't the boss sent me? What was wrong with me? In a few years would I pinpoint this day as the start of a slow and steady decline: first to shitty assignments, then to no assignments, then to imposing my skills on credulous tourists? "Here . . . let me do that. Give me your camera and go stand under the tree together. Of course I don't mind. Yes, I know where to push. Okay, looks good. Smile! Now give me twenty bucks." I would be the photo equivalent of those guys who flag down parking spaces for you. The ones you don't care to engage though you pay them off anyway, lest you return to discover your car antenna wrapped like a bow around your windshield wipers.

I needed to put the brakes on this train wreck, considered taking time off and going to Macedonia on my own, but then thought that might betray my desperation. Or come off as spiteful. And anyway, I didn't have the money; Deirdre and I had just bought a little house in Friendship Heights. I figured it would be better to pursue something the magazine would pay for, something completely opposite what everybody else was doing. And the furthest thing from war, I supposed, was love—or at least good sex.

For years I had tossed around the idea of a project on the porn industry, but I lived on the wrong coast for such an endeavor. And by now it had gotten a lot of coverage, what with the recent release of the movie *Boogie Nights.* Internet porn, on the other hand, had not yet received its fifteen minutes. It was timely, as the dot-com boom was in full tilt, and it wasn't confined to L.A. Cybersex sites were emerging from every state in the country. It also had genuine news value; the Web practically owed its popularity to porn. I cabbed back to the office to do some research.

At the time there were some thirty thousand adult sites, generating a billion plus in profits and comprising up to 70 percent of all Web traffic. E-pornographers were e-pioneers, among the first to turn a profit on the Web, to offer secure online credit card transactions, to offer streaming video. Historically speaking, this wasn't surprising: it's an unpopular truth that porn has driven communications technologies for hundreds of years. It was the smutmongers' preference for the VHS videotape that helped make it the format of choice over rival Sony Betamax. They also helped popularize DVDs, and before that motion pictures, and before that photography. In the nineteenth century, pornography was in such demand that cowboys would shell out more for a nude picture of a woman than they would to sleep with one.

I e-mailed a proposal to my boss suggesting a story for the business section—normally a black hole for photojournalism—and she was interested enough to let me piggyback out-of town shoots onto other assignments. The real question was how to handle this hot potato. As unlikely as it seems, the mainstream print media have never had a strong appetite for sexually suggestive photojournalism. I've never understood it—why a medium so dependent on images of violence for its drama, from wars to riots to natural disasters, is so shy about the culture of sex. One could easily shrug off the dichotomy as a measure of news value: wars matter more than sexual issues. But to do so would be to ignore the puritanical intolerance that helps keep their appetite for these stories low in the first place.

In photojournalism, the old adage "sex sells" seems to have been replaced with a knee-jerk "people don't want to see that at the breakfast table." And I didn't buy that it was okay for readers, particularly of the newsmags, to look at a picture of another human being who's been blown to bits but not a news picture that shows someone's posterior. In this manner even advertising gets away with more than photojournalism, and issues involving sexuality certainly matter more than selling perfume.

I thought this a good opportunity to try and show sex without really showing it, to be there while e-pornographers made their product and photograph the exact same situation, but in a way that wouldn't steam any spectacles. Writers do this kind of thing all the time—use their communication skills to make palatable an unsavory scene. How difficult could it be, making PG-13 pictures of X-rated moments?

▢ While I wouldn't call myself a connoisseur of porn, neither am I one who pretends not to peek. So the sites—and the sights—I encountered during my research weren't overly surprising, though it was satisfying to look at them worry-free at the office. The Web pages fell into two categories, amateur and pro: the latter of the big-haired, bad-boob-job variety we've come to associate with the world of rental porn. Some sites were the creations of ex-porn stars, others of production companies like Vivid Video, whose photo galleries were meant largely to promote their movies, which one could now watch online for a modest fee. Only a few of them had as yet branched into genuine interactivity, where a viewer watching a striptease, say, could tell the model what to take off and when to do it.

The amateur stuff spoke more to the freewheeling, anything-goes culture that made the Net so revolutionary. Some came from mom-and-pop exhibitionists, stripping or getting it on in their homes, their cars, their trailers before a little webcam. Other sites were the full-time job of budding entrepreneurs, enlisting their friends and neighbors for online love-ins. They displayed a genuine savvy for filling niche markets, these homegrown Larry Flynts, posting sites on swingers, sorority babes, biker chicks, lonely housewives, horny Catholic schoolgirls, and women who visit public places without any underwear and allegedly don't know someone is pointing a video camera up their skirt. Yet for members of a subculture accustomed to displaying perversions online, they were oddly standoffish to my e-mailed requests to photograph them for the magazine.

Jen of jen-n-dave.com, a cutesy Maryland couple whose site promised "a boobie guarantee," responded that they'd had terrible experiences with the media, and anyway I came off in my e-mail as "very white collar." Rob, aka Lance Starr on cum2oasis.com, a site featuring an unsavory thing named Oasis who, on designated "slut days," got it on with strangers in bars and bathrooms, among other places, said "extra cameras make Web people nervous" and demanded a guarantee that their URL be published in the article. And their friends' URLs too. Heather of kissus.com, where this Baywatch blond gets intimate with her girlfriends, riffed for a bit about the industry becoming "hippocritical [sic]" before ending with an encouraging "I have so much to share with you." I never heard from her again. Ditto from the folks at Slutclub, Babenet, Liveteen, Youngwives, Besthardcore, Teensteam, Karasxxx, Seemorebutts, and Voyeurdorm. It took another two weeks and seventeen inquiries before an Ocean City, Maryland, man named Jon David, the owner of the wetlands, which advertised itself as the place "where wives get naked," rang me at the office. "Well, goddamn—come on out!"

☐ Jon David (JD) Messner and his wife Cherie had earned much local notoriety of late. Just a few months earlier the mayor of a tiny Eastern Shore town called Snow Hill, the self-proclaimed "Antique Capital of the World," lost his reelection bid after allegedly facilitating one of their X-rated shoots. That mayor, Craig Johnson, also happened to be a sheriff's deputy and was accused of procuring a police car to serve as a prop. Apparently the people of Snow Hill didn't take kindly to seeing Cherie, naked except for handcuffs and a police nightstick, rolling around on top of a Worcester County Sheriff's Department squad car, and Johnson was promptly arrested and charged with two counts of malfeasance.

And just three weeks before my visit, and one day after JD posted a public sign seeking more models for his site, the town of Ocean City cited him for using his office as a photo studio, a violation of zoning ordinances that carried a fine of $500 a day. According to the AP story I read, Ocean City officials were "worried the sign Messner posted will tarnish the city's image." This is a city, mind you, cluttered with signs advertising such class establishments as Hooters, Brass Balls Saloon, Big Peckers, BJ's South, BJ's on the Water, and Bearded Clam. Ocean City is a boardwalk town, a destination where people you probably wouldn't care to vacation with go to swim in above-ground, parking-lot pools, buy T-shirts that say "I'm with Fuck Face," and get drunk on peach coolers. JD's sign was as out of place as a whore at a brothel.

I met JD on a Thursday afternoon at his office, where he was hurrying a model named Jasmine into the studio for a lunchtime striptease. He was short and stocky, with a thin mustache that was disconnected from a second patch of hair that sat Civil War style near the bottom of his chin. I'd never met a pornographer before, and was surprised that this one had the Eastern Shore accent most Washingtonians associate with the good folks who live along the Chesapeake Bay, the ones who wear overalls and rubber boots and make their living pulling up crab pots. And JD was down-home, actually, showing off his setup with the excitement of a man who had never expected all this, but now that it was here was determined to keep it that way. He had started up the wetlands two years earlier after losing his job as a cemetery administrator, and very nearly losing his house. First he posted nude pictures of his wife, then of other wives, then of other couples, and before you could say "immoral" his lewd venture was something of a lewd empire, earning him three million clams a year, which I guess made him the savviest waterman around.

JD's studio was in a small, white back room where a single tungsten hotlight blazed into a reflective umbrella. Next to the door, on the floor, was a thin mattress half covered in pillows, and on the other side of the room was an amateur video camera mounted on an amateur tripod. What looked like black plastic garbage bags were duct-taped over the windows. Jasmine squeezed past me through the doorway, smiling, wearing a tight skirt, high-heeled shoes, and sunglasses Lolita-style halfway down her nose. She was pretty in that Mae West, big-boned kind of way, only she was young, in her early twenties, and her hair was long, black, and curly. JD told me the lunchtime striptease was a big draw for businessmen, and Jasmine splayed herself out on the bed, chatting online with a few fans via a computer that was within reach of the mattress. This thing was starting right away, apparently, so I quickly twisted my 20 mm lens onto my camera, loaded a roll of 400 neg, and stuffed a few more rolls in my pocket.

Jasmine's performance began in the sexless manner of a well-rehearsed striptease, all burden and routine, with much writhing on the bed and pulling off of this and that. JD's assistant moved around her with the video camera, and I moved around him, trying to fit them both in with my wide-angle lens, while at the same time blocking her online assets with various articles in the room—the computer monitor, the light stand, the cameraman's head. This became a bit more difficult ten minutes in, when she straddled a Sybian—a giant vibrator mounted to a saddle-shaped stand on the floor. The room began to feel small, what with the all the bucking and screaming, so I gave her some space. Even from outside the studio, where I tried to photograph through the cracked doorway, her performance was too spicy for the palates of *U.S. News* readers, let alone editors. "I love this thing," she called out. "I'm not getting off it!" Just getting off on it, I thought.

To my dismay she stayed true to her word, even after the show was finished and Cherie and I reentered the room. Cherie wanted to make some still pictures, and when she couldn't find her camera, she and the assistant abruptly walked out, leaving me alone with Jasmine and an uncomfortable hum. Jasmine smiled a little, rocking with the slow and steady motion of someone atop a trotting horse. I examined the hotlight as if it held much fascination, then rooted through my camera bag, looking for some imaginary lens, pulling film out of canisters then putting it back in. I alphabetized the releases I had everyone sign.

"Who are you with again?"

"*U.S. News & World Report.*"

"*USA Today?*"

"*U.S. News & World Report.*"

"*U.S. World News?*"

"Sure," I said and she nodded. The hotlight had warmed the small room enough to make my forehead glisten. Jasmine's cheeks were flushed. Black spirals of hair stuck to her face. She picked at her garter belt. That humming. Finally Cherie and JD charged through the door waving their little digital camera.

"All right!" JD proclaimed, clapping his hands once. "Let's do a girl-girl!" Jasmine relinquished her perch while Cherie, still standing, stripped down to her matching checkerboard bra and underwear. This was photographable and I worked the scene quickly before all the clothes came off.

Eventually the ladies settled onto the mattress, entwining their limbs like WWF wrestlers. I shot the scene from the back of the room, on my stomach, using JD's legs to block the lurid parts. And at the time I thought it worked, the e-porn entrepreneur, a pimp for the nineties, looming over his two sirens, coiled around each other like snakes. But on the drive home, when the relief of having completed my first assignment had faded just enough for me to review my performance, I felt a familiar drag on my psyche: my pictures sucked. Why hadn't I gone outside and shot through one of the cracks in the windows? Or through the viewfinder of the video camera? Why hadn't I used my fisheye lens—create the effect of a peep show? Why had I bothered to show up?

My next opportunity didn't come for a few weeks. The magazine sent me to L.A. to make a portrait of Larry Flynt for a business story on Hustler Hollywood, and I stayed out there a few extra days to pursue the project. After finishing with Flynt, I told him about my story idea and tried to hit him up for access to some of the hustler.com sets. He stared at me as if I were speaking Nepalese. I couldn't tell if he didn't hear me, or if his droopy, doped-out expression was a symptom of his injuries. (As fans of porn, Hollywood, and civil liberties know, a white supremacist shot Flynt twice, paralyzing his legs and impeding his speech.) I repeated my request, louder and slower this time, as one would to the resident of a nursing home. And it got me a reaction: Flynt spun his gold wheelchair in the opposite direction and rolled away.

The next day I headed north to the San Fernando Valley, to Van Nuys, the center of the porn universe. My first appointment there was at the headquarters of Vivid Video's interactive media division. Vivid billed itself as the "world's leading producers of adult films and videos," and its Web site was a well-thought-out online library. Subscribers could watch any of the company's productions, thus eliminating every porn consumer's greatest fear: encountering a friend, co-worker, or cohabitator in line at the video store while holding a copy of *Forrest Hump*. This on-demand access to high-budget porn productions—Vivid still shot some of its movies on film, with budgets as high as $200,000— seemed a good way to put in contrast all the down-home, ma-and-pa stuff I planned to shoot. So I had called Vivid's cofounder, David James, looking to get behind-the-scenes access to one of their high-dollar productions.

"I've got something better," he replied in the soft brogue of his native Wales, telling me to meet him at their offices. When I arrived, he led me to a room that at first glance looked like a production studio, with twenty TV monitors stacked on one wall, in between floor-to-ceiling shelves that displayed Vivid's latest releases. Seated in an office chair next to a computer was a lean brunette named Luscious, wearing a black leotard. The outfit was wired on the outside with electrodes, which looked like the kind doctors use to monitor the chest of a heart patient, rather than one's nipples, navel, and crotch, where Luscious was sporting them. "We're hoping this is the future of cybersex right here," James said. Luscious nodded.

It was a cybersex suit, designed to plug into a computer and receive good vibrations right over the Internet. James had a colleague show me a mock-up of the operating software, which included a photograph of a female model over which one could drag one's cursor, click on the desired body part, and activate the corresponding electrode on one's partner's suit. You could even send different kinds of sensations, like heat, tickle, or vibration. It was genuine telesex, a real-life embodiment of "reach out and touch someone."

"This is kind of off-point." James continued the demonstration as if I hadn't said a word, telling me that once they got FCC approval the suit would be big news, that I'd be glad I had the pictures. Like most photojournalists, I'm standoffish when it comes to flacks, or cofounders, treating me like their very own PR photographer. But at this point in my project I couldn't afford to get James's knickers in a wad—I was just desperate enough to keep the guy happy and do his bidding. After setting up a couple of lights, I photographed Luscious all wired for tele-joy, the twenty monitors in the background displaying semiclad women.

Of my repeated postshoot requests to get on one of their sets, James said "Talk to Matt," referring me to their PR guy. Matt politely told me there was nothing going on at the moment, but that he'd just love to work something out for the future. I told him that this story wasn't going to have a future.

On my third day I arranged a meeting with a young pornographer at a Van Nuys Starbucks. He was tall and handsome and escorted me to the set of *Shut Up and Do Me!* Like the skinflicks at Vivid, this porno would be made available for viewing on its production company's Web site—that of Who Dat? Films. Unlike Vivid's high-dollar productions, however, this was a "gonzo" movie, where a couple of neophytes—in this case two white homeboys, one with a backwards baseball cap, the other with a shaved head, baggy shorts, and oversized sneakers—wielding a handheld video camera tape sex scene after sex scene with little to no regard for such production matters as lighting and sequence, let alone script. Gonzo flicks are as creative as a home movie, though without the heart. But at least these smutmongers were allowing me to stay.

"Don't make eye contact with this dude," Mr. Baggy Pants advised, readying his Sony camcorder to record a ménage à trois. "And don't shoot while I'm taping 'cause you'll mess up my audio." Fair enough on both counts, I told him. We were in the bedroom of a private home, though the crew wouldn't reveal their relationship to the owner. Waiting for things to get underway, which at the moment depended on the "meat" to bring himself to an appropriate state of arousal, I noticed a giant mirror on the other side of the room. Tucked into its wooden frame was a series of pictures—the kind you get at the boardwalk from those coin-operated photo booths—of a yuppie couple exchanging kisses. Finally a picture, I thought. If I focused my lens on these happy snaps, I could contrast the lovey-dovey images with the ménage in the reflection, tastefully out of focus. When the taping got underway, the picture came together, and for a few moments I thought this project might have some life. "Don't be photographing his personal items," the director said, peeved.

I took the redeye back to Washington. Grumpy and unable to sleep, I leaned my head against the cold, plastic airplane window, the overnight flight symptoms of pasty mouth and sour stomach adding to my malaise. Instead of hitting this thing out of the park, I'd have to tell West I had struck out. Swung and missed. Whiffed. The story was DOA. I failed. I landed at BWI at 5 a.m., cabbed home, and e-mailed the boss that the story was looking good, but would require a few more trips out west to nail down the pro stuff.

☐ My next assignment in L.A. didn't come for four months. I swung by Van Nuys afterwards, vowing to give the project one final try, and picked up on the set of a Who Dat? production, which happened to be right where I had left off. This one was called *The House of Seven Stiffies,* and in one day they knocked out five scenes in the same villa. There was much on-set drama, with one guy finishing too fast and having to pop a Viagra to tape more lead up, and another who couldn't get it up in the first place for a scene with his real-life girlfriend. The couple were newcomers looking for a quick buck, and the guy had demanded he be his girlfriend's on-camera partner. When he couldn't deliver, he had

to endure the grand humiliation of watching her enjoy the prolonged and inventive services of a surrogate stud.

In the afternoon I made my first decent picture of the project, shooting through a mission-style window into a bedroom
where a tiny redhead named Mika was enduring a ménage. Mika's
partners looked like caricatures from different decades of porn.
There was Mr. Nineties, who had all the sex appeal of a jailhouse
Aryan. The guy was menacing, his buffed body a graffiti wall of
bad tattoos: a green serpent strangling a naked woman, a swastika
dripping blood, a burning cross. Then there was Mr. Eighties,
who had the boyish, clean-cut appeal of early-porn chic, with a
Dorothy Hamill bob and a slim figure to match. Before the scene,
looking to have him sign a release, I found him outside by the pool
in a white robe, smoking some bud. He signed the release without blinking, whereas Mr. Nineties crumpled it in a ball and
bounced it off my chest. I photographed him anyway. The chances
of that cracker picking up a copy of *U.S. News & World Report* were
as high as those of some aging midwestern Republican picking
up a copy of *Tattooed Skinhead*.

I photographed from outside the house looking in. The room
was lit well enough to balance the goings on inside with the scene
at the pool behind me, which you could see in the reflection. The
geometry of the glass, with its many tiny squares and rectangles,
turned the ménage into a kaleidoscope of limbs and flesh. And
it obscured Mr. Nineties' identity. It looked like poor Mika was
working twice as many men, and from her expression I gathered
that's how she felt.

The next day I drove to a rented mansion in Agoura Hills, the
set of a high-dollar Vivid Video "film" called *Best of Me*. Strolling

through the front door, which was wide open, I encountered a large production crew hanging out in the foyer, eating lunch and staring into an adjacent living room where a bed had been plunked into the corner and where a "Vivid Girl" named Raylene was on her back, digging her claws into the sides of some guy's head and smothering his face with her pelvis. At first I thought he was suffocating, what with his hands clutching the sheets in the manner of a death grip, but none of the crew seemed concerned. I didn't know what was going on down there, but if her screams were to be trusted the guy had a tongue that could tie shoelaces. Half encircling the bed were what looked like railroad tracks, on which a cameraman rolled his dolly-mounted 16 mm film camera to record the carnality; a stand-up set for a screw flick. Though I had my Nikon F5 around my shoulder, I didn't want to start burning frames until I alerted the director, so I stood in the foyer with the rest of the crew, waiting for Wonder Tongue to take ten.

Raylene was one of fourteen über-tarts under exclusive contract with Vivid, their prime attractions. She was dark and chiseled, and it was hard not to stare—even when I realized she was staring back. Ogling back, in fact. Was I imagining it? This kind of thing doesn't happen to me—at least not in real life. But there she was, looking me up and down while her cameraman filmed, her crew gawked, her co-star lapped.

When the cameraman broke to change film backs, Raylene popped off the bed and came right for me, all sweat and smiles. This is how a million fantasies begin, I remember thinking. Or scenes in porno movies. Which made this a porno movie within a porno movie. She extended her hand. "I'm Raylene. Thanks for coming."

"My pleasure," I said.

"Glad you could make it."

"Glad to be here."

"You're the reporter with *GQ?*" Oh dear.

"Actually no. I'm with *U.S. News & World Report.*" I smiled lamely. I then remembered the e-mail the PR guy sent me, the one with directions to the set. It had a second name on the "To" line, apparently that of a journalist she held in higher regard.

"*USA Today?*"

"No. *U.S. News & World Report.*"

"Oh." That was the end of that. She sauntered back to the set, her bare butt jiggling with each step, and I stood there with my pen in my hand wondering what dementia had caused me to correct her.

Permission granted from the director, I started to make pictures and for once had all the time I needed—Raylene worked her partner over for almost an hour. The set was well suited for pictures, as there was a lot of peripheral activity. And frequent breaks to change film backs meant the performers were often in less lewd positions. Ditto for the next set upstairs, a giant bathtub filled with bubbles and brunettes and surrounded by a wall of mirrors. Late in the afternoon another Vivid *fille de joie* joined the party, this one named Devon. A Vivid Girl press packet their PR guy sent me in preparation for the shoot said Devon was best known for "her innocent look," and that she considered "sleeping" one of her favorite hobbies.

I don't know what she was on, if anything, but Devon was having some trouble standing, let alone speaking. Not that these were important characteristics for a porn star. She did a quick scene in the backyard pool with Raylene, and as she climbed out, I tried to reconcile "her innocent look" with what was stumbling toward me. The water had smudged her eye makeup into two black, drippy splotches; she looked like she had lost a fight with a squid. A pink bikini top was pulled beneath her breasts and an unlit cigarette drooped from her lips. She put one hand on my shoulder, for drama or stability I'm not sure, and with the other held out the cigarette.

"Ghatalight?"

"Nope." She stuck her tongue out at me and made a farting noise, her eyes half shut. The next guy she asked, some lowly grip trying to inflate a beach ball, rifled through his pockets with the urgency of someone who thought he had lost his wallet.

Devon's next scene, this one with a yellow-haired surfer dude, was on the same set. It was late in the day, the light was golden, and they humped like heroes, a scrawny, fifty-something cameraman sporting a Speedo, knee pads, and nipple rings recording the ritual not two feet away. When the male half of this beast with two backs grimaced and sighed, dismounted and left, the cameraman followed him. Devon remained right where she lay, alone and naked and staring into space, and I clicked away, thinking this a keeper.

☐ With some decent material finally in hand, *U.S. News*'s new director of photography, Hailey Walker (West having already returned to *Time*), and I put together a show for the top editors of the magazine, trying to get them behind the project with a little sampling. We projected the pictures against a white, pull-down screen in the viewing room before Terry Stilton, the editor of the magazine. Though I had never worked with him before and thus had no experiences to draw from, Stilton didn't have the best reputation within the photo department. He was as well known for dissing pictures as he was for wearing suspenders, which he did every day. And so I held my breath.

There was some snickering among lesser editors. And when the lights came up there were the expected jokes and guffaws. And yet Stilton saw right through the giggle factor, offered that we needed to get some industry figures, determine where the business was heading. I pulled some factoids out of the air, stuff about trend analyses and commerce growth, and did an excellent impersonation of someone who knew what he was talking about. "Well, I think it's great," Stilton said finally. "I think it's a cover story." And that meant I could get down to work for real.

In a nondescript warehouse in a tony Seattle neighborhood, I photographed half a dozen "live" arcades, including an Ali Baba room (with gold satin sheets for walls and a young couple who called themselves "struggling actors" going at it on a mangy mattress), a "girl-girl" shower, a dungeon (with whips and handcuffs mounted to the faux-stone walls and a zaftig blond disciplining herself with a leather paddle), and, strangest of all, a bedroom. In the backseat of a car parked on a pier in the depressed Chesapeake Bay town of Saxis, Virginia, I photographed a young, sad, unemployed couple recording their own coitus—a freelance job they sold to Web sites to make ends meet. In a red-brick maze of low-income housing in Wilmington, Delaware, I photographed a single mom (screen name Hotandwet), her kids away at school, her carpet flecked with cigarette burns, feeling up her neighbor (screen name Blowgirl).

And most depressing of all: at a karate studio in Huntington Beach, California, I photographed an online, pay-per-view event called "Hit and Hump," where porn stars practiced their craft in a cage in between bouts of ultimate fighting. Police broke up the event halfway through (ultimate fighting was illegal, I learned) and I'm quite certain it was my fault. Earlier that day, a Sunday, when I pulled into the parking lot of the studio, I asked a well-dressed Hispanic man directing cars if this was for the cybersex shoot.

"Cybersex?"

"Yeah. And the fighting." I made a boxing motion with my fists.

"This is overflow for the church." And there it was, a big brown church directly across the street.

"That's what I meant," was all I could think to say, which left both of us confused. I drove off with a wave, and in my rearview mirror watched him consult a colleague.

I stayed with the project for eight months, made enough pictures for a small book, and for the first time in my career was satisfied with what I produced. More than satisfied. The images, I thought, were dynamite. Would win awards. Were the best I had ever made. And the photo department was thrilled. In the meantime a writer had put together a superb story, integrating many of the people I photographed. And just as it was nearing publication, while I was in South Carolina covering John McCain's 2000 presidential campaign, I heard secondhand that there were problems, as this is how photographers find things out at magazines. That the top dog had gotten cold feet, that he wanted the pictures reedited, the story revised. I heard that the photo department might be assigning someone to do business portraits.

I pulled over my rental car and pounded Hailey's number on my cell phone. "*Business* portraits?" It wasn't her fault, she explained. And I believed her. The woman had proven herself a fine lobbyist during our first viewing, selecting and talking up to the editors uncompromising photographs. Only now Stilton was backtracking, getting pressure from other editors, Hailey said. As this development involved the top brass, the editor of the magazine, I had a momentary, and uncustomary, lapse of temerity. I wrongly thought it beyond someone of my stature—a common photographer, a foot soldier on another assignment—to challenge official orders.

In the end the cover story did run, though with just five pictures in the spread. And only three of them were mine; the other two were pick-up portraits of CEOs. I was atwitter with outrage. And self-loathing. The whole bloody thing was my fault—I had let eight months of work go unpublished by not involving myself in the postshoot process, by not staying on top of the magazine's interest in my story and attempting to ensure its publication— its publication with *my* pictures. By not being a lobbyist. It was a mistake I hadn't made before and one I vowed not to make again.

ten

morocco

Of the many unpleasant places *U.S. News* was sending me to make pictures—Haiti, Iran, New Jersey—there was one destination I feared above the others. It was a Georgian mansion in the heart of Washington, a mansion that wasn't haunted but beyond whose wrought-iron gates lay horrors just the same. Photographically speaking it was a creative black hole: the uniform lighting, the limited mobility, the lack of access. My fellow *U.S. News* photographers and I spoke of assignments there the way career criminals speak of doing time in the clink. "The Shit House," we called it, though its famed Pennsylvania Avenue address invoked instant regard from less cynical souls.

The majority of our time covering the White House was spent sitting idle in or around the briefing room of the West Wing. This is the blue-curtained room made famous from the press secretary's daily briefings, as well as from those scenes in sci-fi flicks when the president vows to fight whatever invasion has befallen us. Hollywood's portrayal is trumpery, of course, that of a large and well-lit room where the reporters all scream at once and where photographers ignite the room with ancient, oversized Metz flashes. When I first entered the real thing years before for the Clinton/Yeltsin meeting—still an intern and still keen to cover the world's most powerful man—I had the sinking realization that the B-movie version was more appealing.

The briefing room back then was small, dark, and unkempt. Newspapers were scattered over the folding seats, as were plastic cups and wrappers and overworked journalists catching up on the day's reading. It looked like an adult movie theater after the lights come on. The walls surrounding the seats were lined with cameras, those of photographers and videographers, as well as jumbled stacks of stepladders used to gain a bit of height at events in the East Room, but in the meantime making it quite difficult to move around. Television crews were crammed in the rear of the room, the legs of their tripods forming a shiny, silver weave. Behind them, in the next room, writers and photographers shared crowded desk space.

Press events at the White House were—and still are—scheduled with little routine: some days there were five events, others none. They could be held in any number of places: the Oval Office, the Rose Garden, the Cabinet Room. When a pool call came over the intercom ("First and only call for photographers covering the Oval Office event"), all the shooters gathered at a set of internal briefing room doors for an escort. Pushing in a pack to the front of the line were the three wire photographers, AP, Reuters, and AFP, who were allowed first entry, as their pictures had the widest audience. Unfortunately for the rest of us, these photographers also carried the largest loads, their photo vests bulging with enough accoutrements to fill the walls of a strip-mall Moto-Photo: lenses, remotes, monopods, things with blinking lights, things that buzz, things attached to other things. For this, the wire photographers received good-natured guff from us magazine shooters ("Are you going on a five-second photo-op or a five-week commando mission?"), who, by carrying too little gear, often erred on the opposite end of the spectrum.

As between two prisoners sharing the same cell, there was much sniping between the wire and mag photographers. The wires portrayed us maggers as prima donnas—snobbish, self-appointed artists who never shoot night events because we we're too busy exploiting our corporate credit cards at the nearest four-star restaurant. And how to respond—it was true! But by and large we were just fulfilling roles, pretending to be annoyed with each other while deep down, for no other reason than years of proximity, we had grown to appreciate, and even respect, each other's ability.

The wire photographers were fast, tough, and always dead on. They never missed and were thus better suited than I was to that hit-and-run environment. Some Oval Office events lasted ten seconds. Ten seconds! That gave you five seconds to hustle through the white wooden doors, three seconds to frame your picture, and two seconds to hold down the shutter. And all the while a dozen other photographers were jostling for your position, the space allocated for us no bigger than a closet. I was often just figuring out the exposure when the event was declared over and the wires were drifting back outside, reviewing with satisfaction their work on the back of their cameras. Then again, what mag photographer needed a picture of the president locked in a fake, frozen handshake with the prime minister of Burkina Faso?

Unlike the wires, whose role required a hefty task—to provide resolute coverage of each and every White House event—we magazine photographers had it easy, were at liberty to dismiss the intentions of those photo-ops and focus instead on the president himself: to make an image that reflected on the larger White House story that week. So while other photographers had to struggle for that dead-on position, the one offering the cleanest view of the president with this year's spelling bee champs, the head honcho of East Malaria, or other smiling, gussied-up, glad-to-be-there recipients of our commander-in-chief's attention, the magazine photographers were often looking for a different angle entirely, the spot where all these extraneous persons were rendered invisible, or at least less prominent.

There were exceptions, of course, when the events at hand actually mattered to the magazines, when the president gathers in the cabinet room with his staff, say, or in the Oval with the president of Russia, or in the Rose Garden with congressional leaders. Yet even then we had freedom to gamble, to risk missing the safe picture for a more aesthetically challenging one, as we had the wires to fall back on. In theory, at least. The editors at *U.S. News* were so loyal they'd run our own work even when we failed. *Time* and *Newsweek* photographers, on the hand, were more likely to see their images displaced: an act of such treason as to render the victim spitting mad and vulnerable to attack from a group of gloating wire photographers. "That's weird. Didn't we see you at that event? Your cameras go down? Forget to put in film? Or focus? Was it in focus?" Insufferable.

☐ On the frequent occasion of a presidential event elsewhere in Washington, the press pool was hastily escorted to the southern driveway, to two vans parked near the end of the presidential motorcade. The photographers claimed the front rows of both vans as we needed to jump out first, or so tradition held, should the president emerge to shake a few hands, or should his vehicle meet with a more dramatic turn of events. The last to arrive in the motorcade was the president himself, a distant blur ducking into a limousine. And then we were off, tearing through the streets of D.C., paying no mind to such mortal nuisances as road signs, stoplights, and rush-hour motorists. For each and every presidential movement the police stopped traffic on the intended route, providing our commander-in-chief the fastest possible journey and those of us in the motorcade a rolling view of seething commuters.

Upon arrival, van doors burst open and journalists leaped out—photographers, scribblers, videographers, sound people—everyone amped, then running, the press advance person near panic: "Pool! This way! We have to hurry!" The blur of our feet moving through back entrances, up darkened stairwells, down long hallways, past startled onlookers, a stampede of media, a horrible, panting, sweating, stampede, the perfect personification of everyone's worst impression of us, zigzagging through crowds of well-dressed people, bumping into stanchions, abandoning colleagues who couldn't keep up, colleagues who tripped, colleagues who dropped a lens, a laptop, a tape recorder. And for what? So we didn't miss the first ten seconds of another podium picture?

They were all the same, those "in-town" events—held in the banquet halls of the Washington Hilton, or the Omni Shoreham—

the settings supremely dull, the plush curtains, deep red or presidential blue, the tungsten-lit stage with a single podium, the hushed crowd, the movie screens on either side of the stage, projecting a video feed of the president's head. And us squatting in the buffer, the ten-foot-wide border between the audience and the stage, pointing our 80-200s straight up the president's nostrils, then crawling across the carpet like toddlers, on hands and knees, shuffling our gear forward, looking for a better angle, for something different, a shot from behind the video screens, perhaps, or through the water glasses of diners. Or maybe I can silhouette Clinton in a spotlight. It rarely worked. Those sites were so void of visual potential that if the entire lot of us were suddenly, magically, replaced with the most gifted artists to ever peer through a viewfinder—Capa, Smith, Bresson—I have little doubt that they, too, would have made nary a frame, would have dropped to their knees and begged to return to their eternal rest.

Then finally, thankfully, "and may God bless the United States of America," the press advance waving frantically at us, unable to shout, mouthing, "Pool! This way! We have to hurry!" More running, everything in reverse now, the onlookers, the hallways, the idling vans, until we were back in the briefing room and I was scribbling a caption on a *U.S. News* film bag, then calling the courier service to tell them I have a delivery, then jogging up the north driveway and stretching my arm between those black, wrought-iron gates, like a desperate hostage passing a note, and the bike messenger, all muscle and grime, swooping in to snatch the bag from my hand, then pedaling hard to the west, up Pennsylvania Avenue toward Foggy Bottom.

▢ If photographing the president in Washington was stale, con-trolled, and crowded, photographing him on the road was a world of opportunity. Only six shooters traveled, the three wires and three magazines. There was more room to move, the settings were far less predictable, and there was often at least one event where the light was just right, where the president was relaxed and act-ing off the cuff and you had the time and space to move into po-sition and make an actual photograph. That was when you weren't driving, heloing, or flying Air Force One from one place to the next.

"That must be so fascinating" was the usual cocktail observa-tion about flying aboard the president's plane. After just a few years of these flights, I considered it my journalistic duty, if not my patriotic one, to offer a more accurate perspective. There was no retina scan to board, no escape pod to play in, no view of the front of the plane, of the secretary of state sitting pensively in a swivel chair, plotting foreign policy, or of the big man himself, emerging from his study to invite you in for a beer, to play a game of cards, to watch a movie. I made it to the front of the plane only once, and it was well before the president boarded, on a quick courtesy tour with one of the stewards. "This is where the president sleeps," he offered matter of factly. Pushing open the president's bathroom door, he continued, "and this is where he does his thinking."

During Clinton's presidency, we would fly to two, three, four states in a day. And traveling abroad with him was a protracted experiment in sleep deprivation, one that turned the White House press corps into a pack of bleary-eyed zombies. We worked all day and traveled most of the night, checking into our hotels in the wee hours of the morning, then checking out a few hours later and doing it all again. In the midst of one European swing, upon awaking in Florence, Italy, I stared out my hotel window for a few moments, wondering why this most lovely city appeared so dismal. Rusting white Ladas jammed the streets, and in the hotel's courtyard were the red-brick ruins of what looked like a Balkan church. Pedestrians appeared dour and drab. The reason, I learned upon snatching a book of matches off the dresser, was that I was no longer in Italy but in Bulgaria. The Sheraton of Sofia, Bulgaria, to be exact. Then it came back to me: the late-night flight, the mass check-in at the front desk, the overwhelmed hotel staff. And all those other stops—Athens, Ankara, Istanbul, Ephesus. And tomorrow's trip to Kosovo. Then back to Italy, I think.

Road fuzz was an indiscriminate illness; it afflicted all of us. Missed flights, forgotten baggage, bungled photo ops. It was all part of the routine. Once at the Hague I pulled a brand of film from my camera I had never seen in my life. The canister was red and had Cyrillic lettering, and I was convinced one of the wire guys had played a joke on me, had breached the sole provision of mutual detente—"no messing with the other's gear"—and switched the film when I wasn't looking. That is until I realized the roll belonged to the Russian photographer next to me, as did the Nikon camera I had inadvertently picked up and used to shoot the event.

My favorite fatigue-induced gaffe, one that has achieved legendary status among Washington photojournalists, was committed by a good-hearted *Newsweek* shooter named Duke Samuels. It came at the end of a Clinton trip out west, a trip that was unexpectedly extended. The king of Morocco had just died, so the president, and all of us, after making a refueling stop at Andrews Air Force Base in suburban Maryland (where extra journalists like myself were allowed to join the trip), were en route to Africa to attend the funeral. "Yo, Lo," Duke said, trying to wake me just before we landed in Rabat. We had stayed up most of the night drinking, shooting the shit, and now I couldn't keep my eyes open. Duke shook me again. "Lo. Wake up!"

"What?"

"I can't find my gear."

"What do you mean?"

"I mean I don't have my cameras."

"Of course you do."

"I don't. I don't! I left them at Andrews!"

"What? How?"

"Remember we were playing cards and you told me to put them on that seat so nobody would step on them? That's how the brain fart happened."

"That's impossible."

"Well, they ain't here!"

"Didn't you feel a little light getting on the plane?"

"No. I don't know. Fuck!"

"Someone's playing a joke."

"No, man. No. No. No. Everyone's on the other plane." He was right, all our colleagues were aboard Air Force One; Duke and I were flying on the president's support plane. The poor guy had done it, he had flown all the way to Africa without his Nikons.

The plane banked hard, and outside the window all the world was desert, rust-colored and beautiful, like the surface of Mars.

One of the pursers hustled through the cabin, telling Duke to take his seat for landing. Duke stared at me. "What the fuck am I gonna do?" The poor guy—his rugged, Wild West good looks were veiled in dread. His hair was matted in multiple places, like a guinea pig's, and his voice had taken on a defeated dry rasp. He rifled through the pouches on his camera belt, which he *had* remembered, and pulled out a Nikon 28-70 mm lens. I gave him an extra Nikon body. Still, this wouldn't do him much good when the principles were fifty yards out. I told him to stay close to me and I'd share my long lenses with him. He said he was toast.

Upon our arrival at the royal palace in Rabat, we were surprised to learn that President Clinton would walk a two-mile-long funeral procession to Hassan's burial site—surprised not just because Clinton must be tired and it was terribly hot outside but because the streets were mobbed with wailing Moroccans. Two million wailing Moroccans, to be exact, all frantic to get a glimpse of the cortege. They were banging their fists against their heads and rocking cars side to side. It all seemed a tad overdone—and not the safest environment for the president of the United States. A flatbed truck was hastily arranged to drive a few reporters, one wire photographer, and one mag photographer in front of the procession. As it was *Time*'s pool day, they got to ride. Duke and I would have to walk.

And I'm glad we did. Mourners were everywhere, hanging from street signs and standing on lampposts, leaning out windows and from atop buildings, every last one of them wailing their guts out, as if someone had murdered their children. There were so many mourners in the trees that whole branches of them broke off and were swept away in the raging torrent of pushing people. A woman who fainted was passed mosh-pit style to the banks of the flood. It was utter chaos and the Secret Service agents shed their robotron expressions for ones approaching panic, their arms pushing violently at everything that moved, including me. All the while President Clinton pressed on undaunted, just the top of his white head visible, bobbing up and down like a Q-tip in a river of black ink.

And Duke fared better than the rest of us, was light as a feather without all the gear, with just that short lens—all he needed to photograph this mob scene. Yet this story has a post-denouement. On the flight home we were once again too wired to sleep, so we stayed up drinking gin and tonics. And when we landed at Andrews early Monday morning, instead of going home to sleep, Duke headed right out to another assignment. It all caught up with him then, the flights, the stress, the exhaustion, washing over his brain and shutting it off like a switch. Which was unfortunate, as he was doing 70 mph on Route 66. His Land Rover veered across a single lane of traffic, somehow missing other vehicles, and didn't stop until it slammed into a concrete barrier. The car was totaled, though he was unhurt. When commuters ran over to help, opened his door, they found him hunched over in the driver's seat, still asleep.

Never mind he was nearly the first casualty of Clinton's joie de vivre: for Duke, for me, for all us photographers, those grand tours were the saving grace of White House duty. Better photo ops, sure. Though for us it was about the going—that helo ride over the Holy Land, that visit to the Hague, the Kremlin, the Bundestag, that river cruise with President Bush through St. Petersburg, the facades still sunlit near midnight, or the one with

President Clinton through China's Guilin River valley, the limestone cliffs above us, all lush and pretty. And of course that death march through the crowds in Rabat, me and Duke laughing out loud, laughing at the madness of it. Finer memories than presidential pictures, those spectacles, and that was just fine with us.

eleven

russia

Six hours into the driving tour of Moscow, we had all tuned out. Even the American couple the writer and I were following, the couple who had come all this way to adopt a child, were slumped into their seats, their heads resting on one another's. We were still jetlagged. Aeroflot was one of the last airlines that allowed its passengers to smoke, which they did on the nonstop from New York in horrific quantities. It had been a miserable flight.

Moscow was appropriately dark and dismal, this being February. We had to wipe dry the van's windows with our forearms whenever we wanted to see out—a desire that came about with less and less frequency. The driver and facilitator from the adoption agency, acting as tour guides, continued undaunted. "Over here are the Lenin Hills, over there the Pushkin Museum . . . and down that street is where men have sex with horses." Heads perked up. Eyes opened.

"What?" I asked.

"They have sex with horses."

"Where?"

"Down there."

"Who does?"

"Men."

"Men?"

"Men." Everyone in the van shared a glance.

"They don't do this in your country?"

"No!" we shouted in unison.

"You want to see?"

"Yes!"

The driver careened down a road that wound between concrete apartment buildings, then dead-ended in a kind of cul-de-sac. On one side was a poorly lit bus stop, and scattered below its narrow cover a clutch of prostitutes, their lips scarlet, their hair yellow, their legs creamy. All of them smoked. I was the last one to get it, apparently, as the van filled with sighs. "It's pronounced 'whores,'" the writer said.

twelve

antarctica

On the second-to-last day of the twentieth century, when everyone else in the world was planning to usher in the first moments of the new millennium, I flew from D.C. to Miami to Santiago to Punta Arenas, which is on the southern tip of Chilean Patagonia and is just about as far south as you can fly in the Americas. I made it to my hotel room before midnight on the 31st—which in those parts, at such low latitude, arrived in lingering daylight—and watched the festivities on CNN, as well as in the little town square just outside my hotel window. Punta Arenas is quirky and hardscrabble, as most end-of-the-line towns tend to be. Despite the local millennium party, which had attracted less than a hundred people, the rest of downtown felt deserted—no cars, no people, no life. Ditto for my digs, where guests were outnumbered by stuffed penguins, the lobby's most distinctive motif.

In its 160-year history, Punta Arenas has gone through numerous incarnations, including military garrison, penal colony, thriving port, wool capital. More recently it is known, to American scientists at least, as the launching point for National Science Foundation (NSF) ships bound for Palmer Research Station, the lone American outpost on the rough and remote Antarctic Peninsula.

I was on the manifest for the next departure, as were *U.S. News* science writer Peter Neville and several dozen scientists. In two days, after the NSF finished stocking resupplies for Palmer station aboard the blocky, yellow-and-orange research vessel called the *L. M. Gould,* we would weave our way south through the Straits of Magellan, which separate South America from its largest island, Tierra del Fuego, then spend several days crossing the Drake Passage, until we were once again able to reach protected waters, this time on the western shore of the peninsula. Continuing south, we would reach the port of Palmer some time on the fourth or fifth day. There Peter and I would debark, as would a few of the scientists and several tons of mail, fuel, and food, and the *Gould* would head even farther south for three weeks of offshore scientific study. On its return trip to South America, the ship would pick us up.

Peter was based in Northern California, and we hadn't properly met before our arrival in Punta Arenas. I liked him instantly. In his early fifties, he was big and bookish in that Clark Kent kind of way, seemingly reserved, pedantic, yet once you got a few drinks in him, he was effusive and quick to laugh. Waiting to set sail, we felt obliged to exercise our corporate credit cards, which would sleep in our wallets the moment we stepped on the boat, and over plates of salmon and sea bass we giggled like schoolgirls over our upcoming voyage. This was the Big One.

Terra Australis Incognita, the seventh continent, the great white south. For as long as I can remember the mere mention of its name filled my heart with Pavlovian longing. Those four syllables—Ant-arc-ti-ca—so rhythmic and clean, a one-word siren's song for dreamers of distant lands. Ant-ARC-ti-ca. On my boyhood globe the white hurricane on the bottom displayed no names of towns, no borders or geologic features. Just that single word, Ant-ARC-ti-ca. What kind of continent had no place-names? What kind of continent had no people? What would it look like, smell like, feel like? This is the coldest, driest, highest, windiest landmass on Earth. There are places there where no precipitation has fallen in millions of years, places where winds reach two hundred mph, places where the temperature drops to one hundred below. Such an environment shouldn't exist. How could any place on Earth be so inhospitable?

I had often wondered if in some weird, anthropomorphic way the Earth wasn't preserving Antarctica from the fate of its six sisters. If the continent wasn't like some provision thrown into the world's freezer, not to be consumed—or paved, or populated, or Wal-Marted—at least not yet. Nearly the entire continent, a full 98 percent of it, is sealed beneath a thick crust of ice. That ice reaches three miles high in places, and the landmass beneath it is surely the most pristine on Earth. It's never recorded a footprint. The scientific value of such an environment is immeasurable, but it has existential value as well. The mere *idea* that such a place exists, a place that humans can't have, a place that says, I don't want you here and I'll turn your blood to ice to prove it, gives people like me fodder for fantasy against all that has been explored and developed.

Nearly twenty-five hundred years before a Russian naval captain became the first person to see the continent, in 1820, the ancient Greeks conceived of its existence as a means of earthly balance, literally. They believed the Earth was round, and with so much landmass in the north, which they referred to as "Arktikos," surely there had to be an "ant," or "opposite" Arktikos, to keep the world from spinning. Antarctica still provides such conceptual ballast, not with its weight but with its hostile reclusiveness. It reminds us that we are just humans and that there are earthly domains that even we can't tame. Yet we can still manage to fuck them up.

In a tragic twist of fate, the residue of our other conquests, our consumption, has settled over this part of the world in the form of a giant, oscillating hole in the atmosphere, a hole that would reach a record size—11.4 million square miles—the year of my visit. Worse, the ozone hole settled not above just any part of the continent but its ecologic heart: the Antarctic Peninsula. Much of the 2 percent of Antarctica not buried beneath ice is here: a narrow, eight-hundred-mile-long mountain range reaching northward like a limb toward its geologic cousin, the Andes, though ultimately falling five hundred miles short. Sprinkled alongside are hundreds of little islands, home to the wildlife one has come to associate with this part of the world—penguins and petrels, seals and skuas—and more recently a number of concerned scientists.

While temperatures here have always been far more tepid than in the rest of the continent—"Antarctica's tropics" is the peninsula's most common euphemism—the ozone hole overhead had caused things to spiral out of control of late. Since midcentury,

the peninsula's year-round temperature had risen four degrees—
a rate of warming ten times that of the rest of the world. Winter
temperatures there had risen as much as nine degrees. Glaciers
were retreating, ice cover was melting, animals that were supposed to be there were migrating farther south, in search of colder
climes, and species from South America were taking their place. It
was an ecologic disaster on the grandest scale, and that made it
ground zero for the study of global climate change.

Some months earlier Peter had secured us our much-coveted
positions on the *L. M. Gould,* as well as at the research station.
Space at Palmer was tight, very tight. It had a maximum population of just forty-two people, making it the smallest of the
three U.S. Antarctica stations, the other two being McMurdo or
"MacTown" on Ross Island, due south of New Zealand, and the
Amundsen-Scott station at the South Pole. Palmer was also the
least well known. The LexisNexis search I performed to see what
I was getting into returned just a handful of articles. And on the
Web all I found were some dull, depressing snapshots of the station on the homepage of an adventure tourist named Mick. One
of my colleagues joked that when I got there I'd make a picture
of a scientist standing outside with a thermometer reading twenty
below, then have nothing to do for the next month—and I was
terrified that might be true. I knew Palmer was on an island, which
meant restricted movement. I also knew the peninsula was notorious for foul, wet weather, with blizzards socking it in for
weeks straight.

☐ The *Gould* sailed from Punta Arenas on January 3, and we
spent much of the day drifting through the tawny, treeless fjords

of southernmost South America, the water as flat as D.C.'s Reflecting Pool. Peter and I passed the first night sending novelty e-mails from the boat's computer room. Though there was no booze on board, I awoke the next morning with what felt like a vicious hangover. The Straits of Magellan were behind us and seas were undulating around fifteen feet. To the captain and crew, this was bathwater—seas in these parts can reach forty, even sixty feet high. Yet it was enough to keep me in bed for the next two days, drinking Sprite, popping Dramamine, and pretending to Peter that I didn't feel half as bad as I looked. The poor guy was bunking beneath me.

Outside our room's porthole all the world was gray—gray sea, gray sky, gray rain. Yet even out there I saw flashes of life, little brown-and-white birds pitching and rising in our windbreak. They were Wilson's storm-petrels, the voyagers of the avian world, famed for migrating from the Canadian subarctic to Antarctica and back again every year. And on the third day a glimpse of rock, the black face of a distant mountain, fading like a dream behind a curtain of clouds. I grabbed my binoculars and ran to the deck, where other passengers had already gathered. We were hugging the shore of the peninsula, the water calm, my equilibrium restored, my heart racing, the view I had longed to behold for so many years just off our port side—and near-perfectly obscured behind a blanket of fog.

There were fleeting glimpses of gravel banks, of white summits. Somebody thought he saw a whale, though it turned out to be a piece of ice. People drifted back inside. It was raining and snowing at the same time and we had another eight hours to go. But I didn't budge, was delirious with anticipation. It was right there, Ant-ARC-ti-ca, and I couldn't see it. *Lift! Evaporate! Open wide thy cold gray curtain!*

The fog did part, finally, just as we drifted to a stop before Palmer Research Station. It was perched on an outcropping of barren rock: a small collection of corrugated metal fashioned into a half dozen sky-blue buildings. Sprouting from the campus were antennas of various sizes, some tall and lean, others short and disk-shaped, as well as a flagpole displaying the stars and stripes. Numerous trailers, pallets, and stacks of piping were scattered about the grounds, giving the place the appearance of an ongoing construction site, which it was. And farther up the hill were two giant fuel tanks, one painted with an orca leaping Free Willy fashion into the sky. Beyond that, nothing but glacier.

People emerged from the buildings and collected on the dock, waving to the boat and helping with the mooring. Two of these men wore nothing but jeans and T-shirts, and I had the sudden realization that it wasn't cold outside. At least not Antarctic cold. The sun was out and the wind was gone and the temperature was in the upper thirties. And the view—not of a gray, windswept plain but of the most unearthly mountain range, some peaks sharp and fractured, some perfectly beveled, all standing out porcelain-white against a velvet-blue sky; of icebergs so bright it hurt to look at them, their more accessible crags the temporary roost of sunning penguins; of baby-blue glaciers and a half dozen gravel islands, their larger rocks encrusted in fluorescent orange lichen.

The moment the *Gould* was secured, we charged off its deck and into Palmer's galley for orientation and safety lessons. The galley was a small, well-lit cafeteria with cork bulletin boards on the walls and large windows overlooking our protected anchorage, Arthur Harbor. The galley also opened to an outdoor deck, where I noticed a large, black barbecue grill. When the station's lab manager arrived, there was much applause. His name was Sonny Moriarty and he was tall and lean, with a Deadhead's mellow air and long hair and beard to match. He wore a professorial tweed sportcoat over what appeared to be a Hawaiian shirt, and displayed a comforting, Clintonian skill of acting awed to be in *our* presence.

Sonny said everyone would be expected to contribute to kitchen cleanup, as well as to a once-weekly "house-mouse," such as compacting trash or scrubbing the bathrooms. It was a piddly amount of work for the complexity of such an outpost, little more than what a traveler might encounter when staying at a youth hostel. Sonny also said we were allowed to pilot the station's many inflatable motorboats, called Zodiacs, anywhere within a two-mile radius of Palmer, except for two islands that were off-limits for long-term ecological studies. We could visit the penguin colonies on Torgersen Island, the seal piles on Elephant Rocks, the blue-eyed shags on Cormorant Island. We could check out icebergs from a safe distance, or follow a pod of migrating humpback whales. We could go wherever the hell we wanted.

If Palmer's setting was the grand surprise of my visit, this freedom of movement was a close second. Given the climate, the notorious weather, the environmental sensitivities, I had expected there to be much hysteria about venturing off to explore the environs. On the contrary, it's what the staff wanted—for us to experience the ecology for ourselves. And the destinations Sonny rattled off on that first day made my toes curl. All those little

islands I could see through the galley window, awaiting my photographic study. I would have taken a cold shower to contain
myself if I hadn't just gotten a lesson on the importance of mini-
mizing wastewater.

Soon we were distributed among the staff for housing. I would
bunk with a computer tech and a construction worker—quiet,
congenial guys who slept with the shades drawn and the window
wide open. I quickly learned I wasn't well suited to such bedroom
climes, or all-night daylight. On that first night I began with just
an eye mask, then draped my face with a shirt, then sandwiched
my head between two pillows.

The morning routine at Palmer was to rise between 6:30
and 7:00, skip the showers, and head straight to the galley. Because
of the gray water issue, people showered once every few days,
and always *after* being out in the field. Breakfast was served buffet-
style, as were all the meals, and was accompanied with a mini-
version of the *New York Times,* which arrived every morning by fax.
The food was hearty and various, the kind of spread you might find
at an upscale lodge. Eggs, waffles, and French toast for breakfast,
along with heaping piles of bacon and sausage, bowls of yogurt, and
fruit salad. For lunch and dinner there were steaks and Chilean
seafood. And there were always goodies left out for between-
meal grazing: cakes and cookies and freshly baked pies.

After breakfast, teams of biologists, ecologists, and physicists
determined their morning destination(s), as did we journalists
and any staff member with the day off who was up for a little
adventure. Then we consulted the latest satellite images beaming
into Palmer's weather station, trying to get a read on the next five
or six hours. Provided there were no ominous and encroaching

blips on the radar screen, we each signed out a two-way radio, struggled into a bright orange Mustang survival suit, posted our departure time and destination on a chalkboard in the galley, climbed into one of the Zodiacs, and motored off.

For the first week Peter and I spent our mornings with the scientists, trying to get a look at their fieldwork, then went off on our own in the afternoons. By the time I returned to my room each night, I had fifteen or more exposed rolls in my backpack, and I was already worried I had not brought enough film. Despite my productivity, I did have a serious editorial concern: how does one *show* global warming? As with so many environmental stories, its effects are more clearly expressed through the written word. How do you show the lack of a particular species, or the retreating of a glacier? How do you show that it's four degrees warmer outside than it should be? The measure of an affecting photograph is often inversely tied to the length of its caption— a wordy explanation means it hasn't succeeded in telling the story visually. And that was a trap I would have trouble avoiding. For example, warmer temperatures were decimating the local Adelie penguin population, which in the past twenty-five years had been reduced from 25,000 nesting pairs to 7,700. Abandoned Adelie nests were everywhere, yet they were mere piles of pebbles, stained with pink streaks of guano—not a particularly compelling image, nor one that's self-explanatory, unless a lone penguin were to wander through with its flippers extended in a "where the heck is everybody?" kind of way.

It seemed the best way to show global warming was to photograph scientists in the field, studying the phenomenon. With a single umbrella caption, the magazine could group together three or four images, collectively revealing the urgency of the problem. The pictures would be surprising, as these scientists weren't your run-of-the-mill beaker pushers. They were rappelling into glacial fissures in search of microbacteria, launching balloons carrying aerial cameras to measure glacial retreation, corralling penguins into herds to make an accurate census.

On the matter of aesthetics, light was the sole drawback. Though there was plenty of it, the constant cloud cover left it flat, gray, boring. On the few days of sunshine, the soft, orange end-of-day light didn't come until near midnight, when no scientists were working, and then again at dawn a few hours later. It also meant I had to find a Zodiac partner willing to forgo some sleep—and to putz around while I shot animals and landscapes. There was a reward for their service, however. On those few sunny days, when the temperature rose and the icebergs sparkled and the mountains jutting straight from the sea reflected in their snow cover the setting sun, a phenomenon known as Alpine glow, it was easy to believe this was the most beautiful place on earth.

On every outing I lugged a 500 mm lens, which in terms of magnification is equivalent to binoculars with 10x power, though I rarely needed it. This was the only place I had ever been where the wildlife wasn't skittish, was in fact social. Upon spotting me, two-foot-high Adelie penguins would waddle right up, stare me up and down, then slowly disperse. Giant petrels sitting on nests even tolerated the probing hand of Palmer's bird experts, who reached into their warm and hollow brood patch to pull out a single downy chick. The petrels occasionally beaked the ornithologist's arm—not hard, but enough to say "I *could* hurt you if I wanted." We did keep a safe distance from the elephant seals sunning themselves on the beach in blubbery piles of ten or more. They were massive creatures, some weighing four tons, and they demonstrated such an inspired repertoire of farts and burps as to keep all of us, including the men of science, laughing out loud.

The cute little Adelie penguins revealed their own crude habits. They practiced something one of the Palmer biologists referred to as "projectile shitting." Rather then leave their pebble nests to defecate, the penguins would lift up their little tails, bend over, and squirt. Since the colonies were tightly packed, the guano would sail maybe three feet before nailing a neighbor, though the victims never appeared insulted. They'd shake it off with aplomb and fall back asleep, standing upright. Years and years of projectile shitting have lacquered the rookeries a dull pink.

That pink color comes from the Adelies' uniform diet. Like many of Antarctica's predatory species, they eat one thing—krill. These rarely seen, shrimp-shaped crustaceans were of utmost importance to Palmer's ecologists, as well as to the vast Antarctic food web. They drift through the sea in unimaginable swarms, numbering in the billions. In terms of biomass, krill are the world's most abundant species. They are also one of the world's most consumed—a single blue whale can eat four and a half tons a day. Add up all the other whales, seals, birds, squid, and fish dining daily on these little creatures, not to mention all the secondary dependencies—the leopard seals, for example, who dine on the penguins who dine on the krill—and it becomes clear why the health of their population is the kind of thing that keeps biologists awake at night. If their population collapsed, so too would much of Antarctica's ecosystem. And it appeared as if global warming was contributing to just such a scenario. In the first winter of their lives, krill depend on the rippled underside of sea ice for shelter and food. Fifty years earlier, about 80 percent of winters around Palmer were cold enough to produce the necessary ice shelter. By the year 2000, that percentage was cut in half.

To study how many krill the Adelie penguins were eating, and thereby gauge the strength of local krill populations, Palmer's penguin specialist, Roger Williams, implemented an ingenious technique. He would net penguins just after they had finished feeding and flopped themselves onto shore. With an assistant restraining the bird's feet and flippers, he would slide a small plastic tube down the penguin's throat, then pump warm salt water into its stomach. The bird would promptly puke up the contents—half-digested krill—which Williams and his staff would examine back at the lab. When set free the penguins stumbled around a bit, dazed but unharmed, then waddled back into the sea to refill their stomachs.

Williams told me he was concerned about how this action would look on film, and I broke my own "shoot first, decide later" rule by voluntarily not photographing it. I needed Williams too much to upset him. And I would have been devastated if the magazine insisted on publishing the picture, spurring some nut job from PETA (People for the Ethical Treatment of Animals) to come down on Williams and the NSF. As for photographing krill, that all-important species, the best I could get were some lame images in the lab of Williams and his colleagues slowly, methodically counting and measuring what specimens they had extracted from the Adelies.

▢ The first two weeks at Palmer I shot nearly a hundred rolls of film, something I've never done before or since in such a short period of time. I spent what off hours I had in Palmer's computer lab, which had periodic Internet access (the times depended on the path of an orbiting satellite), as well as in their recreation room, which had a billiard table and a video library with thousands of titles. To ward off brain freeze, booze was sold from the station store, which also dispensed the requisite Palmer novelties—T-shirts, baseball caps, postcards. It was station courtesy to store your alcohol at the Penguin Pub, which was attached to the recreation center, for others to share.

The pub was *the* Palmer hangout, and it had the constrained, homemade feel of your neighbor's basement bar. Though people were in there every day, it was most crowded on Saturday nights, when the entire staff gathered to drink and dance. For bar ice they used chunks of glacier, frozen for some twenty thousand years, retrieved from a nearby fissure. Compressed by its own tremendous weight, the ice was crystal clear, like giant rocks of glass—no cracks, no air bubbles, no imperfections. They were glorious to behold, if ice can be so beautiful, and gave off a peculiar fizzing noise when plunked into a drink.

The walls of the pub were lined with color photos of NSF research vessels, and in the hallway outside were photos of each year's winter-overs—mostly men who, despite the beards and boots and flannel, revealed in their broad smiles a park ranger sensitivity, the kind that distinguishes those who have come to a wilderness lodge to see wildlife from those who have come to hunt it. I loved this about the Palmer staff, that the local brain trust, the scientists and lab techs and computer geeks, weren't geeky at all, but were rough-and-tumble outdoorsmen. And conversely, the local muscle, the carpenters and plumbers and electricians, weren't consumed by their crafts, were all students of science, people who sat around the bar talking about lichen, or glacial retreation, or the peculiar flight pattern of a bird they had spotted that day. They were Renaissance men and women, all of them. And the experiences they recounted on Saturday nights were as entertaining as any I can recall.

The two most memorable stories came from staff who had spent time at the South Pole station. There, every winter, they indoctrinated new members into their "300 Club." By "300" they meant withstanding a three hundred–degree differential. First they warmed themselves in a sauna, at a hellish two hundred degrees Fahrenheit, for as long as they could stand it. Then they ran naked outside the station, where it was one hundred below— not counting the wind chill. They weren't entirely naked, actually. They wore shoes, and headbands over their mouths to prevent their lung tissue from freezing. Club members said that the moment they hit the cold their bodies erupted in steam, but that there was enough reserve heat from the sauna to allow them to make it back.

If it seems a ridiculous endeavor, well, that's the idea. And it is quite harmless, at least compared to what a bunch of daredevils attempted near the same spot in the middle of summer. Four skydivers, all Americans, flew down to set a record for the first four-way skydive over the South Pole. Things didn't go as planned, which really isn't that surprising. Three of them augered into the ice, while the fourth was saved by his Cypress, a tiny contraption that automatically opens a reserve chute at a particular altitude. He was the only jumper wearing one. They all had had on altimeters, though, and were veteran skydivers. Did they lose their depth perception over the white expanse? Did they get hypoxia from the altitude? The South Pole sits atop a mound of ice nearly two miles high, and they jumped from another eighty-five hundred feet above that. Or did they fall faster than they expected in the thin, freezing air?

The sole survivor said it was the whiteout that disoriented him, but as for the others, nobody knows for sure. And it really doesn't matter. What matters is what the South Pole staff saw when they got to the impact site: the perfect shapes of three human beings, arms and legs spread wide, cut Wile E. Coyote style into the snow.

Icebergs moored themselves in Arthur Harbor with reliable frequency. Some stayed put for weeks, while others disappeared overnight. They came in all manner of shapes and sizes. Fresh bergs, as in ones that had just broken off from some unseen glacier, were perfect rectangles, while older ones showed evidence of erosion similar to the sandstone Mitten buttes in Monument Valley. We called them the albino buttes. Later in their lives these icebergs would lose the meat in their middles and be left with two hoodoo-like spires on either end, then one spire, then nothing but a dull dome of ice. Peter and I liked to check out these massive freighters up close, close enough even to touch, though boating regulations stipulated, to the point of being annoying, that one must maintain a safe distance. A berg can "roll" at any time. In our first two weeks we were never privy to such a dramatic phenomenon and thereby concluded it was all a bunch of ballyhoo.

On a downright balmy afternoon, on our way back to Palmer, Peter and I boated alongside a particularly dramatic dual-hoodoo berg. We were slowly encircling this specimen, allowing ourselves to be awed by its color and mass, when we heard what sounded like a shotgun blast. I turned around just in time to see a refrigerator-sized piece slap into the water behind us—the initial blast had been the sound of it breaking off. It was just a tiny piece of one of the hoodoos, and yet its loss was enough to destabilize the entire iceberg, which began rocking side to side like a battered ship. I gunned the throttle on the Zodiac while Peter screamed like a stuck pig, "She's gonna go!" There was an awful, high-pitched, whale-like whine: the sound of the bottom of the iceberg scraping the floor of the sea. And then the top and bottom switched places. The newly revealed underside was round and worn, like the hull of a boat, only it had a row of fresh striations from the undersea scraping. Even with the boat going full throttle, the waves the berg generated raced beneath us, littered with foam and bergy-bits.

Peter and I had plenty of time to recover from our adrenaline hangovers; bad weather kept us locked inside for days. Our sentence was broken when a tourist ship docked in Arthur Harbor. Palmer was kind enough to entertain a few of these vessels each year, allowing passengers without a cold or flu to come ashore for a few hours, tour the station, chow down some of the chef's famous brownies, and leave with armfuls of Palmer T-shirts and baseball hats. In return for Palmer's hospitality, the cruise ships would invite Palmer staff aboard for cocktails, or even dinner. These limited invites were doled out lottery-fashion by the station manager, and Peter and I were lucky enough to win access onto the ship, which was an Abercrombie and Kent vessel called the *Explorer.*

When we climbed aboard and got a load of their cocktail hour, which looked like a gathering of aged Georgetown socialites, I felt like one of the three stooges, illiterate and uncouth, doing the bumble-into-snotty-party routine. My hair, which was sticking in about twenty different directions, had been unwashed for days, my face had been unshaven for a month, and my boots reeked with multiple coatings of penguin shit. I also had the sudden realization that I had forgotten to brush my teeth that morning. The passengers looked at me with equal parts displeasure and fear, as if I were a pirate ready to plunder their loot.

If the company was a bit stiff, at least the Scotch was free, and it was twelve-year-old single malt, which was better than the blended stuff at the station. When nobody was looking, I tried to gargle with it, then made attempts at idle chitchat. I zeroed in on a women who seemed particularly annoyed with my presence, feigning interest in her journey. When I asked her if she had visited Palmer earlier in the day she responded, "In this cold?"

☐ With two-thirds of the trip behind us, the weather turned sour for real. Winds kicked up from the west, blowing as hard as sixty knots and periodically clogging Arthur Harbor with a flotilla of fragmented ice, called brash ice. It snowed for a week. I passed the first few days watching movies and sending e-mails, but was quickly reminded that I'm not the sit-around type. By the third day I was pacing the station like an animal in a cage and spending an increasing amount of time in the weather station, checking satellite images of the peninsula in the hopes of discovering an upcoming break in the blizzard. The little white swirl of clouds never moved east like it was supposed to; it just spun like a dreidel over the exact same spot.

With the snow coming down sideways, I also spent a lot of time staring out the galley windows, thinking of the day I left D.C. for Punta Arenas. I had driven Deirdre from our home to her office across the street from the White House. To break our silence along the way, she talked about her New Year's Eve plans, how she'd join some of her friends who were celebrating on the Mall. Prior to my finding out about the Antarctica trip, we had planned to fly to El Paso, then drive south to Big Bend National Park, the site of our first getaway, and spend the millennium camping alone in that great vacant desert. Now she was left to slum with her girlfriends—for New Year's Eve *and* the next five weeks. Before stepping out of the car, she gave me what felt like a forced kiss on the cheek. Then she was gone.

It was happening again. I was putting us through increasingly long separations, and in the process Deirdre was drifting away, taking my satellite calls from Antarctica and other corners of the world with the suspect voice one normally reserves for a telemarketer. And why shouldn't she? All at once I felt like a cheater, like a man skipping out to have multiple affairs, even if those affairs were with places rather than people.

Though it seemed contrite to say so—which perhaps is why I didn't very often—being away from her was the hardest part of every assignment. People who travel like I did—eagerly, and for a living—aren't trying to leave something behind but to acquire something new. New sights, new emotions, new experiences. And though my separations from Deirdre hurt while they lasted, there was always an up side upon return, our newfound togetherness propelling us for a few days or even a week at a time to a union that was inspired, impassioned.

The Palmer staff were far more stoic than I when it came to their separation from loved ones. On Sundays we were allowed to use the station's sat phone to call home. Whenever I signed myself up for one of the time slots, I noticed that mine was the only name. They were a tough and adaptable breed, these characters. Stuck inside, they created their own entertainment—like invoking another installment of their ongoing "lecture series," where a staffer would get up and talk about his or her profession or scientific work, often with slides and charts, or even dressing in drag to celebrate one of their birthdays. On one afternoon I walked into the recreation room to find a group of them watching *The Wizard of Oz* while listening to Pink Floyd's *Dark Side of the Moon*, trying to confirm an urban myth about combining the two, that the songs corresponded with the scenes on screen.

I just drank—happy hour coming shortly after noon and lasting until bedtime. I felt like a depressed Russian in winter, bored into opening another bottle of vodka. A week into my house arrest, I *did* make an effort to get through a day without alcohol. And by 3 p.m. all was well. I was sitting in the galley, eating a piece of cherry pie and reading a book, when I caught a glimpse of something orange and yellow in the distance. It was the *Gould*, gliding back into Arthur Harbor. I went outside and photographed the mooring, then watched all the students and scientists scamper to shore. They had just returned from three weeks aboard the ship, the *dry* ship. I got swept up in all the excitement, and before I knew it I was back in the pub, chipping bits of ice from a giant block that hadn't seen the light of day since the Pleistocene, just to hear them fizzle in my Smirnoff.

Just like that it was over. Peter and I carried our gear aboard the *Gould,* and with equal parts sadness and relief we readied to set sail. On the occasion of a departing ship, it was Palmer tradition for a staff member to leap off the dock and into the drink. We all gathered in the stern to watch the plunge. As the *Gould* began its journey northward, two men climbed dutifully atop one of Palmer's massive black ship-bumpers. I couldn't tell which two had volunteered, and it really didn't matter. Spiritually speaking, the Palmer crew were all the same, curious and courageous and eager to better the world. They stripped to their socks and underwear and saluted the *Gould,* these men of my admiration. And then they stepped off the edge.

alaska

On the eve of what could have been his big break, my good pal Tookie Niles, also known by the sobriquets "Newman" (for his resemblance to the *Seinfeld* character) and "Commander Q" (for his fondness for donning a blue coat emblazoned with the logo "Q"), seemingly consumed with hypochondria, sounded less concerned with the success of his assignment, which involved filming a small population of endangered red-cockaded woodpeckers near North Carolina's Outer Banks, than with the efficacy of his newly built, full-body tick-protection suit. He designed the protective suit himself, had it tailored in Delaware. It was lime-green and made of nylon. I learned this when he e-mailed me pictures of himself wearing it, doing karate moves. He looked like a WWF reject, and I laughed so hard I lost my breath. "Lyme disease is bad news, man," Tookie said when I called him. "I'm not fucking around." Never mind that Lyme disease wasn't exactly plaguing the residents of those barrier islands, or deterring its five million annual visitors. There might be an outbreak tomorrow, or any day he was there. He wasn't going to be a victim.

Tookie needed the work, if not for the money then to boost his self-esteem. At fifty-five, his career had veered off track, his long-time photo agency distancing itself from him. I had been there myself ten years earlier, knew the paralysis that accompanies a lack of work, so I made near-daily attempts to lift his spirits. But he would have none of it, was spending his days holed up in his suburban Virginia home whining to me about his losses and worrying that the neighborhood commission might soon cite him for not mowing his yard. There were ticks there too, he assured me.

Among Washington photojournalists the legend that was Tookie Niles began well before my time, with his appearance at local photo ops. He was a squat, portly, and bearded man with thinning brown hair and a cautious smile. Yet it was this new-comer's occupational quirks, namely his frugality and his fervor, that distinguished him from the established set of shooters. Legend has it that Tookie was so cheap he recycled old shoelaces as camera straps, so zealous he once spent the night in a tree in Arlington National Cemetery. He was hoping to make pictures of Jackie O's funeral the following morning, but was discovered before it started.

By the time I came on the scene in the mid-nineties, Tookie was the subject of full-fledged fascination. When he charged into an event, usually last, usually harried, conversations ceased and heads turned. From a black plastic case that looked like an over-sized lunchbox, he'd carefully remove his gear, which was often wrapped in black duct tape. Nobody had a clear explanation for this phenomenon. Some offered that he had bought new gear with the intention of returning it, and therefore needed to prevent it from being scratched. Others said he was just nuts. When Tookie stormed out of the event, usually first, usually in a hurry, other photographers spoke with zeal of the sighting, as if they had just spotted the last species of bird on their life list.

Tookie was also notoriously disorganized. So cluttered was his car that a homeless person once took up residence inside it. Tookie later explained to me that he had left the car for a few weeks in a Capitol Hill parking lot. The squatter apparently thought all the crumpled newspapers in the backseat would make an ideal nest. But the newspapers did serve a purpose, he said. They were there to conceal any camera gear he might need to leave inside.

I got my first real glimpse of Tookie's infamous thrift at Monica Beach, a small swath of dirt outside the federal courthouse on Constitution Avenue. Photographers had commandeered the turf while covering the Lewinsky trial in 1998. From this spot we could see, perhaps a hundred yards away, the eight-foot walk witnesses made from their vehicle to the side entrance. The beach was so crowded with giant, 600 mm lenses on tripods that when everyone was at their camera we had to stand sideways just to fit. It was a miserable way to spend the spring, the summer, the fall, sitting on milk crates, playing cards, waiting for witnesses and attorneys to come and go. But there we were, day in and day out. And there was Tookie in the courthouse cafeteria, in line in front of me, snatching a bunch of pennies from one of those plastic "take a penny, leave a penny" holders and handing them to the cashier to help pay for his meal. The cashier, a large woman, shot him a look. "That's what they're there for," Tookie said, quite seriously.

Despite these foibles, or maybe because of them, I couldn't help liking the guy. I remember the yarn he spun me that won me over—a prelude to the tick-suit tale. He had just come back from Asia, where he had a change of planes in New Delhi. Concerned a disease-carrying mosquito might bite him during that layover, he said he donned a head net and wore it around the airport as if this were the most normal thing in the world. He laughed about trying to flirt with a fellow traveler, about staring at her alarmed expression through the mesh netting. "I didn't care," he said about his appearance. "If she didn't see the humor in it, then that was her problem." That was precisely what I came to admire about Tookie. He *didn't* care. He was utterly aware of his eccentricities and gave in to them anyway. If somebody thought he was weird—screw them. The guy was his own man and no one could tell him different. And that made him all right in my book.

My photo chums weren't so convinced. They thought Tookie's antics were more disturbing than amusing, and best kept at a distance. They had him all wrong, certainly, and to illustrate their misjudgment I started inviting Tookie to our dinner gatherings at Guapo's in Tenleytown, a Tex-Mex joint. Tookie was the kind of customer who gave waiters nightmares, I learned—or in this case reason to flee back to Chihuahua. There was never enough salsa and always too much ice in his drink. His portions were smaller than everyone else's, and why aren't we getting more chips? On another night, at a restaurant in Georgetown, he waited until everyone tossed in their cash, including their portion of the tip, then pocketed the money and said he'd put the entire bill on his credit card. I didn't like where this was going. After we left the table I walked back and peeked at the slip, which was tucked upside down beneath a condiment. He had shaved off some of our tip and pocketed the difference.

So my friend's opinions of Tookie were closer to the truth than I cared to realize. The man made me laugh. And my stories made him laugh, too. We were kindred spirits that way—two injustice collectors eager to revel in each other's laundry list of faults and grievances. And he had an alias—Max Todd. He never revealed why, but there it was on my caller ID whenever he called. Who else do you know with an alias? I concluded Tookie and I were best suited as telephone friends—he could tell me about the confederacy of dunces trying to do him in, about his hang-ups and hypochondria and penny-pinching without my having to experience them. And I could indulge hang-ups of my own, my temper tantrums and persecution complex, without concern for judgment.

I remember revealing to Tookie my most despicable act, obtaining the home number of a Delta Air Lines telephone rep, one who gave me more attitude than I could handle after holding for eighteen minutes, one who hung up on me when I asked to speak to her manager. She had made the mistake of giving me her name, her location. And in a moment of blind rage I called directory information for Salt Lake City, Utah, got the number just like that. Her husband answered. I told him this was his wife's manager at Delta Air Lines, to let her know not come to work the next morning. We were letting her go.

"You did that? You called her at home? AAHHH! What'd he say?"

"He asked what the problem was, and I told him she was rude to customers."

"That's sick!"

"Yes. I've got a problem." And the truth is we all have problems, though not all of us have fun sharing them. We found it cathartic, these daily rantathons, these expositions of our mutual misery, as fine a way to wind down after work—or in Tookie's case after a day at home—as a good, stiff drink.

☐ If you believe in the theory that for every action there is an equal and opposite reaction, it might help explain how, in the midst of his downturn, a well-known production company offered Tookie the opportunity of a lifetime—the chance to film the afore-mentioned woodpeckers for an upcoming documentary. Wildlife filmmaking was a field Tookie longed to break into. He had just put together a clips tape, culled from years of filming animals on his own time and dime in Death Valley and Canyonlands National Parks. It was impressive footage, and the powers that be at the production company, according to Tookie, suggested the opportunity on the spot. For a fledgling filmmaker, getting such a gig is akin to kissing the feet of Jesus, to walking into the offices of the *New Yorker* with a pocket full of short stories and walking out with a contract. These kinds of breaks don't happen. Only this one just had and I was thrilled for him.

For a time Tookie was sufficiently focused, arranging his itin-erary, renting the necessary camera gear. But as the approaching shoot date brought its burdens down upon his psyche, so too, ap-parently, did a growing list of exotic maladies. Tookie confessed that he cut out red meat—didn't want to get mad cow disease. And that he was avoiding going outdoors when he didn't have to—didn't want a mosquito carrying the West Nile virus to bite him. He was also harping away about bringing his car to the University of Maryland to get it tested for *Stachybotris*—a mold he thought was growing in the upholstery and thus contributing to a recent and unprecedented spate of memory loss. And then there were the ticks.

Something told me the director accompanying him on the shoot, upon realizing that her reputation was in the hands of a man dressed in a giant green stocking, wouldn't find his phobia as amusing as he and I did. But he said he wore it anyway. Standing still in the suit beneath the hot Carolina sun, trying not to move for fear of scaring the woodpeckers, Tookie said he baked like a potato. He claimed he smelled so bad from sweating, the birds wouldn't come near him. But for the entire day he wouldn't take the suit off. Ticks were likely on it, might seize the opportunity to leap to his exposed flesh. He claimed he even kept it on when he stopped at a McDonald's on the way back to the hotel. I would have given my right arm to see it—him sitting in one of those yellow booths, stuffing French fries through the face hole of his prophylactic netting.

When he got to the hotel, he put the tick suit in the washer and it fell apart. He called me to tell me this, and at the time I thought it for the best. But after a few days of working unprotected in the great outdoors, Tookie convinced himself that a bump on his upper lip, one that looked suspiciously like a pimple, was actually a tick bite. He shaved his trademark beard and said he had begun a course of antibiotics. When he came to see me at *U.S. News* a few weeks later, I hardly recognized him. He looked thinner and older, though less stressed. Despite his scare, he was feeling healthy, the shoot had gone well, and now Tookie was returning to his old, slightly less peculiar self, which, in my opinion, was still peculiar indeed.

☐ Tookie enjoyed recounting telephone tales of his amorous pursuits. And I did use these opportunities to convince him that his thrift wasn't helping his social life. Or his career, what with his seeming reluctance to invest in proper gear, a cell phone, enough stocks of film so he didn't have to backwind his rolls to save a few frames. He wasn't biting. On the contrary, he grew angry. And he had a right to. We weren't friends to try and fix our hang-ups. We were friends to indulge them. I dropped the subject, sorry I had ventured across the unspoken boundaries of our relationship. I also knew, from firsthand experience, not to be on the receiving end of his anger. I had once chided him for wanting to charge an MRI to the health insurance of a dude ranch out west, a ranch he had visited a year before. His return rage was so volcanic it nearly ended our friendship—which in hindsight would have been a good thing, as the true denouement was exceedingly worse.

The dude ranch incident began, as so many good stories do, with a bad idea, in this case Tookie's plan to try and teach photo seminars to tourists staying at a clutch of these working ranches, ranches that doubled as tourist lodges. He needed to sell the idea first—had brochures printed, then flew out west to make the rounds. While waiting to meet the owners of one of these ranches, he made the self-admitted mistake of petting one of their horses. The way he told it, the animal used its head to pin him to a fence, and the bone around the horse's eye socket cracked one of Tookie's ribs. In a move that struck me as counterproductive to his business proposition, Tookie said he promptly demanded that the owners use their insurance to pay for his treatment. The ranchers must have smelled what was coming. According to Tookie, they agreed to the insurance request, then had him sign a document stating he wouldn't sue. I don't know which name he signed, but he said he signed it. And now a year later, the photo seminar idea seemingly having fizzled, he was regretting the decision. He said he was experiencing more chest pains, and since he couldn't sue, he thought their insurance should pay for more tests.

I suggested that it was just his hypochondria kicking in. And even if it wasn't, he had gone on *their* property. "Well, that's what they have insurance for," he claimed. "And we had a business meeting!"

"How is that a business meeting—showing up to make a sales pitch?"

"'Cause that's what it's called. A business meeting!" And so on. I had pushed his buttons, and now I was too aggravated to continue. I hung up my cell phone.

The next day at the office I was greeted by six new voicemail messages. Each was two minutes long, the full length of time the system allowed: a twelve-minute tantrum. Which was eleven minutes more than I needed to stay away from him. Then 9/11 happened and with it came a peculiar amnesty, the temporary belief that life was too short to stay mad at people. When the phone rang in my house a few days after the towers collapsed and the Pentagon went up in smoke and I saw his alias on my caller ID, I picked it up.

☐ I suppose I always knew our friendship would end in dramatic fashion. While the grand finale was just months away, its roots had begun to sprout the previous spring as I was preparing to photograph Alaska's Arctic National Wildlife Refuge (ANWR). Like me, Tookie had a penchant for polar regions. Nearly every summer he ventured to Alaska, rented a van that served as his mobile lookout and his sleeping quarters, and wandered the scenic byways of Denali National Park, looking to film or photograph every animal, from moose to mouse, that might cross his path. Now it was 2001 and the congressional debate over drilling for oil in ANWR was making headlines. I proposed to *U.S. News* that I head up there for a few weeks and shoot the place. I told Tookie the same thing—maybe we could go together?

He was into the idea. And at first so was the magazine, though both had legitimate concerns about money. ANWR is not a cheap place to visit, or for that matter an easy place to photograph. You have to deal with long stretches in the backcountry—at least a week at a time—and rely on bush pilots to get you in and out. And trying to put yourself in the middle of the annual caribou migration, the pictures everyone wanted, was a complex task. The caribou don't follow a set path, or timetable. Yet you still had to book your bush pilot months in advance as their schedules fill up with oil workers, biologists from Fish and Wildlife, other photographers. Most of the shooters just risk it—they schedule a mid-June drop-off at a spot in ANWR called Caribou Pass, in the foothills of the Brooks Range, and camp there for weeks on end while waiting for a migration that may or may not come. I had two issues with this approach. First, Caribou Pass was outside the 1002, the hotly contested 1.5-million-acre expanse within ANWR that Congress set aside for possible oil exploration. Second, I didn't feel comfortable asking the magazine to drop five grand to send me to ANWR when there was such a likelihood I would return two weeks later empty-handed. I sweetened the deal, telling my boss I'd pay for anything above the three thousand–dollar mark, as well as use vacation days to shoot the project.

And then I came upon the Web site of a Fairbanks outfitter named Arctic Wild. It was offering an eleven-day rafting trip along the Aichilik River, which marked the eastern boundary of the 1002. The immediate advantage, apart from being in the proposed drilling area, was that you were actually moving. And it was a good way to travel—slowly and without having to carry all your gear. It ensured recreationists to photograph (my fellow passengers), as well as topographic variation (it began in the Brooks Range, crossed the flat coastal plain, and finished at a barrier island in the Arctic Sea). The itinerary was even designed as a course of study on the drilling issue, complete with college credit options, with lectures from officials of Fish and Wildlife and British Petroleum, with stops in Arctic Village, a Gwich'in community largely opposed to oil exploration, Kaktovik, an Inuit community largely for it, and Prudhoe Bay, home to the largest oil drilling facility in the country. It began June 18. It cost thirty-one hundred dollars. I put down a deposit.

And Tookie balked. The price, the dates, the company, none of it seemed to meet his needs. He hemmed and hawed for more than a month, stringing me and the outfitter along, finding fault with multiple details, then officially opted out. I made a few fruit-less efforts to right his perspective, to convince him that the real world would never live up to his own ideals, that it is impossible to tackle such a trip without *some* degree of risk. This was the

Arctic, for Christ's sake. If it were easy to visit, it would be swarming with fatasses in fanny packs. Then I thought better of it. The guy would probably chintz out at the last minute anyway. I flew to Fairbanks alone.

At a pretrip orientation I met my fellow rafters, one of whom introduced herself as a writer for *Audubon* magazine. This was a rare gift from the photo gods. She didn't have an accompanying photographer. And my position at *U.S. News* allowed me to sell my outtakes—those slides the magazine didn't keep for itself—to other publications, provided those publications were not affiliated with *Time* or *Newsweek*. I actually thought that Tookie would look fondly on my good fortune, though that belief soon faded when I called him back in D.C.

"That's bullshit, man! Oh I don't believe this. She's on your trip? I called them and asked for an assignment and they turned me down. That pisses me off. They told me they were using Milos Boynton. That pisses me off."

I told him *Audubon* had hired Milos Boynton, a well-known wildlife photographer, though apparently he would be well west of me, and outside the 1002.

"That's bullshit, man," was all he could say. And I grew irritated.

"Well, that's what you get for not showing up."

▢ When I was fifteen, I began having a recurring dream, a short one, no more than a scene; one that attached itself before and after other dreams without regard for continuity. In it I am walking alone across arctic tundra. It is summer, late in the evening, the grass is yellow, treeless, and tidy, and I can see for miles, can see that there is no one else there, sense that there never has been anyone before, and that there may never be again. In the morning I'd awake with a weird affinity for the place, the way one might for a person. To be in its company, to be the one privileged soul to realize its rewards: warmth when there should be cold, sunlight when there should be darkness, beauty when there should be barrenness. These were not the products of dream-world implausibility, I understood in the sober light of morning, but the fleeting and ethereal realities of a summer far north.

The dream began my sophomore year in high school, the apex of my social awkwardness. In the southeastern corner of Our Lady of Good Counsel High School, a place my parents sent me in the hopes of salvaging my academic interests, there was an outdoor gap between two hallways, one that offered a view of the parking lot, a brief glimpse of freedom. I exploited this architectural flaw one spring afternoon, breaking from the flow of pimply Catholic boys in cloth ties, running up Georgia Avenue to a nearby Cineplex, and plopping myself down before a movie called *Never Cry Wolf*. It was an adaptation of Farley Mowat's narrative of the same name, about a brilliant, bookish biologist alone in the Alaskan outback. He was there to confirm a convenient myth—that arctic wolves were decimating the region's caribou herds. Being a man of limited field experience, he was in over his head, at first. And with his transition to self-reliance came rewards both personal and scientific—that of witnessing the ecologic codependencies of higher Darwinism, and all the ugly truths that go with them.

There has never been a motion picture like *Never Cry Wolf,* with such infrequent dialogue, with such dependence on place, with such realistic, unnerving, exhilarating evocations of what it means to be alone. The emotions it stirred in me were enough to invade my subconscious, apparently, and have hardly abated in the more than twenty years since. Those dreams, less about the Arctic than about the isolation it ensured, the wildness it represented, the extreme distance, seemingly as far as one could go from Washington, D.C., and still be in the States (Hawaii is farther, of course, but held only fleeting power over my imagination). This was an *American* wilderness, *the* American wilderness, one with which I was affiliated, for which I felt a patriotic devotion, a fidelity. And that's what the oil companies didn't get, what none of those soulless assholes had the imagination to comprehend: even for a teenage boy living thirty-two hundred miles away, there was value in nothingness.

It was with much excitement, then, that on our fourth day on the Aichilik we paddled north out of the Brooks Range and onto the arctic coastal plain, the sixty-five-mile-wide, five-hundred-mile-long stretch of tundra that buffered those mountains from the Arctic Ocean. Flat, vast, and tawny, dappled with flowers and braided by rivers, the plain is the ecologic heart of the refuge, what U.S. Secretary of the Interior Bruce Babbitt called "the American Serengeti." If that seems a charitable moniker, consider that the local caribou herd claims 129,000 members, that migratory birds from every state in the lower forty-eight stop here to rest and feed, that countless wolves, polar bear, and musk oxen make it their full-time home.

The date of my arrival was June 22, one day after the summer solstice, the sun not going down but moving in a circle, bounding along the horizon like a plane looking to land. Though I had experienced twenty-four-hour daylight in Antarctica, the sky there was forever overcast, as dramatic as looking at your kitchen light through a piece of Tupperware. Here the sun shone unobscured, and after exploring the environs with some fellow rafters, I hiked west until the camp was out of sight, my shadow stretching ever farther, the temperature dropping slightly, a breeze picking up from the north, bearing a faint though unmistakable scent of the sea. Some time past midnight I perched myself atop a modest pingo—a hump of soil forced up by permafrost—and engaged in no further employment than watching the longest-lasting stretch of orange light I have ever seen.

When the sun reached its nadir, which presumably brought the lowest temperature of the day, a silver band of fog developed rapidly over a distant river, the band as sheer and dense as a piece of pipe, and an hour later evaporated. Caribou speed-walked across the plain, their hides scarred and nappy, though otherwise there was little movement. I made pictures of all this and then slept for several hours. When I awoke the light was sharper, without much of its hue. It was 5 a.m. and there were birds in the sky. I headed back to camp. Along the way I paused to examine little rainbows at my feet, oil percolating to the boggy surface.

We continued north after breakfast, spent two more nights on the coastal plain, then one on a barrier island in the Beaufort Sea. There the legendary Alaskan bush pilot Walt Audi flew us three at a time to Kaktovik, a dumpy Inuit village on the Arctic Sea. Audi owned the closest thing in town to a hotel, the Waldo Arms, where we checked in and took our first shower in a week. With only one night in Kaktovik, I hurriedly set out to photograph the place, and met with little success. It was already late, and the streets were nearly deserted, which made it all the more alarming to hear someone charge up behind me, screaming as if about to bury an ulu in my back. Commander Q.

"Jesus, man! What the hell?"

"I came to surprise you."

"What?"

"I came to surprise you. And do some shooting."

"You're in Kaktovik?"

"Obviously!"

"When did you get here?"

"Today." I stared at him unbelieving.

"How'd you find me here? This is only like the most remote habitation in America."

"I called the Arctic Wild office and got your schedule."

"Ahh, isn't that kind of creepy? You following me."

"I'm not following you."

"The hell you aren't. It's 'cause of *Audubon*, right? Cause you want to shoot for them?"

"That would be nice, yeah." Tookie had in fact already spoken to the *Audubon* writer at the Waldo Arms—where he, too, was staying. Not in one of the rooms. They cost a hundred bucks. He was staying in a shed out back, a shed we went to examine. It was dark and damp, nothing more than, well, a shed. In one corner was a mangy cot, the kind you might find in an urban crack house, and in the shed's center a wood stove, notable less for the amount of warmth it generated than for the amount of gray smoke.

"Why don't you just sleep outside?"

"Don't have a tent," he said.

"You don't have a tent?"

"Nope."

"You came to ANWR without a tent?"

"Yep."

I knew what he was waiting for, the mooch, and as I was already bunking with a fellow rafter there was no way in hell I was going to share my room with him. I offered him my tent instead, though he said he didn't want the burden of carrying it home. And anyway his lack of a tent appeared to be the least of his gear troubles. He had no boots, no parka, no balaclava. The guy was dressed for a spring stroll on the Mall. I pointed at his shoes, some flimsy brown things.

"How are you gonna walk on the tundra with those? The tundra is marsh, man. You need boots."

He eyed the pair on my feet. "What size are you?"

Tookie claimed he wasn't going to overnight in the tundra, but have Audi fly him around to look for caribou, then try to put down for a few hours near the herd. It was a pipe dream. Audi was swamped with other jobs, jobs for people who pay big money. "And what if he gets you out there and you guys get stuck?"

Tookie showed me a bag of food he had snagged at some all-you-can-eat place in Prudhoe, where he'd had a long layover. "They said I could take it," he volunteered, sensing my disapproval.

"And what are you going to drink?" He pulled from his coat two of those little plastic cups of water you get on airplanes, the ones with a foil lid that provide no more than a gulp or two.

At about eight o'clock, all the rafters gathered in the kitchen of the Waldo Arms. Dinner was included with our rooms, a hearty buffet: steak, pasta, rice, greens. We came down on it with ferocity. That first meal after a stint in the wild is without compare, and so busy were we stuffing our faces that at first I didn't notice

Tookie, standing in the corner and eyeing our banquet. Dinner didn't come with the shed. He retired to his cot to try to sleep while the rest of us, stomachs bursting, went to an adjoining room to drink beer and shoot pool. When I went back to the kitchen a few hours later for another helping of chocolate cake, I encountered Tookie alone at the table, pale and trembling. "What's the matter now?"

"I can't go back out there, dude. It's too cold. It's in my bones. I can't stop shaking."

I stuffed the cake in my mouth and patted him on the back. "The boys are waiting for me."

The next morning on my way out, I peeked inside the shed. Tookie was curled up on the cot, his sleeping bag pulled over his head. The fire in the stove was out and it was cold in there, damn cold. I slipped out the door and flew to Prudhoe to visit the oil fields, then home the next morning. Tookie followed me back a few days later. Audi never got him up in the air, and he admitted returning to suburban Virginia with much of his film unexposed.

□ Given both our eccentricities, it had been easy to write off Tookie's surprise appearance, to not see it as a cautionary tale. That opinion changed in February of 2002, when one of my editors asked me to travel to Inuvik in Canada's Northwest Territories. Like Kaktovik, it is an Inuit town on the northern edge of the continent, a little less than three hundred miles east of its Alaskan cousin. The magazine was doing a story on gas hydrates, whatever that was, and needed me to photograph a gas well built atop the Mackenzie Delta. I could hitch a lift there in a helo from Inuvik with some folks from the Unites States Geological Survey (USGS), provided the weather was good. If not, I'd have to drive, which was complicated, as there were no roads. There was the Mackenzie River, however. Frozen. I could rent a truck and drive on top of it for 125 miles, due north, until it reached the Beaufort Sea. The gas well would be on the right—the only visible object in a world of white. This being winter, I'd have to work in serious cold—fifty below, perhaps. The USGS would outfit me with extreme cold-weather gear.

In one of our telephone conversations, I told Tookie I was heading north again. "What! What for?"

"For the magazine."

"Yeah, but for what? What's the story?" The angst in his voice startled me, the ANWR encounter rushing back. I envisioned him showing up in Inuvik in his stupid brown shoes, his Commander Q coat, looking for a place to sleep. He'd freeze for real this time. I told him I wasn't sure just yet.

"Bullshit. What about?"

"They want to keep the story quiet," I told him. The interrogations continued for days. And all at once his eccentricities, his focusing on why I was heading to the Arctic, *his* Arctic, stopped being funny. "Drop it for real," was my request, and he hung up aggravated.

The next morning I got a call from a photographer friend with the *Christian Science Monitor.* He had gone to Inuvik the year before to do a similar story and was loaning me his pair of mukluks. Only now he was calling to tell me Tookie had called him, wanting to know why I was going to Inuvik. An hour later a photo friend from Knight Ridder called—same deal. I flipped, called Tookie enraged, told him his behavior was creeping me out, that it was too damn weird, even for him, that I didn't want to speak to him anymore.

And so it came to be that while sitting in the boarding area of National Airport, eating a bagel, reading the *Washington Post,* and waiting to fly to Toronto, then Edmonton, then Yellowknife, then Inuvik, I saw what looked like Tookie's head pass above the Style section. I lowered the newspaper and watched Tookie park himself in the seat directly across from mine. He placed an oversized carry-on atop the adjoining seat, the Air Canada ticket emerging strategically from the pocket facing me.

"What are you doing?"

Tookie peered around as if he heard someone calling his name but didn't know who. He looked haggard, drained, sucked dry, as if he hadn't eaten or slept in days, his hair sticking this way and that, his eyes webbed with veins, his skin sallow, the color of buttermilk.

"What are you doing?" I repeated.

This time he looked at me. "Oh, I thought you weren't talking to me."

I leaned closer to him. "What are you doing?"

"I'm doing what you're doing. I'm going to Inuvik."

This wasn't happening. How did he know what flight I was on? I saw him queering the whole deal with the USGS. I saw him following me to my hotel in Inuvik, then to the helo pad. I envisioned the look on the scientists' faces when two of us showed up for the flight instead of one.

"Who's this?" they'd ask.

"Ah, well, he's this guy who's following me. I know him from Washington, and he's territorial about the Arctic, and he flew all the way out here because I wouldn't tell him what I was shooting. But don't worry about flying with me, or letting me inside your highly explosive gas well. I'm not a psychopath." And what if the weather was bad. What if I had to drive? Between Inuvik and the gas well was a hundred miles of nothing. Who would see if I met with a sudden, unfortunate accident, was driven off that frozen river, forced out of my car and into the white? I wouldn't be found until the following summer when the river thawed, provided my body hadn't drifted out to sea or washed ashore on some hidden bend and been eaten by muskrats.

"I'm going to Inuvik to photograph a story on gas hydrates. It's a boring story. It's a lousy two-day shoot."

"Ah, yeah. Well. You know. I'm actually going to Tuktuyuktuk. I got some stuff there I want to work on." His knee bounced wildly.

"Are you insane?" He didn't respond. "Okay, here's the deal. I think you've lost it. Mentally. I think you're stalking me. And I'm calling security." He let out a moan. I hurried through the airport searching for a cop, but none were around. Passengers were boarding now. I decided to jump on the plane and deal with this in Toronto. From my window seat I could see more passengers coming toward the airplane. Tookie wasn't among them. A dulcet voice came over the intercom asking passengers to please report any suspicious activity. It was five months after 9/11. Everyone was on edge. I shouldn't ring the call button, I thought, then pushed it anyway.

The flight attendant sent security to look for him, but Tookie had fled the airport. The pilot came back to tell me this, and then politely asked me to get off his plane. "What? Why?"

Another flight attendant, this one male, stormed up, "Because your checked luggage wasn't X-rayed. That's why." I wanted to punch him in the face, the flamboyant busybody, the nancy, attacking me to validate his own miserable existence, his arms now crossed, his lips puckered.

"And that's my fault?"

"We need to X-ray it, and we're not gonna delay the other passengers." He bugged his eyes out for the last half of the sentence, as if it were the most important thing he would say all day.

"But your recording said to report any suspicious activity." Passengers were staring now. Whispering. I was the crazy person. The terrorist. The subject of cell phone calls to friends, spouses. "There's one on our plane!" I've got to shave more often, I thought.

"There's another flight in forty minutes," the pilot said. "I checked. You'll still make your connections." So I walked back into the airport, where an Air Canada representative met me. He alleged Tookie had gotten his attention too. At check-in. According to him, Tookie paid cash for a refundable, one-way ticket to Toronto and had no bags to check. Three red flags. This also suggested that he had come to the airport just to mess with me—without any intention of going to Inuvik. Or at least that's what I kept telling myself.

In a rambling e-mail I received upon returning to D.C. ("rambling" because it contained sentences like these: "So, your low, dirty tactic, formed in a moment of anger, out of an.[sic] warped sense of loss of control and urgency, with no regard for any damage, certainly worked, certainly it took me out of the picture didn't it? . . . Well, you were wrong in your presumption, wrong in your accusation, and WRONG in impulsively doing what you did without regard. You were VERY WRONG!") Tookie confirmed that he had no ticket beyond Toronto. He wrote that he had a second reservation "to arrive in the north in a couple days." Then he informed me that I was mentally unstable, egocentric, and paranoid. And I'm not too proud to admit that there's a little truth to all three.

I ended up having to drive to the gas well. Though the USGS did helo me out the first day, I only got a few hours of shooting time—all in harsh midday light. So the next day I made the drive north, along the frozen river. It was easier than it sounds, had street signs and everything. And the writer came along, in fact did most of the driving. I sat in the passenger seat and looked behind us a lot. I did the same on the return trip. And when I lay in bed in my hotel room with the curtains wide open, hoping to catch a glimpse of the northern lights, I found myself awaiting his portly figure instead, bundled up against the cold, coming toward the hotel in the dark polar night.

st.john

We arrived without an ounce of energy between us, Deirdre run down from covering a Missouri Senate race (where she earned temporary fame when John Ashcroft, the silly tyrant, booted her off his press bus because he didn't like the *Post-Dispatch*'s coverage—this shortly before losing his Senate race to a dead man) and me from covering the Gore 2000 campaign, followed directly by the election contention, those infamous thirty-six days when the forty-second presidency hung in the balance. Every morning during the contention I joined other journalists at the intersection of Massachusetts Avenue and 34th Street, outside Al Gore's home at the Naval Observatory. We sat four to a car to stay warm, me and shooters for *Newsweek,* the *New York Times,* and Knight Ridder, and stayed there all day and much of the night, never sure if and when the Gore staff would give us coverage up at the mansion. News was breaking every day, and on the occasion they allowed us access, it came fast. Contention coverage had been the exact opposite of the campaign, where we saw him all day and night, every day and night. Yet for some reason, perhaps because it was so unproductive, or perhaps because the story seemed it might never end, it felt just as tiring. Finally, on December 12, by a five-to-four ruling, the Supreme Court sealed Gore's fate. Not ten hours after photographing him concede his lifelong dream to George W. Bush, Deirdre and I fled to St. Thomas, then boarded a passenger ferry to St. John.

We rented a villa on the far side of the island, and for ten days did little more than sleep, drink Caribe, and stare at the sea. When I put on my shirt and flip-flops, drove our Suzuki Samurai into town for groceries and learned from a headline in the local paper that Al Gore had followed us down to the Caribbean, was in fact licking his wounds at a secret location on that very island, I actually felt a bout of sympathy for the guy. So he ran a shitty campaign, then allowed himself to be out-lawyered—when it came to travel, he had good taste.

If St. Thomas is the Detroit of the Caribbean, neighboring St. John is its provincial antipode. There are no stoplights or Carnival cruise ships, no schmaltzy singles resorts or buff, prowling college students; just a restrained village named Cruz Bay and twenty square miles of mountains and beaches. Thanks to the late Laurance Rockefeller, that generous benefactor of wild lands, the island is still carpeted in a thick, green arboreal shag. His family once owned nearly two-thirds of St. John, and in 1956 he gave that share to the National Park Service, which renamed it Virgin Islands National Park. And that preserved the forests of kapok and bay rum trees for people like me, who prefer to bird-watch rather than barhop.

St John's north shore, which fronts the Atlantic Ocean, is one long, undulating string of undeveloped beaches. The most famous of these, Trunk Bay, which is often cited in those absurd "ten best beaches in the world" lists, was the sole disappointment. It is a decoy, a prepackaged day-trip destination for those vacationing on St. Thomas, looking for a little adventure. The true treasures of St. John, we discovered, are just to the east, Cinnamon Bay, Maho Bay, Francis Bay. They come one after another, an ever-grander trio of crescent-shaped coves, glowing lunar white in a galaxy of green and blue.

Most days we were alone on their shores, save for the brown pelicans kamikaze diving for fish and the occasional wild donkey standing sad and doe-eyed, though tolerant of a few strokes of their snouts. That water, warm and brilliant and enveloping, its kaleidoscope of alien life; Deirdre's black flippers kicking, then pausing, her hair weightless; that water lured me to her like a potion, to float by her side and web my fingers in hers and renounce forever all the hideous distances I put between us. Leaving her side seemed impossible. I wanted to pitch my Nikons into the sea and spend my life swimming next to her, two happy fish in our own private Eden.

"How long can we keep living apart?" I asked late one day. We were sitting on the deck of our rental villa. I was working through a pile of old *New Yorkers,* she through the local paper. The sun was setting behind a group of green islands in the distance.

She rolled her eyes and sighed, "Holy shit."

"What?"

"Bush made Ashcroft attorney general." She held up the article.

"Did you hear what I asked?"

"I did. Yes."

"Well?"

"I don't know how to answer that and don't pretend it's been hard on you. You got to go to Antarctica and where have I gone lately? Missouri?"

"You haven't enjoyed it?" I asked and she shot me a look. "I'm being serious. You got to live your own life."

"No, it's true. Having the house to myself. Following my career. Sure. It *is* nice. But I don't want to do it forever."

"That's what I'm saying."

She stared at me now, her green eyes glistening in the low Caribbean sun. We had never defined our future, a parental agenda, had only talked about slowing down and having kids "some day," whatever that meant. And yet in that setting, hearing the songs of bananaquits and smelling the perfume of the frangipani trees and absorbing her proximity, her absolute attention, her warmth; what was the point in waiting? "Maybe you should go off the Pill."

She didn't betray the slightest surprise at the remark, as if she had been thinking the same thing. "Are you gonna be able to do it?"

"Give you a kid?"

"Travel less."

"I think so. Why not?"

She smiled. Nodded yes. She reached out and gripped the tips of my fingers, and the decision felt right. For the next few days, anyway. When we returned home, there was a new administration to cover, new people to meet, new places to go. For much of the next year we weren't even in the same time zone on the days she was ovulating. A delivery problem even FedEx couldn't fix. Though I didn't admit it to Deirdre, let alone to myself, I was secretly happy for the delay, to keep moving for another year. Deirdre was sporadically frustrated but never made an issue of it. She knew that deep down I wanted a family and that we'd have one soon enough.

In the meantime we vowed to make St. John an annual event, booked a house for the exact same week the following year. We'd invite our folks along too, escort all four of them to our favorite snorkeling spots. We'd take turns cooking lavish Caribbean dishes. It would have been the perfect sequel had so much not changed in a year.

☐ In magazine photojournalism, as well as in the photo departments of some of the nation's largest newspapers, there exists a peculiar dichotomy between those who edit pictures and those who make them. On the word side there is a natural progression from reporting to editing, and the people who assign, review, and lobby for your work have done their time in the field. But few picture editors began their careers as professional photographers.

Instead, photo editors at these publications are practitioners of their own independently honed craft. A parallel tract with a sovereign role, one that employs a greater degree of research and reporting, as well as selection skills, for which that dichotomy serves a tangible purpose. Choosing what image works for the story rather than the one that works on pure aesthetics (which is often the photographer's preference, as it is harder to produce) is an editor's most valued skill—and the skill I had the hardest time replicating, my vision obscured by emotion, by attachment to aesthetic successes, to what was beautiful rather than to what informed. Pictures that did both, those were what the best photographers produced. I considered myself lucky to have made one or the other.

The editors at *U.S. News* were an inspired and sophisticated lot, and I learned from their proficiency. They could happen by a piece I had been working on for months, the slides scattered all about the light table, and in a series of swift chess moves transform the puzzle into a picture story. A picture *story,* with a beginning, middle, and end. On a daily basis they directed their expertise toward helping me and the boys, toward opening all those doors necessary for us to produce affecting photographs. And to getting them published. They were even kind enough to let me play a role in the postshoot process, pathological control freak that I was.

The traditional procedure for us photographers was to drop our film in the processing lab, from which it went up to the appropriate section editor, who reviewed the take, okayed his or her edit with the director of photography, then "showed," or projected, the images in a viewing room. In attendance were the word editor of the story, an art designer, the art director, the director of photography, and, when appropriate, the managing editor of the magazine. Together they chose what pictures would actually run, and often in which order. Lastly, the word editor would write up the captions and confirm them with the picture editor.

Like many photojournalists who do much of their own research, I had trouble surrendering control of my work after I dropped it in the lab. I saw it as bad journalism, a relinquishment of postreporting rigor, a perpetuation of the stereotype that the photographer's role was a simple, robotic exercise, the pressing of a button, and that we adhered to lesser standards than writers. When a writer hands in a story the editor reviews the work, suggests changes, and returns the material to the creator. Anything less, such as the editor rewriting the piece on his own, would lead to inaccuracies. It would also be fraudulent. The person's name going on the piece is the writer's, after all. Likewise, I considered it my job to oversee my product's passage from camera to page, to review the editor's selects, the designer's layout, even on occasion the color proofs from prepress.

The editors and I didn't always see eye to eye on this, of course. And whenever we couldn't resolve an impasse, felt strongly about different images, say, I had to defer to their judgment. For me this was all part of the process—what mattered was dialogue, open communication, that my perspective was always considered, if not always granted. So what if I didn't agree with every decision they made. The feeling was mutual, I knew, and it never clouded our respect for each other. We were all good friends, one happy, quirky family—with two successive forces in photojournalism at the helm. Finnegan Grove and Madison West were the directors of photography who had put *U.S. News* near the center of the photo world through liberal and innovative use of imagery, bosses who kept photogs on their toes, picture editors inspired, and upper management in check. They were the best in the profession, I believed, and so did others. In the late 1990s, the photo world looked up to *U.S. News* as the premier picture newsmagazine.

It's not that *U.S. News* employed better photographers than *Time* or *Newsweek;* we didn't. It's that the magazine ran better images from our take—and displayed them with brio. So what if some readers—and some word editors, the jealous and red-faced ones who thought photographers worked for them, who saw us as illustrators rather than journalists, who stomped their feet at the amount of real estate we claimed in a particular issue—didn't get why an image was blurry, a subject unlit, a horizon tilted. Exposing people to affecting photography was part of our role— and part of the fun. It also enabled the photo department to thumb a collective nose at the news media's most lazy, if economically sound, practice: that of showing people what they want to see or read rather than what they should.

When Hailey Walker was hired as director of photography, she seemed the latest addition to a managerial trifecta. She was young, in her mid-thirties, drop-dead beautiful in a bright-eyed, first-grade-teacher kind of way. More importantly, she was smart. Refined, friendly; an amalgam of warm and cozy qualities that, for more than a year, clouded my comprehension of a dispiriting truth: my new boss had a great big bug up her ass about me. In the spring of 2001, when I first began to connect the dots of her derision, part of me didn't believe it. Was she really taking control of my contest entries (an annual task for every photographer, entering their year's work in a host of national and international photographic competitions)? Dismissing my request for caption corrections? Forbidding me from color-correcting my pictures in Photoshop? My job, my way, I demanded, and we thus clashed with reliable frequency.

Hailey saw me as hotheaded and confrontational, as independent-minded to the point of skirting her authority, and those were fair assessments. I had a dangerously low tolerance for other people's imprudence. And yes, if someone pushed me I pushed back, even if that person happened to be my boss. Which is to say I *was* a pain in her ass. But I also produced—and didn't that productivity, not to mention my tenure, entitle me to some spouting off? Don't get me wrong, on a personal level I really liked the woman. So did most of us. And I so wanted her to like me— to find me smart and funny and talented. The model employee. The apple of her eye. But I couldn't curtail my righteous persona, surrender those liberties I held as inherent to me as a photojournalist. It was the *photographer's* job to choose his contest entries, to decide what computer he carried, to ensure the captions were correct, the color corrections accurate, the space commensurate.

Yet Hailey was stripping me of those tasks. Worse, she was delegating them to a trio of young and uninspired protégés, a trio she had overpromoted from digital imaging (the department that, among other tasks, scanned the photographer's slides and negatives into the computer system). A trio that was collectively known, in the lazy parlance of inner-office scorn, as the "digi-chicks."

The digi-chicks' offenses were ever-aggravating, a maelstrom of minor fuckups that gave me an intermittent eye twitch. Too many assignments from them came last minute and weren't researched. Too many photos didn't get entered in contests. And getting a picture story up on the Web, that venue with the greatest amount of vacancies, and the easiest ones to fill, was now only slightly more likely than winning the Powerball. One of them called in sick nearly every Monday. Another was such a little snot to me—easily the least pleasant person I have ever worked with—

I had recurring fantasies of pushing her off the Georgetown water-front and watching her drown in the Potomac.

When one of the digi-chicks published a picture of mine in the magazine from Antarctica for a story on the Arctic National Wildlife Refuge, I had had enough. I stopped her in the hall-way. "Are you bipolar?" I asked and I meant it in the kindest way, was trying to make light of the mistake. Though her expression failed to register the double entendre of my jibe. "You used a picture from Antarctica for the Arctic Refuge story."

"You didn't like it?"

This wasn't happening. "Antarctica is in the Southern Hemi-sphere. The Arctic is in the north." Still the glazed expression. "They're two different places. Holy crap!"

Her smile evaporated. "Well, I guess I fucked up, then," she snapped before marching off.

My photo department colleagues would sigh and roll their eyes at these offenses, then get on with their jobs, their lives. I didn't see the rewards of such clemency—found it preferable to file every blunder and platitude, every missed meeting and unre-turned phone call in my mental collection of affronts and injus-tices. And then to huff and puff with embellished outrage. Because doesn't everyone see that these three were ruining the photo de-partment's credibility? That they were diluting the talents of the senior editors?

Of course, I was loath to admit that these issues had as much to do with me. With my open disdain for anyone I perceived as lazy. With my sense of entitlement. With my growing resentment at having ignored the elements of a happy and rewarding existence—a beautiful wife; a beautiful family—for the now-questionable recompense of working at a national newsmagazine. For the privilege of taking direction from these three! No way. I was the victim here, and the whole thing depressed the hell out of me. And further distanced me from Hailey, the digi-chicks' stalwart supporter.

The only way to alleviate my angst, I knew, was to leave— something I lacked the courage to do. I might have survived the freelance market, but at what price? Working in Washington? Covering the Shit House? Handing over my wings, my supreme desire, my self? The diversity of destinations the magazine placed under my feet didn't exist elsewhere. And photographically speaking, I couldn't exist without it. I was a manic, East Coast, type A travel-holic, and the *U.S. News* photo department was my link to the road, the dealer for my addiction, the propellant on which I was emotionally, physically, and spiritually dependent. Nope— I'd have to stomach being the boss's bête noire.

Hailey's and my worst clash came that summer, after I returned from the Arctic Refuge. Four days after finishing the trip, I handed to the Web picture editor—one of the digi-chicks— a completed package: twelve photos with detailed captions, and a two hundred–word story summary. Upon receiving the ANWR project, all she had to do was get the text fact-checked and hand it over to the Web team. A simple task, yet one I feared was beyond her. I had visions of the work being filed away in the dark netherworld of her office. Of it being placed atop the tall and dusty pile of other Web projects I had given her, a pile that was visible from the hallway and that raised my blood pressure every time I walked past. And so I commenced a two-day-long campaign of fierce and scurrilous lobbying—okay, bullying—until the poor creature promised that my project would be posted by the following Monday. And she came through! The story went up and I thought myself all the shit—not for producing a project on the Arctic Refuge but for getting a digi-chick to do her job.

Both of us had informed Hailey of its impending appearance, myself on several occasions. But apparently we hadn't done so in a way that an overworked manager would remember. At the weekly editorial meeting, known simply as the "Monday morning meeting," when our new and amiable editor-in-chief, Gerald McGee, found out about the posting of my essay, whose subject was a political hot potato after all, he turned to Hailey and in front of all the powers that be said he didn't know anything about it. Hailey responded that neither did she.

Then Hailey called me at home where I was packing for a summer vacation with Deirdre to Africa. "McGee looked at me in the morning meeting as if I don't know how to do my fucking job!"

"What are you talking about?"

"I'm talking about you going around me and doing whatever you want and just putting up your picture story on the Web. McGee didn't know anything about this. And neither did I." The tenor of the conversation was already heated, and instead of cutting my losses and backing out, instead of letting her get away with what seemed a lot like selective memory (a practice that really pushed my buttons), instead of admitting my own involvement—that I had coerced one of her hires into putting my project up quickly, too quickly, apparently—I dug in my heels. Worse, I fortified my outrage with such heaping amounts of injustice and innuendo that I quickly lost sight of any way out. Civility be damned—I wanted a fight.

"You can't be serious. Didn't know about it?"

"Yes. Didn't know about it."

"That's bullshit. We had a conversation about it on Friday. In your office." There was a long pause on both ends. "And so what if I wanted the pics up quickly? There was a shooter for *Newsweek* in the refuge at the same time as me, and I wanted to beat her to the punch. Jesus. If anything, you should be *thanking* me."

"Why is that?"

"Because I shelled out sixteen hundred bucks of my own money to do this project. I edited eighty rolls and cranked out extended captions and a story summary all by my goddamn self because your Web editor doesn't do her job and everyone knows it. I mean, here I went out and busted my ass and gave you a great project and in return you kick me in the nuts."

"I know you wanted to beat *Newsweek,* but the magazine isn't yours. These people don't belong to you. You can't just put your pictures on the magazine's Web site."

"How would I do that? I gave the essay to your Web editor. And for once she actually put the thing online."

"Who edited the pictures, Jim?"

"I did."

"Exactly! That's not your job."

"Like she would have done it?"

"And who had it fact-checked?"

"She did."

"She didn't! She did not have it fact-checked!" Oh, Christ. I should have known.

"Well, why are you telling me? Tell her. It's her job. I mean, first you're pissed off at me for doing things I'm not supposed to do. And now you're pissed off at me for *not* doing things I'm not supposed to do."

"You can't just put pictures up on the Web site without consulting me."

"Aren't you listening? I didn't put them up myself. I gave them to her and she put them up, and anyway I did consult you. We both did. Last Wednesday. Last Friday. In e-mails."

"E-mails don't count in my book!" she shouted, and that was all I could take.

"E-mails don't count in your book? Okay, that doesn't make any sense. None of this does. You calling me and yelling at me. It's not my job to have the text fact-checked. That's your Web editor's job. And it's not my job to tell McGee that I have a picture story going up on the Web. That's your job. Right? Is it not? So back off!"

Her response was aggrieved and accurate. "Nothing's ever your fault, Jim." I hung up, then pitched my phone against one of the radiators in my family room.

The next morning I swung by the office before heading overseas, and in my mailbox was a white envelope with my name written in a woman's hand—my annual review. It was dated ten days before, though now rewritten, as it highlighted yesterday's allegations, namely her innocence and my guilt, as well as my role in a myriad of other atrocities. She called me a puppy. In my annual review she called me "a puppy nipping at [her] heels," and I figured I would soon be fired. I put the review in my pocket, Deirdre and I flew to Namibia, and while we watched two wild leopards chomping down an impala, I grew increasingly envious of their ability to act on primal impulse, to tear flesh from bone and make no apologies about it because they're leopards and that's what they do. Hell, maybe Hailey's canine comment wasn't so off the mark. A license to maul, to bare some teeth—we all want one from time to time.

Hailey and I didn't speak to each other for four months. When she finally called me, I was in Puna, Hawaii, working on a travel piece. I had just smoked a fatty with one of my subjects, a lomi lomi masseur who insisted I try the home-grown. "Puna butter," he had called it. And the moment I felt my cell phone vibrate in my pocket, saw Hailey's name on the caller ID, I was glad I had accepted the offer. She was calling to tell me the magazine was tightening its financial belt, that all those making over $50,000, a figure I was marginally above, were getting 10 percent pay cuts.

I didn't care about the decision. If cutting back now meant *U.S. News* would be around in the future, then why not? What bothered me was how we'd gotten to this point. Yes, the economy was in the shitter. Yes, advertising was way down. But promoting people who did a half-ass job? People who called in sick nearly every Monday? Wasn't *that* contributing to our demise? For God's sake, be a boss! Pitch the dead weight and save those of us who never stopped rowing.

If ever there was a time for the photo department to rally, it was now. In the previous months the Twin Towers had come down, the flags had gone up, and the grand shell in which the media was residing—that had been the summer of killer sharks and a missing congressional intern—was rattled. This was our chance, an obligation born on the incineration of three thousand lives. Watching the Pentagon burn was like watching a bad special effect, a scene scripted from some nationalistic summer block-buster, one that thought it excellent to make the Capitol dome visible through the smoke, glowing like a beacon. It was too improbable to be true. But there it was. And there were the wail of sirens, the smell of burning rubber and metal and brick and bone, and all the journalists gathered seemed to know that that fire was a mere flicker, the tiniest of flames compared to what was to come. There would be hell to pay. And to cover.

Americans were now on the verge of bombing the crap out of Afghanistan, and I wanted to go. I had never made a name for myself as a war photographer. And we had a contractor who was one of the world's best. Nevertheless, Hailey agreed to make me second shift, to send me and a staff writer in the coming months, and I was grateful for the opportunity. In the meantime Deirdre and I decided to keep our second date with St. John.

☐ With a big story before me rather than behind me, my office troubles hovering around my head like a cloud of gnats, I found myself thoroughly incapable of escapist enjoyment, of losing myself in surroundings that, while not new, were sufficiently exotic. I was wound tighter than a tick, and things that should have rolled off my back stayed put, weighed me down. Little things, it was always the little things with me, skewing my perspective and now turning me and my wife's long-awaited excursion, our gift to ourselves and our parents, into a laundry list of burdens and disappointments.

On the ferry from St Thomas, some bug-eyed and bearded Rastafarian, an employee of the ferry company, slammed another passenger's vehicle into ours. "No way, man," he said as he hopped out of the car, and whether that meant "no way was that my fault" or "no way am I paying for that shit" was irrelevant to me because they both ensured the same consequence. Denials and paperwork and checks made out to Budget car rental, that's what was now in store because some dumb, doped-up idiot couldn't drive. Then there was the house we rented, different from last year's, more cramped than last year's and too close to Cruz Bay. And the weather. It rained constantly, a battering, Biblical downpour that flooded the roads and swept the plants off our sundeck and kept us inside that house that was too small and too close to Cruz Bay, staring out the wet, fogged-up sliding-glass doors at a world of whirling gray. I caught a cold.

While everyone else made the best of it, playing board games and renting movies and cooking extravagant seafood feasts, I made a desk of the dining-room table and disappeared into my work, trying to learn how to use the magazine's digital cameras, a task I had successfully avoided for two years, and e-mailing the UN in Pakistan for flight schedules, my doctor in D.C. for prescriptions, my colleagues in Kabul for advice. If overseas assignments get easier with age, in my case it was only because pretrip planning had grown more burdensome. When you know firsthand of the multitude of possible mishaps—gear stolen, computer fried, fixer incompetent, visa expired, stomach spent—it leads to a flurry of preparations that, once begun, only seem to grow more fruitless as they reveal far more potential problems than they resolve. It is a curse, really, a slow and steady self-torture of envisioned dramas and worst-case scenarios. Conditions in Afghanistan promised to be pretty rough.

The first obstacle was getting there. The road west from Peshawar, Pakistan, through Jalalabad to Kabul was passable in a 4WD, but overrun with Talibs and bandits. West of Jalalabad four journalists had just been shot dead trying to make the drive. The UN was starting up twice-weekly flights to Kabul from Islamabad—an hour-long trip that cost $2,300 each way. No matter—the magazine would have to pay it. Getting on those flights was another story. The latest I heard was that there was already a two-week waiting list, and you could only sign up in person, in Pakistan.

Then there was where to stay. The one hotel open in Kabul, the Inter-Con, had only a few floors that were operational. Journalists were camped out in the lobby, which wasn't a great alternative as bandits were charging periodically onto the grounds and robbing people. Some journalists were renting private homes in town, the only reasonable alternative. But there'd be no way to do that in advance. I'd have to wait until I got there to hunt for a room.

And how to get my film back to the office? Shipping was out of the question as there was no mail service. I'd have to shoot digital, something the magazine and I loathed, and transmit the files back to the office. Since there was no phone service, I'd haul a satellite phone capable of an ISDN-speed connection. Of course, sat phones, computers, digital cameras all had batteries that required electricity—in short supply in Afghanistan. I'd bring a power inverter that I could hook up to a car battery for emergency juice, and try and buy a diesel generator there for my room. I'd also buy some electric heaters to stay warm, as I got word from other photographers that buildings weren't heated and it was downright freezing.

Then there were issues of food (or the lack thereof), translators (in equally short supply), money (no credit cards accepted, I'd bring $14,000 in cash), bathing (no showers, just buckets of water), and visas (God knew where to get those—was Afghanistan even an official country?). Whenever I had one issue resolved, another took its place. And I had it easy compared to the photogs who went before me, as I had access to their advice. Those intrepid souls, having gone in through Kazakhstan and Tajikistan when the country was still up for grabs, risked their lives to cover the conflict.

☐ On the flight home from St. John, I felt the cold, sober day-after realization that my grumpy and distant mood had successfully ruined the vacation for myself, for Deirdre, for our parents, and now that we were hurtling northward, there wasn't a thing I could do to take it back—a fact that depressed me further still. "Great vacation," Deirdre offered when we landed. "Maybe next time we can just go to your office. Sit there and watch you work. Would you like that?" She was furious, could barely look at me. I had it coming.

The cabby from National Airport dropped me off at the magazine, then took Deirdre home by herself. The office computer guys were about to flee for the holidays, and I needed to pick up the sat phone from them. About fifteen minutes into their briefing, Deirdre called me on my cell phone to tell me my camera bag was missing.

"It's in the trunk of the cab," I said. There was a long pause.

"The driver pulled all the luggage out. It was dark."

"He's gone? You don't have it?" She didn't respond. She sighed. "Do you have his name?" Silence. "The name of the cab company?"

"I don't remember—wasn't it orange-colored?"

"I think it was orange." I squeezed my eyes tight, trying to remember something, anything, about the cab—a color pattern, an insignia, a phone number, a license plate. Nothing. I couldn't even recall if the tags were D.C., Maryland, or Virginia. I'm a photographer, for Christ's sake—I look at things for a living—and I couldn't remember what I saw half an hour ago. I did a quick mental inventory of what was in the bag. It was *crammed* with gear—lenses, camera bodies, chargers, filters—gear I needed for Afghanistan, gear I'd never get replaced in time. It was the holidays! And Hailey. How could I tell her about this, that I screwed up so royally? "This isn't happening."

"What do we do?"

"Start calling cab companies. Maybe they have lost-and-founds. I don't know." I cabbed back to National, but when I got there it was already empty. In the post-9/11 security frenzy the airport was operating on limited hours, and we had caught one of the last flights in for the night. I headed home.

Opening the front door, Deirdre looked more miserable than I did, had exchanged her anger for worry, her eyes red, her lips pinched. It wasn't her fault, of course—the guy had removed the bags from the trunk himself. Either he didn't see it in there or he robbed us. And yet I couldn't bring myself to say this—or anything else. She did recall one piece of information about the driver: his wife was from St. John and now taught special education at Ballou High School in Southeast.

Ballou is well known to Washingtonians, and anyone who reads the *Post,* though not for its academic excellence. It is a Metro section mainstay for repeated closures, student brawls, improper incidents between students and teachers. Early the next morning I called the principal at home. He said there were probably a dozen special ed teachers, but he could only recount the names of three. He was sympathetic, though, and promised to call his assistant and track down a list. In the meantime we got from information the number of one of the three teachers he mentioned. I rang her up and explained the situation—looking for the cab-driving husband of a Ballou special ed teacher from the Caribbean because I had left ten grand in camera gear in his trunk—and there was silence on the other end. "Hello?"

"How am I supposed to know if my husband has your cameras? I ain't seen my husband in twenty-three years!"

I hung up the phone and turned toward Deirdre. "We're screwed." Two days later, at noon on Christmas Eve, I reached the last of the teachers from my office phone. The Ballou connection was a dead end—the woman didn't exist. The gear was gone.

The *U.S. News* offices were empty except for me. It was one of our dead weeks, a week we don't publish, and all the staff was home with families and friends. Outside my office window last-minute Christmas shoppers were strolling up and down Thomas Jefferson Street (the magazine had relocated to Georgetown from Foggy Bottom a few years before). I felt like the Grinch looking down upon all the happy residents of Whoville, holding hands with lovers and children, yapping on cell phones, sipping coffee from tall, all-white cups—the nonlogo of the café up the street—their arms draped with shrunken shopping bags from Prada, Armani,

Dean and Deluca. I felt lifeless. I felt like I'd gotten it all wrong, my raison d'être, and now it was too late to turn it around. I felt like I'd spent all the years of my youth gathering speed, moving faster and faster, and now that I had achieved the desired orbit and was hurtling through time and space, there was no way to slow down, nothing to grab onto, no inertia. A body in motion stays in motion, says Newton's first law, unless acted upon by an unbalanced force. An unbalanced force. I wasn't sure what Newton meant by that, but knew in my case it meant having a child.

Deirdre had been off the Pill for more than a year, and when we were together and she was ovulating, we had made gallant and repeated goes of it, yet without reward. I was starting to worry that my subconscious was affecting my chemistry, not allowing me to father a child until I was emotionally able to surrender all the rest: the ambition, the drive, the get-up-and-go. I did want a child, I know I did, but it was also true that I was terrified about the consequences, about sacrificing my job.

The industry was changing fast, moving from film to digital and in the process creating a glut of cheap labor. You couldn't throw a rock in D.C. without hitting a struggling freelancer, one born of the digital revolution, of the technology that put a television screen on the back of his camera. Suddenly everyone was a photographer, able to forgo the exposure skills the rest of us had taken years to perfect. Those newly empowered masses, firing their do-everything digitals on full automatic, where did they all come from? Every day a new face, it seemed, younger and willing to work for less.

I wished I could say they were all hacks, nothing but pixels and playback. That we mag photographers were on the side of the righteous, having learned to shoot without "chimping"—the industry verb for reviewing your work on the back of your camera. Having learned on chrome, on slide film, where if you screwed up an exposure it stayed screwed up—and you felt such humiliation for it. That we were better because we still shot film when we could. Because we believed zoom lenses were trash and strobes were for wimps. That prime lenses, the ones of a single focal length and wide aperture, the 24 mm 1.4, and 85 mm 1.2, these were what *real* shooters carried in their camera bags, were far sharper, if less convenient to use. And strobes? That natural lighting was not to be messed with, or only in the most dire instances. That it didn't matter if things went a little dark, if your subject went a little blurry. That a picture's flaws were as valuable as its virtues. Just like with people.

But these were differences of style, not ability. Many of these young and desperate wannabes were enormously talented. Too many, in fact. Every week the editors received portfolios from aspirants—and the work I reviewed made my stomach ache, gave me an ulcer, was moving and sophisticated and lovely. I stopped looking. We magers were going the way of the dodo bird for sure. There were now just three of us left at *U.S. News*. This digital progeny would surely speed our demise.

How had I become this person, I wondered, sitting alone in my office on Christmas Eve and fretting about my existence, fearful that if I stayed put too long my career would be handed to others? I was bound to my travels, of course, could at any moment rattle off the top five destinations I had yet to visit. But even nomads need sabbaticals, want a family. I wanted to be one of the shoppers outside my window. I wanted to have the time, the life, that would allow me to surrender to Christmas schmaltz, to peruse Georgetown arm-in-arm with my wife and child, checking out the same lame Christmas décor the city puts up every year—wreaths around the streetlights and two giant Christmas trees perched on either end of M Street—just for the sappy fun of it.

Deirdre had been patient with me for so many years, and what had I given her in return? Anxiety. Anger. Depression. My frustrations were forever mounting—my office troubles, my career fears, my fertility concerns all hung over our relationship like a death shroud. Even our vacations were strained. I had made a fool of myself in St. John, and in southern Africa before that. Driving across Namibia, I casually mentioned to her that our rental truck was a Toyota. She replied that it was a Nissan, and I said she was totally wrong because I'm a photographer and I notice these things. She pointed to the word Nissan on the steering wheel, and I looked at her and proclaimed with a straight face that somebody must have replaced the original steering wheel with one from a Nissan, because this was damn sure a Toyota. Deirdre was speechless. But her return stare was eloquent enough; it said I had become an insufferable tool.

I closed the window shades of my office, picked up the phone to call Hailey, and then slammed it back down. Screw it; I couldn't deal with her at the moment. I was halfway out the door when my phone rang. It was a man named Jonathan. He said he had my camera bag. "Found it in the cab this morning."

"Where are you?"

"At home. In Maryland. Took my wife to Eastern Market, opened the trunk to put in the groceries, and said, what's this bag doing back here?" He said that we were his last fare on Friday and that he had taken off for the weekend. He could bring it by my house in half an hour on his way to the airport.

Speeding toward my house up Rock Creek Parkway, empty for once, I felt a measure of relief from the previous hour, from the previous three days. The parkway is the prettiest road in the city, largely because it doesn't look like the city but the country, wending like a river through towering strands of oak and hickory and Virginia pine. I rolled down my window and felt a slap of cold air, the smell of dried leaves and distant chimney fires. When I jogged up my porch steps and went in the front door, I peered instinctively behind me. And there he was, getting out of a black-and-orange cab with Maryland tags, carrying my bag. I raced through the house looking for some kind of reward, and yanked a bottle of Clicquot from the fridge that we were saving for my departure dinner. I also grabbed a box of chocolate-covered strawberries given to me the day before, which I had planned to regift to the mailman, and a hundred bucks from my wallet. We exchanged our goods on the porch. He was tall and thick and smiled a lot, and staring at him so did I. We sat down on the front steps.

"You don't know what we went through, looking for your wife."

"My wife?"

"Your wife. You told us she taught at Ballou. We got the principal to help us. We spent three days trying to find her."

"She is there," he laughed. "They've got problems, you know." He had a Caribbean accent himself. I hadn't noticed it before, maybe because we had just flown back and I was accustomed to the cadence.

I told him about my fertility fears. Sitting there on our porch steps, I opened up to a complete stranger, told the guy I was worried that some selfish part of me wasn't letting go, wasn't allowing it to happen because deep down I was afraid to stop moving.

"Do you think it's possible? That my body is somehow messing with my sperm count so we can't conceive?"

The cab driver shook his head. "Man, you're *all* messed up."

afghanistan

In-flight service on the UN charter flight from Islamabad to Kabul consisted of a single Hershey's Kiss, distributed with a wink to each passenger by a pretty, black flight attendant with a British accent. In return she got lots of nervous laughter, which I suppose was the point, as the terrain below us was raising a few heart rates. We were above the southern reaches of the Hindu Kush, bald, brown, and imposing. Though crowned with snow at their peaks, which reached fifteen thousand feet, the mountains looked too arid to sustain life. From the time we entered Afghan airspace, I didn't see a single tree, not to mention a town, building, or road.

Sitting next to me was Calvin Stellenbosch, a smart and upward-moving writer for the *U.S. News* World section who, at twenty-eight, wielded a passport already fattened with two dozen supplementary pages. We skimmed each other's blue books during the flight, and I saw stamps for Iraq and Macedonia, Rwanda and Zaire, Vietnam and Cambodia. Collectively we realized we had much of the Third World covered, yet our long-shared common interest, discovered and reveled upon in countless hallway run-ins, was Afghanistan. A few years back, during the heart of the Taliban reign, we got a green light from the magazine, but Calvin was unable to secure visas from the consulate. Today we were getting our due.

Recent American airstrikes had destroyed the runway at Kabul's airport, so we put down thirty-five miles north of town at Bagram Air Base, which the Soviets built prior to their occupation in the 1980s. Looking through my window as we taxied, I counted eleven MiG-21 fighter jets, bullet-ridden and rusting, strewn about the runway like props from some postapocalyptic movie set. Those that weren't decomposed to their steel skeletons revealed a camouflage of green, yellow, and brown and displayed on their tails the bright red star of the Soviet empire. A dozen years before, in a true tale of David conquering Goliath, tens of thousands of tribal militia, known as mujahideen, sent the mighty Red Army back to its motherland. Of course, the muj *were* armed with $6 billion in aid from the United States, including nine hundred Stinger (surface-to-air) missiles. But that was peanuts compared to the overwhelming firepower, and $45 billion, shelled out by the Soviets.

Civil strife followed the Soviet expulsion—warlords, rival muj factions, and former government forces all fighting for control. Out of this country-wide brawl emerged the Taliban, an army of simple and idealistic Islamic students hoping to rid the country of its factionalism. And the populace welcomed them, at first—the Talibs brought security, an end to ethnic fighting. Refugees returned from *madrassa*s, or religious schools, in Pakistan to join them, and the Talib ranks swelled to twelve thousand soldiers. It wasn't until 1994, after seizing control of the southern city of Kandahar, that they implemented the draconian social policies for which they would became infamous. Then they headed north.

Numerous muj forces aligned to stop the movement, but they were too late. The Taliban had momentum and spread across the country like a plague, taking Kabul in 1996 and the northern city of Mazar-e-Sharif in 1997. By 2001 they held 90 percent of Afghanistan and were on the verge of squashing for good the resistance forces, now known as the Northern Alliance. Then came 9/11, two months of American shelling, and, shortly before I arrived, the retaking of Kabul, and most of Afghanistan, by the Northern Alliance.

Twenty-three years of unrelenting war. The social cost of such a trauma was hard to fathom—estimates ran as high as 2 million killed, 6.5 million displaced abroad as refugees (though 4 million returned under the Taliban), and another 2.5 million displaced internally. The country was in ruins. Half of Afghanistan's villages had been obliterated, reduced to rubble. Life expectancy was forty-five, and infant mortality was the highest outside of Africa. The country had few hospitals, little infrastructure, and an untested government. It did have a lot of landmines—was the most heavily mined country in the world, in fact—and its only real export was raw opium.

Into this fray, Calvin and I bummed a lift. A photographer from the *Boston Globe,* whose company was renting a house downtown, was on our UN flight, and we piled in his ride, hoping we might be able to slum at the *Globe* house for a few days until we got on our feet. Rambling south across the Shomali

Plain, which five years before had been the frontline between the warring Taliban and Northern Alliance, I was surprised to see vineyards, miles and miles of them, withered and untended, along both sides of the road to Kabul. Certainly the Taliban hadn't tolerated wine-making. "Not for wine. For the grapes," the driver responded to my inquiry. "But no more. No rain three years." As if two decades of war hadn't devastated Afghanistan enough, the country was in the midst of a horrific drought. The landscape was a symphony of browns, a picture-perfect example of desertification. There were deep brown tree stumps, all that remained of fruit trees chopped down by the Taliban to better see the enemy; and light brown villages, dry and crumbling. Even the charred remains of Soviet tanks, some on their sides, others completely overturned, were brown. The place looked like the end of the world, lifeless were it not for a group of nervous-looking Afghan men, trying to locate landmines alongside the road with small metal detectors. They wore undersized flak vests and clear, wraparound facial visors, their arms and legs unprotected.

We were able to overnight at the *Globe* house, and the next day moved into a small, newly reopened hotel called the Mustafa. Journalists and NGO workers were its sole occupants, and a colorful thirty-one-year-old car salesman from New Jersey, Babur Fatima, its manager. The Soviets had taken the Mustafa from Babur's family back in the seventies, and the muj had shelled the crap out of it in the '90s, but Babur and his hired team of helpers had worked miracles. Though there was no heat, it had electricity most of the time, and faucets in communal bathrooms that produced clear, cold water.

Glass walls divided the rooms at the Mustafa, a modification made by the muj when they turned the place into a currency bazaar. Babur and his construction team had painted the glass walls white, which did little to block light from adjoining rooms, and nothing to block sound. Our neighbors were smokers, and every morning Calvin and I awoke to their immodest attempts at extricating heaps of lung butter. In truth, the coughing fits weren't entirely their fault. The air in Kabul was as clouded as those smoking booths you see in airports. Sand, dust, charcoal fires, and tons of exhaust had mixed into a bluish, airborne smog; taking a deep breath was like wrapping your lips around a tailpipe.

My first night at the Mustafa I left my sat phone hooked up on the balcony, and when I pulled it in the next morning it was coated in black soot—the kind you get on your hands when you open the flue of your chimney.

"Look at this!" I said to Calvin, displaying the once-clean sat phone.

"That's what the inside of our lungs are gonna look like," he offered.

"We'll be hacking like a Holiday Inn waitress," I said. Indeed, within a few days, we too developed the "Kabul cough,'" an omnipresent dry hack that made our bodies convulse and our faces turn scarlet.

Our room at the Mustafa was directly above the dining room, the social center of Kabul. Babur had somehow managed to supply it with a TV, complete with a satellite connection, which attracted journalists from throughout the city. Though the satellite got the BBC, it was more often tuned to the fashion channel: twenty-four-hour-a-day footage of models jiggling up and down runways. It was hypnotic in that repetitive, campfire kind of way, especially when you consider every other woman in the country was covered in a head-to-toe burka. The young, all-male Afghan help stared endlessly at these lurid images through the dining room's clear glass walls.

The dining room served the usual suspects: kabobs, rice, and the blistered Afghan flatbread called naan, as well as a few pasta dishes. Coke and tea were available, as were illegal libations. Smuggled Russian beer was going for nine dollars a can and Tajik vodka for eighty dollars a bottle. Not that Calvin and I had to pay for booze. Every evening between six and seven, Babur would slip into our room carrying whatever contraband he had managed to acquire that day, pour it into three glasses, and shoot the shit while we drank. The poor guy was so lonely for home, for Americans his own age to socialize with. He was thick, dark, and tough, Babur, with a tight haircut and a flat, boxer's nose. And he was hot-tempered, which didn't bother me as it was always directed against Afghans. The way I saw it, the guy had a right to be stressed. Leaving a comfortable, well-paying job in the States to build a business in this mess. That took stugats.

In the coming weeks we learned that Babur was something of a neighborhood don. He tooled around town in a vintage Camaro convertible, protected by a gaggle of armed goons, one of which we nicknamed "Jaws" after the similarly sized James Bond villain. When Babur stepped out of the driver's seat, people either got out of his way or kissed his feet. Whatever Babur needed for his hotel, the neighboring merchants had gotten too—protection, electricity, running water, not to mention extra business from all the foreign journalists. When the electricity went out in the neighborhood for longer than usual, Babur rounded up some of his muscle and sent them down to the electric company. There they encountered a disagreeable staff—the electricians were refusing to work because they hadn't been paid in six months. So Babur hired them to do their jobs: to come to the neighborhood, find the problem, and fix it. The next evening, when Calvin and I returned from the field, the juice was back and Babur was proudly brandishing the remains of the electrical bypass: a blackened, ancient-looking transmission cable, three feet long and a half a foot thick. "Found the motherfucker!"

"You brought electricity to our village," I said. "How can we thank you?"

"You can help me mount this bitch. I'm putting it on the wall as a plaque."

For all those who loved the guy, Babur claimed there were an equal number who wanted his head. Bandits and ex-Talibs were still about, aware Babur would fetch a hefty ransom. Then there were the government forces and rival clans who were pissed off they weren't getting a piece of the Mustafa's profits and were constantly threatening to storm the place and shut it down. You don't just restart your business in Kabul without paying some people off—only Babur claimed he had, saying he'd put a bullet in the head of anyone who didn't like it. "They fuck with me, I'll fuck with them," he said, showing me the handgun he kept hidden on his waist for just such an occasion. "That's the Afghan way."

His goons out front were even less subtle, standing in the entranceway with Kalashnikovs around their shoulders, menacing grimaces on their faces, that is, until they got to know you and greeted you with bear hugs. House rules forbade Afghans, including translators, from passing above the second floor, where the guest rooms were, for Babur's safety and ours. There was just no way for the goons to distinguish between a translator and an anti-American Talib with an axe to grind. When one translator ignored this rule, pushing his way past Jaws and other security, he was beaten to a bloody pulp in the stairwell, beaten into a coma, in fact, and was henceforth referred to as "coma boy." A few weeks after the beating, I happened to see Babur in the hallway, accepting gifts from a teary old man.

"Who was that?" I asked Babur later, during his nightly visit.

"Coma boy's father. He's worried we're going to kill him in the hospital."

☐ For our first story, Calvin wanted to produce a "postcard from Afghanistan," a quick and broad primer on the mood of the country, before diving into deeper issues. This was fine by me, as it offered leeway photographically. My only concern was that it was already midweek and we had to have the piece back to the office by Friday. "No problem," said Jungal, my newly hired translator and fixer. "Friday is Afghan holiday. We will go out for the clicking."

In the morning, I visited the dogfights. They had been banned for the past five years under the Taliban, not for their brutality but for the betting they inspired, and the Afghans seemed thrilled to have them back. A thousand or so people crowded together on a dirt field to form a large ring, made ever more wide by a group of black-turbaned groundskeepers who flogged people back with short, leather whips. Men holding giant brown dogs by their

scruffs pranced their contenders through the crowd, giving everyone a good look. The dogs looked rough, wild, and mangy like
wolves yet without that wolf-like skittishness. They were ready to
rip to shreds anything, or anyone, they could get their fangs on.

The actual bouts were short, with two dogs charging each
other from opposite sides of the ring, then disappearing in a cloud
of fur and dust. The owners stayed close to the brawl, trying to
get a good look, as did a referee and several out-of-control spectators. Trying to photograph in the melee was challenging at first.
People practically trampled each other, and me, to get a look,
and the only way I could get a clear shot was to move inside the
ring. The groundskeepers were kind enough not to flog me for
my indiscretion. Soon enough they were smiling at me, even beating people back who got in my way. Fine photo assistants, these
thugs. I fantasized about bringing them back with me to D.C., to
the White House, where that most annoying of demands, "Get
behind the rope!" would be met with a merciless flogging, leaving the offender whimpering on the marble floor and me and my
colleagues free to make pictures for once.

Apparently, dogfight rules call for ending a match when one
canine has pinned the other, though the dogs didn't fight with
such structure. They tore at each other's necks mostly, and the
back of their heads, and all the bouts I witnessed were called
when one of the dogs was too injured to continue—the dogfight
equivalent of a TKO. The losing owner would lead or carry his
mutt out of the ring and disappear over a surrounding ridge to
the jeers of those who had lost money.

Later in the morning Jungal drove me to the cockfights, held
in yet another dry and dismal field, though Jungal claimed when

he was a boy the place held "green gardens so beautiful." As with the dogfights, a large crowd had created its own ring. I wormed my way into the front to photograph, which nobody seemed to mind, and for two hours watched the same pair of roosters claw and peck each other into a bloody, broken-feathered mess. It made the American method of cockfighting, where razors are tied to their talons, seem civilized. These birds weren't equipped for killing. Going at each other with beaks and bare talons, as the pair were in front of me, was like watching two people trying to kill each other with those little pencils you get at the putt-putt golf course. After an hour they'd finally pecked each other blind and the owners had to hold the birds in front of each other to fight.

In the second half of the bout, the owners had to keep stopping the fight to clean off their birds. They poured water from a kettle into their own mouths, then sprayed it in their bird's face. Finally, mercifully, one bird slumped in his owner's hands, and the crowd gasped. We could stay for the next match, Jungal suggested, or move on to a different species. The afternoon promised sparrow fights, cow fights, even ant fights.

"Ant fights?"

Jungal nodded yes, laughing with me at the absurdity of it.

"How do ants fight?"

"In the ring," Jungal said. "They're special fighting ants. They have horns." I stared at him. "It's true. But hard to see." While I was tempted to verify his claim, we decided instead to check out rumors of a greater spectacle across town. Supposedly, there was to be a match of *buzkashi,* or "goat-grabbing," where twenty horsemen fight for possession of a beheaded fifty-pound goat carcass. As spectator sports go, buzkashi is Central Asia's *pièce de résistance,* or used to be before the Taliban. The sport is a relic of Genghis Khan and his Mongol army, who instead of a goat were said to use the carcasses of unlucky Afghan prisoners. You'd think the Taliban would have appreciated such a history, even revived it as a way to dispose of their enemies, but they deemed the sport un-Islamic.

The objective of the game is to grab the goat by the leg, gallop with it downfield, round a post, gallop back, and drop it in the center of a circle. If riding a horse while carrying the *boz,* or carcass, isn't hard enough, realize there are ten others on the opposing team trying to fight him for it. And fight they will, with kicks and punches, even elbows to the face.

After several dead ends and numerous shoulder shrugs, we located the upcoming match at a little stadium behind the British military compound. Parwan Province was to take on Kabul Province, and the bleachers were spilling over with spectators, all Afghan men and boys. It was late in the day when they started; the light was yellow and sideways, the scene medieval. An official dragged a limp brown-and-white goat carcass, gutted and headless, into the center of a giant ring outlined with lime. Suddenly horsemen charged from every direction, surrounding the boz like a rugby scrum. After much pushing and whipping, a rider emerged, boz in hand, then thundered downfield. He rode at full speed without holding on—the reins were in his mouth! The weight of the goat was pulling him halfway off his horse, and his other arm was outstretched rodeo-style for balance.

As he rounded the post and came back toward me, I motored off picture after picture. In the corner of the frame I watched another rider catch up with him, grab one of the goat's free legs, and yank. He pulled with such force I thought the boz would split in two. It didn't, and while I photographed, the riders leaned ever farther off their horses, galloping at full speed, the boz straining between them. Then yet another horseman caught-up with the would-be boz thief and beat him over the back with his leather horsewhip. The challenger let go and the goat was heaved into the ring. Goal! The crowd went ballistic. They charged onto the field to congratulate the player, who, still on his horse, spread his arms wide. Officials chased back the crowds with sticks and straps, and so it continued until dusk, such a wild affair, the horsemen looking all brave and elegant in their tribal garb. Watching them rear up on their horses and shout their battle cries, it was easy to forget the city that surrounded us: brown, dusty, destroyed.

Back at the Mustafa I reviewed the day's work on my computer and felt that familiar nag of disappointment. The dogfight pictures were dramatic, though I feared too graphic for the magazine, and my cockfight pictures didn't translate the scene well. The midday light was harsh and those cheap-ass Nikon D-1s, an early-model digital camera, couldn't handle the contrast—the whole thing looked flat, muddy, ruined. Had I shot chrome, they would have looked beautiful. The light in the buzkashi pictures, on the other hand, was gentle and warm. But each of what would have been my best shots had some distracting element encroaching on the aesthetic—fans running into or out of the scene, a horseman in the background who overlapped with one in the foreground, making them hard to distinguish, a rider with an arm raised out of the frame. In scenes like those, with a lot of activity, the difference between a good and great picture is in the details, the moment when everyone or everything is positioned just so in the frame. It's often an issue of pressing the shutter a millisecond later, or leaning an inch to your left—something the best photographers know instinctively. I wasn't one of them.

I transmitted fourteen pics back to the magazine in Washington, then went on the roof of the Mustafa to smoke a cigarette with Babur. He, too, was in a grumpy mood, something about the electric company jacking him around again, and we sulked in the cold for half an hour, watching the journalists moving about the roof with their handheld sat phones, trying to find that exact spot that would get them a connection home.

☐ "For sure, we will go today. We will go today. I am 100 percent certain we will go today." For three days I had been trying to accompany the fledgling Afghan police on one of their alleged foot patrols in downtown Kabul. For three days I had followed the same routine: arrive at their commander's office at 10 a.m., drink tea, stare at the cracks in the wall for two hours, plead for information about the patrol, have more tea, decline invites to his house, and, around two in the afternoon, be told to come back tomorrow. But not today. "I am for sure certain," Commander Razaq said, "today we will go."

Calvin and I were trying to finish a piece on the local gun culture before heading south to Kandahar. It was proving more difficult to photograph than it sounded. Though I found plenty of guys with guns to picture up on the Shomali Plain—people ate with them, prayed with them, even slept with them—it was a different story in Kabul, where Calvin's reporting was focused and where the weapons had gone underground. The country's interim president, Hamid Karzai, in a desperate attempt to create some semblance of security, had proclaimed guns banned from the city, which is like trying to ban tea in China. So the country's ministers were actually talking of physically disarming residents, of taking their weapons from them in random house searches.

According to Commander Razaq, the police force was doing just that during foot patrols of the city. It seemed a great picture, the only picture really, so I waited. But after three days of staring at my watch I was starting to wonder if Commander Razaq, and the whole disarmament program, wasn't a crock. I had never once even seen a foot patrol in Kabul, let alone a police officer. And how could they just barge into someone's home—they'd get their heads blown off. It was all bullshit. Or was it? On what I predetermined was my last day of trying, the phantoms appeared. I was in my usual chair in Commander Razaq's office when he charged through the door and pointed out the window. There, standing at attention, was an uneven line of police officers, waiting for the truck that would take them, us, on our foot patrol. "I told you see," Razaq said, all smiles. "We go."

And we did, sort of. I piled into the bed of what looked like a dump truck with eighteen of Kabul's finest—or should I say Kabul's worst. Their helmets were about three sizes too big, and tilted on their heads at odd angles. Some wore boots and a uniform, others a *salwar kameez*—which looks like loose-fitting pajamas—and flip-flops. Across their chests they wore vests that held extra banana clips, which they decorated with a softhearted selection of stickers, including a Hello Kitty face, a heart with an arrow through it, and a mug of Leonardo DiCaprio, among others. In the truck they sat on opposing benches with their Kalashnikovs between their legs, the butts of the weapons on the metal floor, the barrels pointing skyward. When the truck started up and we rattled out the front gate I noticed the guy next to me was scraping the plaque from his teeth with the sight of his rifle. I moved to the other bench.

According to Razaq, the police were going to patrol a village on the outskirts of town, but our truck broke down a mile from the station. There was nothing around but an ugly concrete Soviet-era apartment building, draped with clotheslines of drying laundry, and a few roadside fruit kiosks. Passersby stared up at the police. The police stared back. "We will patrol here," the commander said. The police seemed confused. No one moved from the truck. The commander slapped the side of the truck twice, which apparently was code for "Get off your ass." Men headed out in various directions. I followed two who walked like robots, their eyes frozen forward, seemingly fearful of interaction. They weren't even talking to the public, let alone disarming them. I tried to make pictures, and they stopped in their tracks, staring at me. This was terrible.

I ran toward the housing complex to try to find a different pair, and for a time followed an officer who, I soon noticed, was growing more and more annoyed with a swarm of children following him. Having been in his shoes many times, I knew that the thing *not* to do was show your aggravation. Kids read it like an invitation to grow more aggressive, to keep pushing your button for the amusement of their friends. Indeed, the moment the policemen shouted at them to scram, the rocks started to fly. One hit him in his oversized helmet, and he picked it up and threw it back. The little offenders thought this was the funniest thing they had ever seen, as did I, and they grew bolder. They started slapping him on the butt and running away, and he swung his Kalashnikov at them like a baseball bat. It wasn't the finest display of dispersement skills, but at least it gave me a gun picture.

The commander called us back. The truck was fixed. We piled in and rattled away. Only instead of going to wherever it was we were supposed to patrol, we climbed up and up a hillock, to a medieval fort where the commander said he wanted to take possession of a mobile artillery launcher. This sounded promising—taking someone's cannon was even better than taking away his gun. His men banged and banged on the fort's giant front door, which creaked open at the hands of three guards who pulled with all their might. There in the doorway was the launcher, or what they claimed was a launcher, though it wasn't from this century. It looked like something out of the Civil War.

"Is that it?" The commander nodded and smiled. "How does that thing shoot?"

"Oh, it doesn't work, I don't think so. We want it for the decoration, to put in front of the headquarters." The whole patrol thing *was* bogus, done for my benefit. The real reason the policemen had left the station was to act as movers, to haul this stupid piece of artillery in front of their building.

The owner of the cannon, another police commander, wasn't around, and his guards refused to give up the goods. There was some shouting, followed by a compromise. The police could take the cannon's wheels now and come back later for the rest. Everyone appeared happy about this, and the wheels were rolled into the back of the truck. We returned to the station. The commander seemed proud. He shook my hand for the longest time. He asked me to please come to his house for dinner. I was pissed. Instead of being straight with me, he'd wasted three days of my time.

But there he stood, all smiles and glee. I supposed in his mind, as is often the case with these kinds of shoots, he gave me just what I was looking for. How could I lay into someone who just wanted to make me happy? I said thanks but no thanks, gathered my gear, and fled.

☐ I liked Kandahar the moment I saw it. Afghanistan's second-largest city had all the rough-and-tumble trimmings of a frontier town, with armed, bearded, black-turbaned men, their eyes rimmed with kohl, their fingernails dyed with henna, prowling the streets with the self-assuredness of a species that knows it is on top of the food chain. Compared with Kabul, the weather was warmer, the food was better, the air was less polluted, and there were far fewer journalists.

Though Kandahar was just a three hundred–mile drive southwest of Kabul, bandits still stalked the road linking the two cities, making it too dangerous for Calvin and me to travel. We had to fly back to Islamabad, then down to Quetta, in the south of Pakistan, where we hired drivers, translators, and some armed security to move us west, overland, back into Afghanistan. All told, it took four days, though the detour was worth it for the Islamabad Marriott alone, where I enjoyed my first shower in three weeks and where we descended on the all-you-can-eat buffet like a plague of locusts. We also had to get our Pakistani visas renewed, and were helped through the befuddling, six-step process by a similarly burdened *Wall Street Journal* reporter named Daniel Pearl. He was reserved and well dressed and made an impression, guiding us with the patience of one who seemed in total control. The next day, as Calvin and I left for Kandahar and Pearl for Karachi, he would be kidnapped by Al Queda operatives and subsequently, famously, murdered.

Our first night in what had once been the Taliban stronghold, I ran into Jacy Byrd, a young freelance shooter and fellow Missouri alum. He asked a peculiar question: "Been goosed yet?"

"Goosed?"

"Goosed."

I shook my head no, and he exchanged smiles with his translator. We were in a restaurant just down the street from our new digs, or should I say dive, the Noor Jahan Hotel, devouring a side of fried chicken with French fries. "Well, be ready."

More journalists made the same inquiry in the coming days. But for a week, no goosing. Ditto for Calvin, though we were out and about every day. We first did a story on warlords, then one on the opium trade, which was in full swing, and full view. I watched in awe as farmers lugged twenty-pound bags of the stuff, raw and tar-like, in clear plastic bags into a row of ramshackle stalls locally referred to as Opium Alley. Upon seeing my camera, buyers in the first two stalls, who sat on giant throw rugs, barefoot and genie-like, while doling out bricks of Pakistani rupees to smiling, toothless farmers, told me in no uncertain terms to take a hike. But the third stall was a charm. While my new fixer, Tahir, pacified their growing discomfort with my presence, I photographed. Quickly.

Though the Taliban first used the drug trade to help finance their meteoric rise, they later banned production under international pressure. Now, ironically, after Americans liberated them, the Afghans had made the growing and selling of opium legal again, though consumption was not. Farmers were eager to unload their long-hidden stockpiles of the narcotic before international pressure mounted and the ban was reimposed. On this day, farmers were getting 41,400 Pakistani rupees a kilo, or $314 a pound, a princely sum for men who hadn't seen a penny in three years.

As I made pictures, the buyers plunged dipsticks into the farmer's bags, then pulled them out, sticky and opium-laden. They rolled the goo into BB-sized pellets and ate them. This being Afghanistan, they offered their Western guest a sampling, which I tossed into my mouth. They tasted unctuous and bitter and offered no body-numbing rewards, at least that I could tell.

After conceding to the quality, the buyers weighed the giant bags, with both parties paying much fuss to the primitive scales. When all seemed in agreement about the heft, out came the calculators. The farmer in front of me had brought in four nine-kilo (twenty-pound) bags. I saw the figure 1,490,400 on each of their calculators. It couldn't be—I looked again, and already the buyers were stacking ungodly amounts of cash before him. One and a half million Pakistani rupees, or $25,000. The farmer said the opium gum came from his fields and those of his three sons. He said that had they used their land for wheat they would have earned just a few thousand rupees in the same period of time, and used twice as much water. He stuffed the blue bricks of cash into a giant white sack, which he threw over his shoulder like Santa Claus, and hustled out.

The merchants told me they shipped the opium to Iran, Russia, and Pakistan by car, where it fed countless heroin habits. When

I asked them if they felt bad about contributing to someone else's addiction, one buyer laughed, "They send us their guns. They send us their alcohol. Why should I feel bad?" Another asked me how much one of these bags would go for in the States. I had no idea, but looked into the matter when I got back to D.C. According to the Department of Justice, at that time nearly all the heroin sold on the streets of Washington originated in Colombia. Nevertheless, one ounce of heroin was going for about $3,000. According to the Drug Enforcement Agency, that ounce was probably only 50 percent pure, which meant a pure ounce would fetch $6,000, and a pure pound $96,000. Now, it takes approximately ten pounds of raw opium to make one pound of heroin. So my farmer's four twenty-pound bags of his cash crop would make eight pounds of heroin. And that would have fetched $768,000 in our nation's capital, more than 30 times what he was paid.

After leaving Opium Alley, I went back to the hotel to review my pics and transmit them to the office. My room at the Noor Jahan faced north, which meant it wasn't good for a satellite signal. I went to the roof, unfolded my sat phone, and angled it skyward, east-southeast, toward that magic spot in the cold, nether reaches of outer space that registered on the tiny monitor of my Nera World Communicator as two full bars—the sat phone equivalent of pay dirt. As I stared at the stars, waiting for my opium pictures to complete their space travel and feeling somewhat envious of their opportunity, a writer for *Newsweek* approached and held up the index and middle fingers of his right hand. "Get it yet?"

"Get what?"

"Violated."

"What's up with this?"

"Their fingers," another filing photographer said.

"So you haven't gotten goosed?"

"I don't think so."

"You'd know."

"He looks too much like an Afghan," the photographer offered lamely. "They like white meat." I was starting to get suspicious, even a little offended. What was wrong with my ass?

"Calvin hasn't gotten goosed either," I said, sounding like a defensive fifth grader, and they raised their eyebrows.

The next morning I photographed a mob of moneychangers at Afghanistan's answer to Wall Street—a small, jammed-to-the-gills courtyard of screaming traders who, on this day, were selling off Afghanis (the local currency) for Pakistani rupees. Spectators sat on porches above and overlooking the trading floor, their legs dangling in midair. I thought myself clever to shoot the scene from one of those porches, with a slow shutter speed, which turned the traders' pushing and shoving into a colorful current of turbans, and was reviewing the results on the back of the digital camera when someone jammed a rod up my ass. I leapfrogged into the air and heard the sound "Wuh!" blurt from my mouth. When I landed, I was eager to hurt somebody. That was no goose but a full-force, two-fingered jab, right up the middle. For a split second I thought it might be another journalist, playing a joke. But there stood three turbaned Afghan men, smiling and blinking like a group of schoolgirls.

Apparently, among Afghans, Kandahar has long had a reputation as a gay town. Right before I left Kabul for Kandahar, a picture editor at *U.S. News,* who happened to be Afghan, e-mailed me the warning "watch your backside." I thought she meant as in "be safe," but when I e-mailed her of my rectal probe, she left little room for doubt. "I meant because they're gay," she wrote. I also soon learned of an Afghan saying—whenever crows fly over Kandahar, they use one wing to flap and the other to cover their ass.

How could it be? How could this conservative, masochistic town, the one-time cradle of the Taliban, be home to a group of armed, bearded queens? After all, two months before my arrival the punishment there for admitting you were gay was having a wall bulldozed on top of you. Then I realized I had it wrong—that such a repressed, all-male environment, not unlike prisons or the priesthood, was in fact *ideal* for the spread of homosexuality. I posed the question to my translator and knew even before he answered, from his unembarrassed, matter-of-fact considera-tion, that this was true. He said that homosexuality had simply become acculturated—that everyone did it. He said that was be-cause they were taught from childhood that women are ugly, dirty, subhuman. He said the only woman he ever laid eyes on growing up was his mother. The translator of a colleague con-firmed Tahir's theory when asked the same question. "Because boys are beautiful," he said.

By "boys" he did, in fact, mean children. Same-sex pedophilia among Pashtuns, the ethnic majority of southern Afghanistan, and of the Taliban, was so prevalent there was even a term for a boy lover: a *haliq*. In fact, it was the abundance of haliqs in Kandahar that helped the Taliban rise to power. They famously rescued one haliq fought over by two muj commanders, earning them wide public support. And when they took Kandahar in

1994, they officially tried to suppress the tradition with severe punishment, though rumors abounded that they, too, had their own boys on the side. Now that the Taliban had been run out of town, the pedophilic practice was open. Men, usually married, would approach a boy between the ages of twelve and sixteen, offering him expensive gifts such as jewelry or a motorbike, until he agreed to be the man's haliq. According to a *New York Times* article published just after I left Kandahar, the problem had already become so widespread that "the government had issued a directive barring 'beardless boys'—a euphemism for under-aged sex partners—from police stations, military bases, and commander's compounds."

I tried to persuade Calvin to do a story on the matter, but he was dubious that Kandahar was coming out of the closet. So was Anthony Turbino, another *U.S. News* reporter who had recently arrived in Kandahar with the 101st Airborne Division out of Fort Campbell, Kentucky. Anthony, a young talent, as handsome as he was easygoing, was staying with the American soldiers at their base at Kandahar Airport, along with several dozen other reporters, photographers, and cameramen. All the media were sleeping on the cold, filthy floor of the airport, whose windows were blown out, and were serenaded through the night with the sound of C-130s taking off two hundred yards from their heads. I joined them for a few nights to photograph the troops for Anthony's stories.

Among the menagerie of press traveling with the 101st was a local TV news crew from a city in the southeastern United States. I learned this within hours of arriving at the airfield when their on-air talent, tan and effeminate in that TV reporter way, with sparkling eyes and can-do smile, handed me a black-and-white glamor shot of himself. In the picture his expression was all surprise and delight, his hair perfectly coifed. In real life his hair looked thinner, the casualty of infrequent showers, perhaps. And his teeth were less white. I flung the gift into a trash can already overflowing with MRE (meals ready to eat) boxes. The photo landed on top of the pile, putting my crime in full view of anyone who walked past. I was too lazy to move it. What did the guy expect me to do with it anyway, put it under my pillow?

It took several days of pleading with the public information officer (PIO) just to get on a simple off-base patrol with the American soldiers. When he finally gave me the nod and I collected my cameras, ran outside, and got a look at my ride, my heart sank. Between two humvees was an open-backed truck, already occupied by Glamor Boy, decked out for his viewers back home in a bulky, camouflaged flak vest and helmet, though we were still on the base. His cameraman rolled tape from a few feet away.

For three hours we rattled through the desert, not passing more than a handful of people. I was cursed—another patrol from hell. Except to take a piss and check their maps, the soldiers didn't even get out of their vehicles. Our movements took on a lazy aimlessness, as if just passing time. My gear and face were coated in sand, I was freezing, and I wasn't making any pictures. I was in a foul mood. Eventually we did stumble upon a little village, the rumble of our vehicles luring out herds of children, who promptly gave chase. They ran alongside the convoy and even jumped on the back of our truck. Finally a photo—the free-riders laughing, clinging to the truck with little brown hands, their shawls fluttering in the wind, the third humvee and the rest of the children kicking up dust behind them. I had just brought the camera to my eye when the local news cameraman from Kentucky flailed at the boys with his hands. "Get off the truck! Get off the truck!" he shrieked at them. They jumped off.

"What the hell are you doing?" I asked, but his attention was on another group of young daredevils trying to fill the vacancy.

Again he shrieked, this time "No! No! No!" Again, they jumped off.

"Would you shut up. SHUT THE FUCK UP!" I screamed it at the top of my lungs, and he stared at me as if just slapped in the face. The boys disappeared in the dust behind us, as did the picture, and for the next half hour while we rode back to the Kandahar airfield, me staring homicidally at the cameraman, the cameraman not daring to look at me, nobody spoke a word. My temper was on a hair trigger, waiting for the slightest peep from him or from Glamor Boy to seek vengeance on them, rationale be damned, for the whole worthless day. Then the cameraman gave me my chance.

"Remind me why I shouldn't have said anything?"

"'Cause it's not your job. If the soldiers don't want the kids there, it's their job to tell them to get off. Your job is to sit still and shut the fuck up and record what happens! You ruined the one picture I could have had from this FUCKING SHITBALL RIDE-ALONG!" Again the slapped-in-the-face look. Earlier in the trip he had voiced some idiotic, B-movie notion about Afghan kids packing plastique, and now I was begging for him to repeat it. He didn't.

When we got back to the base, I ran into Anthony, who was eager to get word on how it had gone. "We should have done gay Kandahar," I said to him. Anthony did have a cool little story for us on the back burner. He found out that a group of young American soldiers were living miles out in the desert with a group of equally young anti-Taliban forces (ATF), jointly protecting the perimeter of the airfield. Anthony had gotten permission for us to spend the night out there, and we arrived late one afternoon, just as the light was turning soft. From our past experiences with American soldiers, we expected there'd be little if any unofficial interaction between the two groups. What we encountered surprised us both—a group of young Americans eager to go native. The two groups were bunking in a medieval-looking mud hut with a giant, fortress-like door. They ate together Afghan-style on the floor, with their hands. They wore each other's hats, taught each other board games, shared lessons on each other's weaponry, even schooled each other on their languages.

I photographed until it grew dark, when we gathered for dinner in a room lit by a single lantern. Almost hidden in a dark corner were two young Afghan boys helping to prepare the food. I asked the soldier sitting next to me who they were, and he said he didn't know, but that the boys lived there with the ATF. I asked him if he knew what a haliq was, and when he said no, I told him. He responded with an interesting story, saying he heard from a sergeant on the airbase that 80 percent of men in Kandahar have engaged in some sort of homosexual activity. He and the other men had written it off as an army scare tactic, a way to keep them from interacting with the locals. It was a likely theory. Still, I suggested to the young soldier that the 80 percent figure may not have been far off. "No way," he said. "Look at these guys." I had learned in the past few weeks that looking tough had nothing to do with it, but didn't want to belabor the point.

After we ate dinner, the ATF cleared our plates and poured us tea. Then they entertained us with "love songs," the first one a long, undulating melody that lasted some ten minutes. They used cooking pots as percussion and sang with such passion I thought they might break out in tears. I rolled some video while the soldiers clapped along. When the song finished, we all cheered and asked what it was about. "It is about the boys," they said.

texas (reprise)

If each presidential administration brings upon the White House press corps its own signature suffering, President Clinton's being sleep deprivation, then President George W. Bush's scourge is a place: Waco, Texas. Dubya's Lone Star estate, the Prairie Chapel Ranch, better known as the "Western White House," is nearest the central Texas town of Crawford. There are no hotels in Crawford, let alone traffic lights that do more than blink, and on the occasion of a presidential visit, the press are stored twenty miles to the northeast, in the relative abundance of chain hotels in and around Waco.

On the days the White House offers coverage at the ranch, to photograph the president with a visiting head of state, say, the protocol is to drive one's rent-a-car to Crawford Middle School, which sits beneath the town's tallest structure, a shiny, silver water tower emblazoned with the name "Crawford Pirates." The school's gymnasium doubles as our press file, the basketball courts now obscured beneath long rows of tables, scattered newspapers, black tresses of computer cords. From here the White House staff drive us in vans seven miles north, onto the president's ranch, and deposit us outside his guest cottage, or sometimes outside the house itself. The president likes to arrive for these events behind the wheel of a white Ford pickup, hop out wearing a cowboy hat and cowboy boots, then use his cowboy hat to brush the dust off his cowboy boots, and did everyone see he's wearing a cowboy hat and cowboy boots?

My first extended visit to Waco was in August 2001, during the president's month-long hiatus. *U.S. News, Time,* and *Newsweek* divvied up the month, word from the White House promising little to cover, and that left each magazine responsible for ten days. I was first to go and was eager. With the president officially down, I wouldn't have to spend my time sitting idle in the press file. I could explore central Texas, a bird-watcher's bonanza, could shop for some boots of my own, do some personal photography, go on barbecue safaris. I could do whatever the hell I wanted, and that freedom would make tolerable even a place as challenging as this. Or so I thought.

I have explored almost every niche of this country, and what impresses me most is that every region has aesthetic value, its own topographic character, which in some immediate, if not lasting, way appeared to my eyes as distinct and beautiful—the slick-rock deserts of the Southwest, the sad hollows of Appalachia, the manicured mountains of New England. Even Midwestern states, those like Iowa and the Dakotas, long the butt of barrenness jokes, display in their stark, sprawling vistas a curious pull, like an ocean without the waves. It is a stunning country, this one, unmatched in the breadth and variance of its physical qualities. Yes, the Himalayas are grander than the Rockies. Yes, the Sahara is vaster than the Sonora. But no other country has so much of everything: mountains, deserts, canyons, plains, prairies, pastures, islands, rain forests, volcanoes, bayous, beaches. And that leaves me all the more astounded that our forty-third president managed to find, and reside in, an anomaly such as this: the only place in America, or at least the only one I've ever seen, that is void of visual rewards.

The Waco area sits on the border of two prairies, the Grand and the Blackland, though the tall and midrange grasses that once distinguished these provinces were long ago devoured by cattle. All that is left, save for the occasional swath of cedar and oak trees, are pebbly fields the color and consistency of kitty litter, a few sand loams, and patches of dark clay referred to locally as "black gumbo." Which is to say there is a lot of dirt. The land looks exhausted, sapped of life. It is dry. It is brown. It is shrubby. The surrounding homes are ugly, the towns relics. Waco is dust. If the area blooms every spring with bluebonnets and Indian paintbrush, as I was told, that was still not enough to resurrect the rolling fields from eleven months of unsightliness. And if President Bush really believed this a "spectacular" setting, as he was fond of saying, believed his sixteen hundred–acre spread, his limestone home, his man-made, bass-stocked pond lifted this landscape from the banal, it was less an accurate endorsement of the topography than further evidence of how life in the bubble can limit one's perspective.

Waco in summer is mercilessly hot, a day-after-day, never-a-cloud-in-the-sky kind of heat. Television weather outlooks were unwavering—five orange suns radiating above three-digit numbers. Moments after checking in to the Waco Hilton, with its sad, eighties-era decor, I stared disbelieving at the weather report. I had trouble hearing the accompanying commentary, for from just outside my window, in the branches of an oak tree, was coming quite a racket. This live oak was indeed alive, quivering, full of grackles, a black, Hitchcockian swarm, fighting, squawking, shitting, swirling around the tree like neutrons around an atom. How many were in there? Hundreds? Thousands? And will they squawk at night? I rapped on the window and they didn't blink a yellow eye.

This wasn't the kind of bird-watching I had in mind. Nor was it the only plague passing through Waco, apparently. At check-in I was handed a letter, on the bottom of which was a cartoon drawing of a giant, smiling cricket, wearing a sweater with the Hilton logo. "Dear Guest," it began. "Welcome to the Texas cricket migration!" It warned that there was a proliferation of these critters this time of year, that they would in fact be bounding through the front doors and sharing the hotel with me. It called them our "cricket guests." I was in no way opposed to visitors, in fact was quite sure I would soon crave them. Though any with six legs, I warned the bubbly receptionist, would soon meet with an unfortunate accident—that of a telephone book falling upon them.

Without the ability to watch TV, or, more precisely, to hear it, I set off for a day on the town. I visited the Dr. Pepper Museum and Free Enterprise Institute just across the street, where I learned about the evolution of the soft drink. I bought a Dr. Pepper float and a T-shirt for my editor that said, "Be a Pepper!" I also bought a pair of cowboy boots at a store called Cavender's, though

I wasn't sure I wanted them. Then I drove east, down Double EE Ranch Road to the Branch Davidian compound at Mount Carmel, site of the 1993 FBI siege and home to a few Davidian stragglers, a burned-out school bus, a lonely church. There was a one-room visitor center, unlocked and unmanned, chronicling the day seventy-six Davidians lost their lives. There were pictures of the dead, and by the church a plaque for the dead, and in the yard a crepe myrtle tree for each of the dead. A woman named Amo Bishop approached me while I photographed, handed me some Davidian literature. A hot, dusty wind blew her hair in her eyes. She looked homeless and hungry, like a Depression-era mother in a Farm Security Administration photograph. She said she liked my boots.

On the way back to Waco, I stopped at Wal-Mart to buy some DVDs and, shame of shames, ate dinner in their cafeteria—at 5 p.m. Back at the hotel the grackles had moved to another tree, one in the parking lot, and were doing a thorough job repainting the oversized pickups below. It wasn't yet dark, was still my first day, and already I felt a severe depression descending, one whose gravitas would shackle me to that miserable room if I didn't wiggle free. I grabbed my cameras and headed back out, driving west this time, because west couldn't be worse than east.

At a place called Gatesville I came upon a drive-in theater, joined several dozen other vehicles for what turned out to be a talking animal movie, one where cats and dogs waged an ever-escalating war behind their owners' backs. When the movie started, people left the air-conditioning of their vehicles to sit on blankets, lawn chairs. Couples cuddled in the beds of their pick-ups, their faces glowing blue, the sky behind them red as a ruby.

An excellent image. But how to get that sky, those faces, and the movie screen in the same shot? I decided to turn my rental car around to face them, to shoot them through my windshield with the movie screen reflected in my rearview mirror. And conceptually it worked, though I was now the weird guy facing the wrong way, the focus of a gang of distracted teenagers. "The screen's behind you, douchebag!" And so on. Screw this; tobacco-spitting, pickup-driving, backward baseball cap–wearing yahoos scoring off me. I drove back to the Hilton and, in a move I would repeat in the evenings ahead, called it an early night.

seventeen

iraq (reprise)

The desert between Amman and Baghdad was dull and featureless, less interesting even than the J Lo video CD that my driver played over and over on a TV mounted to the dashboard of my GMC. From my camera bag I dug out a picture that Deirdre had snuck into my luggage, a picture I first discovered in my hotel in Amman. It was of the two of us at the White House Christmas party. We were in the East Room, dressed up and beaming, holding glasses of eggnog. Behind us was an elaborate buffet, mountains of shrimp and lamb rib chops, other journalist couples smiling, eating, gazing at the Christmas trees. Deirdre was a few weeks pregnant in the picture, I suddenly realized. A hopeful end to a shitty year.

The first miscarriage had happened seven months before. She had gotten pregnant shortly after I returned from Afghanistan, and my euphoria caught me off guard. It felt like fantasy; I went about my daily routines with the hushed and methodic intensity of someone fearful of acknowledging his good fortune.

Of someone in a trance. It was a destiny I had never allowed myself to contemplate, let alone fulfill. And yet it was happening. This *was* happening. I had created a life. I had made my wife happy. I had made myself happy. It felt right, and the fears of slowing down evaporated. Just like that. Not because my wanderlust was satiated, I hoped, but because the open road would always be there, would invite me back when the time was right.

Then that life lost its way. Though the autopsy was inconclusive, I knew it was my fault, that my reproductive DNA was flawed, defective. I just knew it. My subsequent semen analyses at GW supported my belief; low count, slow motility, poor morphology. "Ever had mumps?" the doctor had asked.

"Mumps? No."

It wasn't until later that same evening, lying in bed and drifting between consciousness and sleep, that I remembered that I had. I was in the sixth grade, and my parents had rushed me to Holy Cross Hospital in Silver Spring, Maryland, my testicles swollen like a peach. My memory of that experience should have been more clear—I was eleven years old—yet it was vague, repressed, a collection of dark and distant images, like those from a nightmare: the look of concern on the face of a young nurse, a doctor taping my penis to my belly and sticking a long, gleaming needle in my nuts, my friends asking me where I had been and me being too embarrassed to answer.

All those years I had never allowed myself to contemplate the illness, as well as one of its potential side effects: sterility. I had filed away the experience, the hospital stay, in some hidden corner of my brain. Only maybe I hadn't as I'd long held an unspoken, nagging fear that I couldn't have children. Even now it was hard for me to equate the two, to resurrect those memories and lay them square on the table as the cause of my infertility. It was hard to accept that this wasn't my fault.

Deirdre and I decided to ignore my medical history, and the doctor's diagnosis, and tried to conceive throughout summer and fall. Then just before coming here, another pregnancy. A fool's hope. A second life lost. I held the photograph of Deirdre and me against the window of the GMC and watched the Jordanian desert passing behind it. I had to stop fretting and focus. The toughest assignment of my life was fast approaching.

☐ The driver of my GMC, whom I had hired in Amman, said the trip between capitals would take nine hours. And up until reaching the Iraqi border, where a squat Iraqi agent rifled through my luggage and promptly relieved me of my helmet and flak vest, we were making good time. "No allowed in Iraq," he said of the items, which he was now trying on.

"Yes allowed."

"No allowed."

"I'm taking them with me," I said, reaching for the helmet.

"No, no. No allowed."

I tried the usual routine, asking if there was a "fee" I could pay to resolve the issue, or if perhaps I could exchange the goods for a brand-new watch, a handful of which I had brought on the street in Amman for just such an encounter. Nothing. I slipped a wad of twenties into his shirt pocket, but he flung the money to my feet.

In other developing nations—India, say—that are known for their creative and prolific means of separating foreigners from their property, the piracy comes with a wink and a nod. Everyone is in on the game and knows their role—they're the grifters and you're the mark, and on the occasion you nab one of them in the act, discover a little hand reaching into your pocket, or an extra credit card slip tucked beneath the one you're about to sign, or a border guard removing items from your bag that you're pretty sure you're going to need, that's your cue to throw a coarse and sustained shit fit, followed if necessary with a small contribution to that person's retirement fund, until you get your property back. Those are the rules—and they work. Never once had I encountered a place, even in countries destabilized by war, where a thief confronted with his crime couldn't be talked, shamed, or threatened into returning the goods.

But in the weeks before the second Gulf War, words were for the weak. The only way to get stolen property back, I quickly learned, was to open your wallet—and empty it. I slipped the guy a crisp, new hundred-dollar bill for each piece of gear, which he abruptly returned, and then to my surprise told me that his three-week work shift was up, that he needed a ride home to Baghdad, and that he was coming with us. The little swindler jumped into the passenger seat and locked the door. I climbed into the back and off we went.

"You very angry," the guard said, turned around in his seat. He was all smiles now.

"And you're a thief."

"No, no."

"Yes, yes."

"No, no."

"Just admit it. Admit you're a thief."

"Not a thief."

"Really? Whose money is in your pocket?"

"Mine."

This was pointless. I told him to "turn around and rob some-body else," which didn't make much sense.

"No rob," he said.

An hour later, we pulled into a rest stop, the first sign of life since the border post. I thought it best to stay in the car with my gear while the other two went for tea. When my driver returned and climbed into the GMC ahead of our hitchhiker, I locked the doors and told him we were leaving.

"Habibi, habibi," he said, pointing to the tea house. "Friend, friend."

"Drive or you don't get paid!" That was enough for him, for he opened the passenger side window, tossed out the guy's shiny, blue duffel bag, and took off.

That night I checked into the Al-Rasheed Hotel, famed as the Baghdad hideout of Peter Arnett and the CNN crew during the first Gulf War, and the following morning registered at the Ministry of Information (MI). Technically speaking, in order for foreign journalists to visit sites in Baghdad, or anywhere in Iraq, you needed permission from the MI. The stated protocol for photographers was to show up each morning with a list of destinations, whereupon one of the Ministry directors, a corrupt, distracted pair named Mohsen and Khadum, would peruse the list, approving or, more likely, denying your choices. I came to revile those two men with every ounce of my being: their autocratic air, their open and avaricious need for deference, their vanity. It was an open secret that they were spies for the Mukhabarat, the Iraqi intelligence service. And yet I still couldn't bring myself to feign reverence. Bribe them, yes. But fall to their feet like some other journalists, offering gifts of food and flowers and tailored suits, no way. If there was any satisfaction to be had in the coming war, for me it was that these twin tools would get what they had coming.

The MI was also where all foreign journalists were issued their oversized credentials (which we were supposed to wear around our necks at all times, like cowbells), had their sat phones unlocked and registered (border guards used a metal crimp to seal your sat phone in its case when you entered the country; you then had a few days to have that crimp unlocked at the Ministry of Information in Baghdad, the only legal place to use and store your sat phone), were assigned a "guide" (a government minder who followed your every move, told you who or what you could or couldn't see, photograph, or interview, and reported daily on your actions to the Ministry), and, apparently, were charged out the ass in mandatory fees ($350 a day, to be exact). There was the $100-a-day "journalist's fee," which they claimed was for the privilege of using the Ministry as a work space, though I didn't have a work space; the $100-a-day "sat phone fee," which I guess was for the privilege of sending transmissions through their atmosphere; the $75-a-day guide fee, which didn't go to the Ministry but to the minder himself, whom the Ministry wasn't paying properly and who was therefore charging journalists independently; and the $75-a-day driver fee, though the driver was also paid on the side. And that was just the beginning.

While all these official fees made you legal, allowed you to stay in-country, they didn't help get the job done. If you actually wanted to work, wanted to get out in the field to interview and photograph instead of sitting around the MI waiting for permission to do so, you had to dole out twenties and hundreds like a Mafia don at a made man's wedding. Want to visit the Al Dora Oil Refinery? A hundred-dollar bill to one of the ministers will make it happen. Want to check on your colleague's visa status? A hundred will open the file, another hundred will get you what it says. Want to get your sat phone unlocked without waiting all day? A twenty should do it, or maybe a hundred. Want to get a visa extension, to get a permit to visit Basra, to get Mohsen and Khadum to actually look up from their paperwork and acknowledge your presence? A hundred, a hundred, a hundred. Slipping a folded Thomas Jefferson into an Iraqi palm was like slipping it into the hand of a magician—so practiced were they at making it disappear.

Even the uniformed peons at the Al-Rasheed, where I was paying $45 a day for a room and $35 a day for the "mandatory" breakfast, were getting into the act. Late on my first day I asked to switch to a south-facing room. That was the direction I needed to point my sat phone to make a connection, and like most journalists I wanted the option of transmitting on the sly. I slipped the concierge a TJ, which he openly examined, then returned. I doubled it and got the same response. "What, then?" He held up five fingers.

◻ The first minder the MI assigned to me was a tall, broad-shouldered, mustachioed man named Abdul Rachman. He bore a resemblance to Hussein himself, though I doubted the tyrant shared his castrato voice. Rachman sounded like a woman pretending to sound like a little boy, which troubled me. On our inaugural morning I told him I wanted to make pictures of people stockpiling food and fuel in preparation for war. He took me instead to a giant statue of Saddam in Firdos Square, the very statue that American forces would famously topple seven weeks later.

"What are we doing here?"

He turned towards the statue and pretended to make a picture with his hands. "Very nice statue," he said in his she-boy voice.

"It is a nice statue. But I need to photograph real people." We climbed back into the car and tooled around town for a bit before stopping at another statue.

Switching minders was a surefire way to piss off the MI thugs, Mohsen and Khadum, though I didn't really care. Rachman was already working for the AP, which seemed to me a good enough excuse to dump him. And Khadum seemed to agree. "Take this one," Khadum said, motioning with his head to a scrawny, goateed man with a lit cigarette pinched between his lips.

"How's your English?" I asked. He winced at me through cigarette smoke, then said something in Arabic. They both snickered.

"Moonee," he said to me finally.

"What?"

"Moonee, moonee."

"He wants money," Khadum said. "You pay him $100 a day."

"Any others available?"

Khadum gave me a look that said he was growing tired of this exchange. "This one," he said, pointing to the same man. Just then through the glass behind Khadum I noticed my driver, waving his arms and pointing to a little man in a plaid suit. The guy was old, in his late sixties perhaps. He looked like one of the comic villains in the early James Bond movies. His hair was slicked back, he wore a silk ascot and was smoking a cigarette from a long, black holder. He had kind eyes, though, and smiled and waved.

"Oh, my guide is here." I motioned for him to come in. "This guy was my first choice but he had to see if his schedule was free."

"Mr. Jim telephoned me at home to see if I could work," the little man said, taking the cue. I supposed my driver had told him my name.

"We don't like the people choosing their own guides," Khadum mumbled, waving the man away with his hand.

"Relax," I snapped, getting up to leave. "He and I are gonna work together." Khadum stared at me and I stared right back. That arrogant little shit, I so wanted to hurt him, to grab both his ears and drive my knee into his forehead. To make him bleed. Scream for mercy like a little girl.

"Who do you work for?"

"*U.S. News & World Report,*" I said, and he wrote my answer on a scrap of paper.

My new guide's name was Saadiq. He asked for $50 a day while in Baghdad, $100 a day outside the city. He said we could start first thing in the morning. "I just screwed myself with the MI to get you," I said. "So don't play me."

☐ Photographing in Iraq during the last days of Saddam Hussein was a lesson in compromise. The MI was eager to direct journalists to the antiwar protest du jour—usually a collection of unshaven, tattooed foreigners in "Human Shield" T-shirts, sitting lotus style outside some government building and chanting for peace; or a parade of middle-aged Iraqi men, proclaiming devotion to their mustachioed madman. This theater never drew in the masses who gawked from the sidelines as if Ringling Brothers were passing through town. And it was utterly void of news value. Yet you had to attend from time to time, and appear happy about it, in order to get more suitable subjects approved. Ditto for the dreaded "hospital tour," where a sullen doctor escorted you to his or her pediatric wing of horrors—bed after bed of deformed and dying babies. The doctors blamed these displays on UN sanctions imposed after the first Gulf War, claiming they barred medical supplies from entering Iraq, which wasn't entirely true. Medical supplies were allowed in, yet it was the UN sanctions that had left much of the country destitute, and as many as eight hundred thousand children chronically malnourished. But standing in the sour miasma of certain death, with teary mothers pulling on your sleeve and pointing to what was left of their children, who was going to argue?

In the field, photographing anything to do with the military was a definite no-no, as were beggars, Saddam's palaces, and most oil fields. Naturally, these were the things I wanted to photograph. Saadiq's way of dealing with these forbidden fruits, on the occasion we stumbled upon one, was to pretend they didn't exist. Up in Mosul, for example, when we came across a missile battery aiming due north, a missile battery that was well inside the no-fly zone, and that, for the moment, was unmanned, I told Saadiq to tell the driver to pull over. "I have to shoot those things."

"What things?"

"The missiles."

"Missiles?"

"The ones right there."

"I don't see anything."

"They're right there." I put my wide-angle lens on the camera and reached for the door handle.

"If you care about my life, you won't get out of the car."

"Quit being so dramatic. Just drive up to them and I'll shoot them from the car."

"Shoot what?" And so on. These matches usually ended with me pestering the poor guy to the point of him clutching his heart and popping one of the little nitroglycerine tablets that he kept in a small tin in his coat pocket. He had had three prior heart attacks and with me in tow appeared well on his way to a fourth.

Our driver, who was also named Saadiq, took us up and down the country in his black 1987 Monte Carlo SS—though we spent most of the next three weeks working in Baghdad. The city was lively and well laid out, and—with Saddam's goofy mug everywhere—surprisingly photogenic. He stared from traffic circles and from shopkeepers' windows, from building facades and from car windshields. In each incarnation, be it sticker or statue, painting or photograph, the shit-eating grin was the same, though there were quite a few costume changes: Saddam in camos, waving his soldiers into battle; Saddam in shades and *kaffiyeh,* or Arab head-wrap, surveying some barren piece of desert; Saddam in suit and fedora, firing a shotgun with one arm. Outside the Kamal al-Samarai IVF Clinic, a setting that apparently called for a more sensitive visage, there was even a painting of Saddam picking flowers in a meadow.

My favorite picture of the trip incorporated one of these portraits, a popular black-and-white profile of Saddam from the

1960s. A vendor on al-Rasheed Street, Baghdad's answer to Fifth Avenue, was selling the visage in a gold frame and had it leaning up against the outside wall of his shop. Walking past, I noticed you could see al-Rasheed Street reflected in the glass, reflected right across Saddam's face, and it appeared as though the tyrant's ghostly mug was superimposed on the city, a black-and-white mirage in a world of color. I knelt there for close to three hours, photographing the reflection, as images like these are wholly dependent on the random and ever-changing pattern of passersby. The image I liked best had a bright red double-decker bus abutting the right side of Saddam's profile and a young, attractive woman in a scarf below Saddam's left cheek. Silhouetted on his forehead were the distant domes of a mosque, and in the background, beneath his left ear, bearded men were drifting in opposing directions. I make a picture like this, one I'm real happy with, maybe once a year. At about twenty thousand frames a year, that's not a great batting average—.00005, to be exact—which meant I wasn't getting into Cooperstown.

I gave the two Saadiqs the rest of the day off, as I had some serious visa problems to tackle. Iraqi visas were good for just ten days. While most journalists were simply bribing or begging their way through multiple extensions, I wasn't as lucky. Switching minders had so pissed off the MI thugs that they had offered me only one extension—for four days. This being Iraq, I bribed a well-connected guide named Hamid to skirt their demands and get me a proper ten-day one. I figured the MI thugs were so overwhelmed by the demands of the journalists that they'd simply forget they'd told me to leave, and by all appearances that's what happened. But with my second extension things had become more complicated, as Hamid thought the black market for visas strong enough to quintuple his rates, from $100 to $500. He also neglected to tell me of his price hike until he had had my passport for a week, the visa now expired for six days. He was now demanding the money, new visa or not, for the safe return of my blue book.

I soon realized I didn't like being extorted and offered a proposal to a hulking young man in a leather coat. His name was Ali and he worked in the Ministry, though apparently he did a little freelance work on the side. On my first day in-country he took a liking to me, due in no small part to the fact that I mistook him for the sat phone guy and slipped him a TJ. When I learned of the mistake I wasn't concerned—the guy had such an air about him, looking and dressing like a million bucks, that I figured he was some well-connected son of privilege; a good person to have on my side. Indeed, Ali was eager to return the favor. One day I made the mistake of complimenting him on his leather coat, and he removed it immediately. "You want it? It's yours. I demand you take it," and we had to go through a silly song and dance— "Thanks, but I don't want it," "I insist you take it," "No, please, I can't"—before he finally relented. "Anything you want, habibi," he said then, "you come to me."

"A guide has my passport and I can't get it back."

"Who?"

"His name's Hamid. He drives a green Mercedes. He's holding it hostage for five hundred bucks."

Ali nodded his head, threw me a placatory gesture. "I know this Hamid." Now, I don't know how this kind of thing is done in the States, but I assume some calls are made, some goons are hired, some shirts are ruffled. The Iraqi method, which I greatly admired, was more hands-on. Ali walked out of the his office to the front of the MI, where the said gentleman was leaning against the said car, and promptly throttled him around the neck with a single hand. Hamid made a sad little "Gaa-ha," then turned maroon, the back of his head pressed against the roof of his car. Ali squeezed so hard he was bending at his knees for leverage.

Hamid emptied passports out of his pocket—Italian, Japanese, American. When I saw one hit the ground with a familiar yellow sticker taped to the cover—a method I used to ID my passport from afar—I shouted, "I got it! I got it!" Ali let go and straightened his leather coat, the job accomplished without his speaking a word.

I still didn't have a valid visa, but no longer cared. With the war only days away, I figured I could bribe my way out of anything. It was by now mid-March, and most journalists believed it was about to start "raining" in Baghdad. Foreign embassies had withdrawn their staff, and there were rumors Bush was to offer Saddam a forty-eight-hour ultimatum—leave the country or face his wrath. When I called Washington, the picture editor of the magazine's World section, Romeo Cerecola, told me the editor of the magazine was adamant I leave Baghdad immediately, which gave me a pang of self-satisfaction that my welfare had reached such a level of concern. I'd like to be able to claim I executed his order reluctantly, yet the truth was I was ready to leave.

It wasn't "Shock and Awe"—the much-advertised forty-eight-hour bombing binge that the Americans claimed would leave the Iraqi leadership, and much of Baghdad, in tatters—that worried me. On the contrary, I thought it would be quite the show. It was the Iraqi reaction to Shock and Awe that made me nervous. With the end to their regime in sight, I figured there was too great a chance they'd seek vengeance for their impending demise on foreign journalists, either killing them, holding them hostage, or using them as human shields. Already, the mood in Baghdad was growing portentous. The MI was on the verge of assigning us new minders, and there was talk of everyone having to move into the same hotel, "for our protection." Trusting Iraqi officials required a level of bravery above my potential, and my pay grade. Instead I'd follow orders and drive to Jordan, stash up on food, money, and fuel, recross the border as soon as the war started, and return to the Iraqi capital in the windbreak of American troops.

I headed for Jordan at 5 a.m., sharing a ride with a bald Australian photographer named Nolan Jones. We made it to the Iraqi border complex in four hours and handed our passports to an angry-looking Iraqi agent. He returned them abruptly and said something in Arabic to our driver, who led us to a room with a wooden plaque above the door that read "Doctor." Inside were a few chairs, a TV on full volume, and a little man with a violent cough and a greasy, black comb-over. He was severely bucktoothed, and that made him look a bit like a capybara, one of those giant Amazonian rodents you see in *National Geographic*. He was sitting behind an oversized desk, empty except for a green telephone. The moment he got a load of us, his left leg started bouncing.

The driver handed the rodent our passports, which he reviewed with much ceremony, pausing at each and every page. He coughed incessantly. He picked up the receiver of the telephone and shouted as if he were talking to someone on the moon.

"Amerakee" was the only word I could make out. When he hung up he placed our navy-blue passports on his desk, arranging them squarely in front of him, one next to the other. Apparently the symmetry was unsatisfying, as next he arranged them on top of each other, using his fingers to make each side perfectly flush. Than he covered them with his right hand. Nolan and I shared a glance.

"You must take AIDS test," the rodent said, his left leg bouncing so hard it made his whole body twitch. "You take test for the AIDS. Than I stamp passport and you can go."

"AIDS test?"

"Sorry, mate. It ain't happening."

"You must. You pay 150 Euros. You give me 20 cc's of blood, and then I stamp the passports." He slapped them with his palm.

There was simply no way in hell I was letting that man stick me with a needle. "I won't do it," I said

"What's the point?" Nolan said. "We're trying to leave."

"It is required for every foreigner staying longer than fifteen days. You stayed longer than fifteen days. You were supposed to give the blood in Baghdad. But no problem—you can give it here." He pointed to the next room. I had heard sporadic reports of this "requirement," and figured if I was unlucky enough to encounter it, I'd throw some money at the problem and be on my way. But now other people were in the room, attracted by the sight of foreigners, by the rodent's volume, and I couldn't slip him the dough.

"We'll pay the fee only," I said. "And you give us the stamp and we'll go."

"No. You must take test."

"You're not sticking me with a needle. We're gonna pay the fee. We'll even pay a penalty fee, and than we're gonna go."

"Where's your diploma?" Nolan asked, which seemed the wrong direction to take the argument. Diploma? Who the hell cared? Anyway, the rodent ignored the question.

"Why problem?" he said, looking at me. "The needles are clean." He stood up and led us into the adjacent room, and the entourage followed. This room had the filthy, white-tiled walls of a Hollywood torture chamber. Glass vials were strewn about the counterspace, as were syringes and needles. Some needles were wrapped in plastic, some were not. He grabbed a handful of ones that were wrapped. "See. Clean." Their packaging was sun-bleached and frayed and looked tampered with, like letters that had been opened and resealed. A short, stocky Iraqi with a face and forehead full of hair tried to push up my left sleeve. I yanked my arm away and he laughed. "Its okay," the rodent said, "he is my helper."

The hairball motioned for me to sit down in a green pleather armchair. Draped over the armrest was a thin plastic tube, the kind nurses tie around your bicep to make your veins swell. I opened the pack of Dunhill cigarettes I kept in my front pocket for petty bribes. I needed a stress smoke. "Fine," I said. "I'll do it." I pushed everyone out of the room, sat in the green chair, and the hairball went right for my sleeve. I pressed a folded hundred-dollar bill into his palm and he let the bill drop onto my chest. "La la," he said. No, no.

"Yes, yes," I said, and tried again. He waved his finger at me and called for the rodent, who quickly entered. "This is messed up. Okay. You wanting my blood. It's messed up and I won't do it."

"Then we lock you in room for one month." The rodent wrapped his fingers around his wrists in case I didn't get the message.

"Fine. We'll go back to Baghdad and get the test there," I said. I walked back into his office, snatched my passport off his desk, and headed for the car. Nolan soon followed.

"Look, mate. I know you had to walk out to save face but I ain't going all the way back to Baghdad 'cause these cunts want 20 cc's of blood. Let Doctor Death have his way and we'll be off."

"No way. No journalist does it. Its just intimidation. It's extortion. And I'd like to leave Iraq *without* getting AIDS."

"I saw the list, mate. A bunch of Japs had to do it yesterday. I asked Doctor Death if we could use our own needles. He said we could." I stared at Nolan, defeated. "You got any needles?" I did have some, as well as syringes, had brought them in case of a medical emergency. I pulled them from my luggage and handed them over.

"I'll do this as long as you're the one that takes my blood. I don't want that guy touching me."

"No worries—and you do me."

"I can't, dude," I said. "I'm sorry. I have a needle phobia."

"All right. I can do it myself."

"What about alcohol wipes?"

"You don't need 'em, mate. Smackies don't use them."

"Smackies?"

"Drug addicts."

On our way toward the rodent's office, Nolan suddenly reversed course. "I'm gonna grab my camera."

"I don't think that's a good idea."

"I'll just bring it with me and see if they mind."

We waved the bag of needles at the rodent from his doorway, and he jumped from behind the giant desk. I was first to assume the position in the leather chair, and the crowd of gawking, foul-breathed truckers quickly regrouped. There were arms all around me, it seemed. The hairball and some other roughneck were trying to push up my sleeve, which wouldn't go past my forearm, while the rodent was trying to tie that rubber tube around my bicep. Everyone was shouting directions to everyone else, and I felt on the verge of freaking out. I yanked my arm away, my sleeve unable to go any farther. I took off my shirt, and the men squealed like schoolchildren. One pointed repeatedly to a tattoo on my right arm, a brown bear drawn in the totemic style of the Tlingit Indians in Alaska, then started poking it with his finger. I looked up at Nolan, who was making pictures of me, of the men, of the room. "Hurry it up, dude."

Nolan put down his Canon, screwed a needle into the syringe, and pushed it into my vein. "How much?" Nolan asked the rodent. "Tell me when to stop. Is that enough?" Everyone offered an opinion.

"Just pull it out," I said. Nolan obliged and we switched seats.

"Make some pics of me," he requested, and I made frames as he drew his own blood. Then we got out of there. The last thing I remember seeing in the room was our vials of blood, frothy, unlabeled, and already forgotten, lying on the counter in direct sunlight.

Our next stop was the gear-inspection room, where two Iraqis rummaged through our camera bags and confiscated all the flash cards they could find—three of mine and eleven of Nolan's. "What the fuck is this?" I asked.

"These must stay in Iraq."

"So now you're robbing us?"

"Why did you make pictures here at border? No pictures here."

I glared at Nolan and he turned pink before my eyes. "You cunts!" he screamed, "you swore to Allah you wouldn't rob us! You're thieves . . . THIEVES!" The Iraqis stormed out of the room and he turned to me. "Fuck, I'm so sorry, mate. I feel horrible."

"This is the part where I leave you," I said.

"I'm not leaving without those cards. Those are worth $3,000."

"I don't care. It's gonna be our gear next." Nolan came to his senses and left with me. At the next stop, the one where they inspect the rest of your luggage, the customs inspector robbed Nolan of his oversized souvenir carpet. Right in front of us—he took the carpet out of our truck and announced that he was keeping it. This brought me modest pleasure. Nolan's head turned pink again, though this time he didn't say a word, and soon we were back in the car and driving past two giant paintings framed in concrete—the first of Saddam Hussein waving goodbye, and the second of Jordon's King Abdullah smiling hello.

☐ After a couple decompression days at the Grand Hyatt in Amman, comprised largely of Dead Sea salt baths, mini-bar binges, and extended catch-up phone calls with Deirdre (we had communicated largely by e-mail while I was in Iraq), I began arranging my reentry into Iraq, teaming up with Terrence Palani, a fast-talking, well-traveled photographer for the *Los Angeles Times;*

Melina de Koning, a well-connected South African writer for *USA Today* who carried three phones (two cell, one satellite) in her purse and was often on two, even all three at one time; and Ali Hafiz, a young and genteel Jordanian driver/translator who shunned the prevailing fashions of his fellow countrymen—macho shades, yellow chains, chunky watches—for a more restrained ensemble—jeans, sneakers, and a T-shirt. All three were team players—smart, focused, and eager to move—and I couldn't think of a better trio to go to war with.

Melina scored a rental house for us in the eastern Jordanian town of Ar Ruwayshid, a vile backwater whose one redeeming quality, if you can call it that, was its proximity to the Iraqi border. The three-room home was outfitted with a dozen bedframes on which to sling our sleeping bags, a satellite TV, and a kitchen and bathroom, which was all we needed, really. The idea was to wait there until the war started, when we assumed the border would become porous, and bolt for Baghdad. We all thought this thing would move quickly, that by the time we got to Baghdad the city would have fallen. But just in case the war moved slowly and we'd have to linger on the outskirts of the city, we stocked up on supplies—enough food, water, and gas to sustain us for a month. Thirty-six hours after Bush issued to Saddam his get-out-or-be-bombed ultimatum, we hauled everything in a rental van to our border hideout.

The American invasion began early the next morning. And the Jordanians kept their border sealed tight. "For your own safety," one guard claimed. I called the sat phone number of a *U.S. News* contract shooter who was hoping to enter Iraq through Kuwait. His name was Michael Yellow, though everyone at the magazine had combined his first and last name into a portmanteau nick-name, one that fit his laid-back, California groove: Mellow.

"I'm in," Mellow said.

"You're in?"

"I'm in. We crossed the border this morning no problem." I was beside myself with jealousy, having been overseas for six weeks and missing opening day. Why had I chosen Jordan instead of Kuwait? Why hadn't I just stayed in Iraq?

There were rumors swirling that the Jordanians would let us cross early the following morning, rumors most of us wanted to believe, and we readied our gear, food, and fuel for another at-tempt. The next morning border guards turned us around once more. I grew spitting angry, felt an irrepressible urge to throttle somebody—to take vengeance for my situation on some unlucky soul just for the ugly and irrational pleasure of it. The opportunity arose when we got back to the rental house. There the photo half of a duo from a well-known midwestern newspaper—a clueless pair who had spent close to two months in Amman allegedly try-ing to get into Iraq, though whose unprovoked recitations for not making it had served to distance the rest of us—had, in our brief absence, moved his gear onto my bed, claiming it for himself.

"What the hell is this?"

"You left."

"For an hour!"

"You said you were going to Iraq."

"Yes. We tried to get into Iraq."

"Well I want to be in this room. It's warmer."

"Well, I'm back, so fuck you." He stared at me and didn't budge, didn't remove his gear, and I was on the verge of going nuclear. "This isn't your house, dude. We were nice enough to put a roof over your head."

"Hey . . . you left."

"You're trying to take my bed? Jesus Christ!"

"You left!"

"Yes! We left! We're trying to cover a war, you know. And what are you doing here—you and that reporter? Come to hang-out in Ar Ruwayshid? To sit on your asses while the rest of us go to work? You're like two indoor cats, staring out at the world." His nostrils flared and his fists clenched and I figured I pushed him as far as I could. "You know what . . . take it."

I stormed into the den, where Palani was laying on his back and staring at the ceiling. "This is like an episode of a bad reality show," I said. "I can't take this."

"Fifty clicks from Iraq and we're watching the shit go down on CNN," he said. "I'm so depressed I could kill myself."

"Shock and Awe is a bunch of bullshit—it ain't happening. This thing's gonna last awhile, and the longer we stay here the more we're gonna miss. They ain't gonna open that border."

"Every journalist in Jordan is fucked," Palani said. "Fucked!"

"Which is why we should head to Kuwait and go in from there."

"I'm not going through Kuwait. We already have somebody trying that."

"So does *U.S. News.* But what's the alternative—miss every-thing? Hang here with the likes of those two?" I pulled my pass-port out of my money belt to examine my Kuwaiti visa, which I had gotten back in D.C. as a precaution for such a scenario, and was surprised to see the thing had expired just four days earlier.

"I'm going back to Amman. I'm getting a new Kuwaiti visa and flying there."

The Kuwaiti embassy had other ideas. "No more journalist visas," came a voice from their intercom system, and I taxied back to the Grand Hyatt and decided to alter the one I had. The visa had been valid for three months from the date I received it, which was handwritten in blue ink as "Dec 17 02." Changing the "1" to a "2" would buy me ten days, keeping the visa valid until March 27—just enough time for me to get in-country. I spent a few hours finding a pen that offered the same hue, followed by another several hours practicing the alteration. Finally I just grabbed the passport and made the change—and it looked good, actually. Upon exhibiting my workmanship to a group of journalists in the hotel lobby, themselves bemoaning their presence in Amman, one revealed a scenario I hadn't foreseen.

"I think their customs is all computerized. They'll punch in your visa number and see it's expired. They'll see you forged it." A discomfiting vision popped into my head—that of myself clutching the bars of a Kuwaiti prison. What the hell. At least I'd have a better excuse for missing the war.

☐ The customs line at Kuwait's airport was long and disorganized, and for a few moments, until a uniformed agent ordered all foreign journalists to follow him, I thought that might offer me an advantage. A dozen of us marched behind the man into a private waiting room, where he collected our passports and handed them to another official, who sat behind a computer, typing in people's visa information with a single finger. About every five minutes, Fingers handed a passport back to its rightful owner, setting the lucky soul free. When my turn finally came, when I saw Fingers reading the passport with the familiar yellow sticker on the cover, he made his usual pattern of typing, followed by a not so usual scrutiny of my visa, followed by an even more distressing consultation with two other agents. They flipped to the front page, the one with my photo on it, and turned the passport horizontal. I looked down immediately, pretending not to have a care in the world while, I assumed, they scoured the room for my likeness. When I finally looked up again, I saw my passport moved to the side of his desk. Fingers was working through the rest of the pile, and a half hour later I was the only journalist in the room.

"Mr. James?" I presented myself before him. "Your visa is expired. You'll have to go back to Amman."

"Expired? When?"

"Two days ago."

"No. It's fine." He opened my passport and pointed to the date on the visa, the very one I altered. He pointed to it as proof. "So?"

"It says 22."

"It doesn't say 22. It says 27." He looked at it again. The guy wasn't challenging the digit I forged but the one after it, the one that actually was a seven. I pointed to another seven in a different line for a comparison. "All the sevens are like that." With an abrupt slam he brought his entry stamp down on my visa, which I guess meant he agreed with me. I slung my camera bag around my right shoulder, my computer bag around the left, and got the hell out of there.

On my way out of the airport I rented a 2002 Mitsubishi Pajero from Thrifty Car Rental, signed a $30,000 waver promising I wouldn't take the vehicle into Iraq, then promptly had it outfitted in Kuwait City with a roof rack, 150 liters of spare gas, two spare tires, and enough food and water to last me a couple weeks. Then I drove across the Iraqi border.

Getting into Iraq wasn't difficult—the challenge had been getting out of Kuwait. Armed with some expert advice on routes from other journalists, including Getty photographer Victor Ruiz, whom I picked up in Kuwait City and who was now riding shotgun with me, we quickly made it into the DMZ, the twenty-mile-wide no-man's-land between Iraq and Kuwait. There we met up with Mellow Mike, my *U.S. News* colleague, who had left Iraq the day before due to car trouble, and a photographer freelancing for the *New York Times*. British Forces at the next checkpoint had already turned Mellow back, so there was no sense in our pressing forward. We drove our three Pajeros west, across the DMZ. The Iraqi border was just to our right, not a quarter mile north—a giant, twenty-foot-high berm followed on the other side, we had been told, by a trench of equal depth. There were periodic breaks in the berm through which you could stare straight into Iraq. Kuwaiti soldiers were stationed at each of these breaks, guarding them with apparent indifference.

We scouted a break that looked promising, where the Kuwaitis appeared particularly apathetic about their duties, lounging some thirty yards from their post beneath a makeshift tarp, drinking tea. There was some concern as to what we would find on the other side of the berm, namely whether or not the Iraqi desert, through which we'd have to drive before reaching a paved road, was mined. We drew straws to see who would go first, and I lost. I laid my flak vest out on the driver's seat, so I could sit on it. After redistributing some of my camera gear, as well as my passenger, who smartly opted to ride in another car, we headed off. Approaching the break at a casual speed, I watched a Kuwaiti guard drop his tea and jog toward our caravan. I saluted, not slowing down. He returned my gesture with a confused wave, and just like that we were through.

On the other side I made a sharp right, following some day-old tire tracks on the north side of the berm toward Um Qasr, a small Iraqi port town, and soon enough we were there, with desperate-looking men and children surrounding our convoy, waving empty buckets before our windshields and shouting, "Water, water!" One man shouted, "Water for baby! Please!" We drove to a secluded spot where we could have a brief roadside congress, then tailed a British column north for several miles and onto their base. They booted us out a few minutes later. I wanted to push north and see what we could see. The others thought it too late, and so we drove back toward Um Qasr and made camp outside a British- and American-occupied port, laying out our sleeping bags beneath a giant concrete statue of an eagle, the Iraqi military emblem. Throughout the night there were explosions in the distance and strange red lights zipping through the sky. At about 5 a.m. a soldier woke us up and told us to get our gas masks on. Ten minutes later he gave us an all clear.

Late in the morning, Ruiz and I tried to photograph some NGO (nongovernmental organization) distributing clean water to the people of Um Qasr. The town's supply had been knocked out during the first days of the war, and judging from the way residents assailed my car every time I drove through town, begging for water, they had grown desperate. A white water truck parked itself near the local hospital, and Iraqis climbed over one another to reach a single, rear hose. I pushed into the crowd, raised my camera over my head, and had just gotten off a few frames when people turned on me, whacking me in the head with their plastic buckets and trying to yank my camera from my hands. "No pictures! No pictures!" one man screamed, inches from my face. I beelined back to the car, where I found Ruiz, looking similarly stunned. "That didn't go well," I said.

"Fuck, dude. I'm not going back in there."

We bagged Um Qasr for the time being and made what would become a daily commute to the southern outskirts of Basra, to a bridge held by British troops. Iraqis were still in control of the city, and there were pictures to be had of the Brits exchanging machine-gun and mortar fire, and of civilians fleeing the fighting.

☐ There were two equally important categories of journalists covering the war in Iraq: the embeds, those traveling with the U.S. military; and the unilaterals, or unilats, those, like me, traveling on their own. While the former enjoyed obvious journalistic advantages (access to American troops and their conflicts), as well as logistical ones (food, transportation, and military protection), their window of coverage was far from comprehensive—confined, in fact, to the immediate movements of their unit. That's where the unilats came in. With more freedom of movement, we were better able to report the humanitarian side of the war, the consequences of the military's actions on the very people they had supposedly come to liberate. Unilats did have a major operational disadvantage: it isn't easy to move around a war zone in a rental car. Already, four unilats had been killed—two of them by U.S. Marines. Many of the coalition forces I encountered, their guns forever pointed at me through my windshield, were quick to point out that they could have me sent back to Kuwait. This was their show, and unembedded journalists weren't even allowed to enter Iraq.

For media outlets in the States, which I reviewed online with my sat phone, the war had become something of a football game, their coverage rich on play-by-play and short on consequence; go team go and all that. Which meant the embeds north of us, at the tip of the military spear, were enjoying most of the coverage, as were some unilats who had crossed early and successfully leached onto a military unit, making them partially embedded as well.

Most unilats in the south of Iraq were car camping, and the outside of the Um Qasr port, which had become the overnight address of choice, soon looked like a gypsy camp—dusty, bearded travelers sitting in the dirt, eating canned peaches and telling tales of that day's ventures. At its most crowded there were maybe twenty Pajeros pulled off the side of the road, and three dozen sleeping bags scattered in the sand, curled in the morning chill. Food consisted of whatever packaged goods you brought in from Kuwait, as local supplies were nonexistent, and people were already resorting to desperate means to mix up the menu. One morning I watched Mellow and another photographer scrounging through a garbage dump outside the port for discarded MREs. "Got two!" Mellow proclaimed.

Hygiene wasn't real high on the agenda, obviously. By now so much desert had accumulated in my hair that it looked like I had dreadlocks, only ones that stuck straight up: an ever-elevated Rasta-do which Mellow referred to as "the unilateral." I knew my presence was crowding him, though he was too kind to admit it. The south of Iraq was too small for two *U.S. News* photographers, so I tried repeatedly to push north. The first two times American troops turned me around at a roadblock three hours out, near the city of Nasiriya. "What the hell you doing out here by yourself?" both lectures began. Trying to cover your dumbass war, I wanted to respond.

I knew it wasn't smart tooling solo around Iraq, yet I didn't have much choice; other journalists were content to stay near Basra. On my third attempt to move north, when I saw the highway ahead was still blocked, I put the car in four-wheel drive and rambled east through the desert for a half hour, until I reached a road that linked to Nasiriya. There I drifted around aimlessly, biding my time until I could figure out what to do, when I stumbled upon a small convoy of American soldiers tearing down paintings of Saddam. I jumped out and photographed their effort, than tailed them onto their base. They were Marines with the 15th Expeditionary Unit, and their PIO (public information officer) agreed to let me camp in a corner of their base for a few days, until the road opened. He also told me they were just beginning some humanitarian operations downtown, and suddenly it was clear why he let me stay.

Early on a Saturday morning my hosts opened a field clinic for injured civilians, and one of their first visitors was a handsome man named Khadim, wearing an elegant red keffiyeh, sporting a well-groomed salt-and-pepper beard, and pushing a burned teenager in a wheelchair. The skin was missing from the boy's face and back, from his arms and his hands, and when the Marines lifted him onto a stretcher, he shrieked in the horrid, high-pitched tone of someone adrift in unimaginable agony. Two weeks before, an errant American missile had destroyed their home, Khadim explained, and sprayed his son with molten shrapnel. The boy's body had caught fire and Khadim couldn't put him out.

While I photographed, the Marines injected the boy with morphine, scrubbed clean his burns, and rolled him in gauze squirted with iodine. They did this in the shade of a tree, with wind kicking up clouds of dirt and dust. Two weeks without medical treatment must have been rough on him, they agreed. Khadim presented another boy then, this one older than the first, though displaying a similar pattern of burns. And when that one was being cared for, Khadim brought forth yet another, this one a girl. He carried her in his arms, a dark beauty in an orange dress, her mouth open, her arms limp, her legs seared a sickening shade of yellow, as if dunked in a deep fryer. The Marines cleared a third stretcher and looked at Khadim curiously. "Are there any more?" a medic asked.

"No."

"Thank God."

"The rest are dead."

The Marines looked at each other. "How many?"

"Ten."

"All your children?"

"My children, yes. And my wife, my parents, my sisters, my brother."

"All you can say is 'Fucking Saddam,'" a Marine offered. I stared at the Marine until he looked up at me, then I walked away.

When the whines of Khadim's daughter were numbed with morphine and the man sat by himself beneath a tree, I asked him how he could be so calm, so forgiving. He said the lives of his children depended on it. And the Americans were just children too; they didn't know what they were doing. Then he invited me over to see what was left of his house. I took him up on it, swinging by a few hours later with a reporter from Al Jazeera, the Arab news network. They spoke for some time in Arabic, and upon noticing I was left out of the conversation, Khadim made a simple, eloquent motion to the ruins around us.

▢ On April 6 I bid farewell to the Marines and headed north from Nasiriya. The road was now clear and I had been moving for two hours when a photographer with the *Washington Post* called to tell me to get my ass back to Basra—the city was falling. I pounded the steering wheel over and over, then pulled to the side of the road. The Americans were still days away from taking Baghdad, which meant I was days away from making pictures there, though it would be helpful to try to get into position now. On the other hand, there'd be enough work for two *U.S. News* photographers down south. I could risk it and go back to Basra, shoot for a day or two, then push north immediately. Shit! I made a U-turn, drove south for five hours, and by the next morning was glad I had. There were pictures everywhere.

The Red Crescent was lifting the lifeless bodies of soldiers, stiff and hollow, from their dying places and loading them onto the backs of flatbed trucks. At the hospital, dead civilians were accumulating in a tiny morgue, wounded civilians in the wards. Sitting upright in one bed was a man who had been shot in the face and was trying to speak, though the swelling garbled his words. "He's saying he came to Basra to find work and can't go home like this," a doctor translated. Another civilian, this one without a shirt and with red stains dripping down his blue jeans like candle wax, wandered by, sat on a bed, then thought better of it and left. He had a little bullet hole just beneath his throat, and when he walked past, I saw a giant exit wound on the back of his neck, exposing the upper reaches of his spinal column.

All-male mobs were looting much of the city. Outside Basra University men scurried off with desks and chairs, with lightbulbs, ceiling fans, and Xerox machines. One looter wore a mortarboard on his head. Other photographers told me looters had ransacked the Basra Sheraton, where I had stayed a month earlier; and when I arrived, the hotel looked like the remains of a mauled animal. All the windows were smashed and lobby furniture was spilling out the front doors, like guts. Water cascaded from the balconies of rooms.

The British forces were still engaging Iraqis here, in the northern half of the city, and the sound of gunfire and exploding mortars was pronounced. Whenever I pulled over to photograph British soldiers, I tried to park my car next to one of their giant Challenger 2 tanks, backpedal for a time with their column as it marched through the streets, then hustle back to my car, leapfrog it forward, and start again. When one of the tanks I used for protection opened up with its chain gun, firing bright orange rounds down an alley and into a building, I ran back to the Pajero to get it out of the way. Starting the engine, I glimpsed to my left, just as two men in civilian clothing, maybe eighty yards out, attempted to dash across the alley. The first man's torso exploded like a water balloon, a red-and-black burst of clothes and organs. The tank kept firing and I sped off, trying to ignore what I had just witnessed. With engagements escalating and the sun going down I drove back to Um Qasr, ate a can of tunafish, and transmitted a dozen pictures. Unfortunately, it was a Monday, and as the magazine's deadline wasn't until Saturday, I wasn't optimistic the coverage would survive the week.

The next day Basra was quiet, and after an unsuccessful morning cruising for pictures, food, and fuel, I contemplated making a resupply run south of the border. I was in decent shape with water, in bad shape with everything else. My gas gauge was near "E," and the spare fuel on top of my car, bartered for two cases of water from a taxi driver in Nasiriya, was of such shitty quality that a single tank of it had left my engine sounding like a sputtering lawnmower. My food box, too, was down to the undesirables: some spare parts from MREs—crackers and brownies and squeezable jalapeño cheese—a couple cans of fruit cocktail, a bag of pink cookies with white filling, and a dozen cans of tunafish. More bothersome to me at the moment, though, was that I had no clean clothes, was in fact no longer wearing socks and underwear, only my sneakers, a pair of black camo pants, a flak vest over a wife-beater, and a green bandanna over my head to ward off the sun. I was ripe and couldn't waste my drinking water doing laundry.

I emptied all my spare gas into the sand, crossed the border at Safwan, and managed to stay in Kuwait all of eleven minutes, which was how long it took to find a station, fill every tank I had to the brim with high-test, then get waved back across the border by Kuwaiti guards, who, having just seen me come from Iraq,

offered me amnesty from the normal can't-cross-here routine.
Already the car sounded better, and I was eager to head for Baghdad. That city was still the prize, was now on the verge of falling.
I went back to the camp to try and find like-minded journalists,
and my Baghdad-or-bust appeal raised nary an eyebrow. Someone said a writer/photographer team from the *Chicago Tribune* was
thinking of heading north the next morning, though, as was a
photographer with the *Rocky Mountain News*. When I spoke to
them they seemed noncommittal. I wanted to leave at the crack
of dawn and not stop until Rasheed Street; they were talking of
leaving at nine and stopping for a day or two in Nasiriya. I forced
myself to be patient and wait the few extra hours for them.

In the morning we got a late start as expected, though were
joined in our journey by a Pajero full of likable Brits. Our four-
car convoy made it to Nasiriya quickly, and there, upon learning
that Baghdad was about to fall, my travel companions agreed to
keep moving. Polly Patterson, the shooter for the *Tribune,* hopped
in my car for the next portion, while her colleague, a brave and
savvy blonde named Aria Heckerling, drove with their translator
behind us. The road to Baghdad was near deserted, a half-dirt,
half-macadam highway that passed through not a single city or
village—just untold stretches of dull, brown sand. For five hours
the only evidence we encountered of any conflict, apart from several slow-moving American military convoys, was the blackened
shells of Iraqi tanks and trucks and an occasional blown-up camel.

Nearing the outskirts of the city, two scorched Iraqi tanks
blocked the road completely. I was the first to drive around
them, and just as I brought the car back on the tarmac and began
to accelerate, there was a staccato crack of machine-gun fire, a

near-simultaneous lifting of dirt to the front right of the Pajero. Polly and I ducked at the same time toward the center of the car, and I think we clunked heads. I slammed on the brakes, turned the car around, and headed back around the tanks, all the while bracing for a second barrage that never came. The other cars in the convoy had heard the gunfire and were already heading the opposite direction. We sped several miles down the road, then pulled over to discuss what to do. The last safe spot we had passed, an American base, was sixty miles south, yet Baghdad lay just thirty miles north. It was getting late. An Iraqi car came speeding toward us, a white flag whipping from one of its windows. The occupants said they too had been shot at, just up the road in the same place. They said it was Americans, and so we decided to risk it and move forward. "I'm not going first this time," I said.

"I will," Aria volunteered without hesitation.

We pulled back around the charred tanks going maybe a third my original speed. Our flashers were on and each car held something white out the window. Rolling forward, several American tanks came into view, then a black soldier walking toward us, smiling. "Sorry to scare you like that."

On a tank behind him, a young white guy with a machine gun spoke up. His voice had a southern lilt. "That was me. Didn't know who y'all were."

"So you just start shooting? You shoot at people two hundred yards away before you know who they are?"

"They were just warning shots."

"They hit five feet from my car."

"They were fuckin' close. Glad I didn't hit you. After you left I was like, maybe they were media. I'm glad I didn't hit you."

We continued north and arrived in the city just after sunset. There were great clouds of black smoke rising from the horizon, and pieces of cars and tanks strewn across the roads. The closer we got to downtown, the emptier the streets became, and we could hear fighting in the distance. Coming over a rise, myself in the lead again, we encountered more warning shots. We held up our hands, Polly and I, and in the darkness I could make out the shapes of American helmets moving toward us. The soldiers were kind enough to let our caravan stay for the night on their compound, which was on the grounds of one of Saddam's palaces. There we learned that Marines had just brought down a statue of Saddam outside the Palestine Hotel. We also learned that Marines had cordoned off a perimeter around the Palestine and neighboring Sheraton, and that embedded journalists were moving into the hotels. I felt simultaneously exhausted and exhilarated. After weeks of living like an animal, of being shot at, eating shit food, and sleeping in the dirt, I was back in Baghdad, just in the nick of time, and believed in my heart that the next few days would present before me a refund for my suffering, a giant, unharvested field of photographs, from which I could reap all the images I wanted.

In the morning our four vehicles pushed off for the Palestine Hotel, where we hoped to find rooms to ditch our gear before working. What we saw on that short drive made me realize I had overestimated the photographic potential. The streets were deserted—not a soul in sight. Just mangled vehicles and plume after plume of black smoke, much of the city still smoldering. Crossing a bridge over the Tigris River, we saw buildings with giant holes in them, heard the pop pop pop of gunfire to the north, the distant rumble of American tanks. We drove slowly, weaving around chunks of metal and glass, Polly holding a dirty white T-shirt out the window. And still nobody. No celebrations, no tearing down of Saddam statues, no Iraqi people. Just the remains of a ravaged city.

The hotel was full, the desk clerks claimed, pointing to groups of journalists camped out in the lobby. Ditto for the Sheraton next door. Though the *Tribune* folks were somehow able to nab a few rooms, and generously offered me one. It was a corner room on the fourth floor. There was a giant bed with a brown blanket, and a shower that worked, which was more than I expected.

We regrouped in the lobby and tooled around the east bank of the Tigris, the omnipresent cracks of sniper fire keeping our range in check. Some Iraqis were posing with the severed head of a Saddam statue, the one that Americans had brought down the day before. There was also some scattered looting, though nothing to compare with what I had shot in Basra, and by and large the downtown remained dull and deserted.

Over the next three days things grew more lively, though it still wasn't the photo free-for-all I had hoped. I zipped around in my car from dawn to dusk, saw Iraqis tie a chain around the neck of a Saddam statue and bring it down, saw a man try to stab another for looting his shop, saw thousands upon thousands of Iraqis returning single file to the city. On a street near the Palestine I even encountered Hamid, the MI "guide" who held my passport hostage. He looked thin and his mustache was shaved. He put his arms around me, as if we were old friends. He kissed me over and over on the cheek. "Beat it," I said, pushing him away, and he whispered something to a photographer friend of mine for the *Christian Science Monitor*. "What did he say?" I asked.

"He said, 'Please tell him I'm sorry.'"

By now the journalists from Jordan had arrived, their hair washed, their clothes clean, their vehicles shiny, and Baghdad was becoming something of a scene. On a Saturday night, after transmitting that day's pics from the parking lot of the Sheraton, my sat phone and computer set up on the hood of my car, I called the office. I learned from Romeo that I was only getting modest play in the magazine again. Basra was old news, of course, trumped by the fall of Baghdad. And other photographers here had made better pictures than I had—of looters and morgues and destroyed palaces in other parts of town. I hung up and pounded my fists against the hood of the Pajero, then lit a cigarette. I felt ill and embarrassed. Craven. My talent wasn't on par with these world-class war photographers. I had been outsmarted, out-braved, outphotographed. And it seemed the most searing of all defeats, to reach the limits of your ability and still come up short, to realize you were never going to be one of the greats, that your work would never carry the weight of legend, no matter how many risks you took or miles you drove. No matter how hard you tried. No matter how many days you stayed away from home, from the people that loved you, needed you. That cool April evening in Baghdad, the air thick with burning oil and munitions, with triumph and ruin, I accepted this for the first time. In the world of photojournalism I would always be a man of minor accomplishments.

I walked up the hot, darkened stairwell of the hotel, walked straight to my shower. The water came out yellow at first, then cloudy brown, then clear. When I emerged, I stared at my naked self in the mirror, the water dripping from my hair and down my chest. My body looked estranged, not my own but that of a man much older and leaner, sadder; a vagabond whose neglect had worn thin his outer self. I had missed dinner again, which was offered for only a few hours in the Palestine Hotel, and in my room opened another can of tunafish, draining its water over the balcony. The smell of it made me sick, and I flung the tuna can toward the Tigris River. It curved like a Frisbee around the hotel and out of view. I grabbed my Thuraya sat phone and walked back outside, across the street to Firdos Square, to the base of the Saddam statue that American troops had pulled down a few days before. The statue's torso still lay in the dirt a few yards from its pedestal. The head was long gone and American soldiers had peeled pieces of the copper skin from its raised right arm. Pocket keepsakes. I called Deirdre's cell phone, and when she answered, I lost the desire to speak. That day we parted, sat in the spare bedroom and clung to one another other, it seemed so long ago. Lovers from a different lifetime.

"I'm ready to come home now," I said.

◻ A week later we were driving south on Route 522 into Berkeley Springs, West Virginia, a spa town in the simplest sense of the term. It was drizzling and the streets were empty and I still felt out of it—dreamy and someplace else. We stopped for a time in the town square, on the way to our rental cabin in the woods, and Deirdre insisted we get massages. She led me into a small building where the lobby smelled of lavender and the walls were lined with kitschy soaps, Kama Sutra oils, and books on

Tantrism. I lay before a young masseuse who placed smooth black rocks on my chest, some hot, some cold. Then she put her hand beneath my neck and asked me to close my eyes.

We drove farther south, past the local high school and signs for Bucky's Used Cars, Adult World, and Terry's Taxidermy–Wildlife Museum, before turning left onto a road that, to our relief, was more pastoral. It climbed and pitched with the modest thrill of a children's roller-coaster and dead-ended at the bottom of a lush, wooded hollow before a little log cabin, which itself fronted a spring-fed pond. Everything was green: the grass, the bushes, the trees. I felt like I was seeing the color for the first time.

We left the groceries in the car and went to inspect the grounds, and I don't think I've ever heard so many birds. There were red-winged blackbirds calling from the cattails, their liquid shrill more insect-like than avian, and a pair of yellow-shafted flickers calling from the treetops, their voices a satisfying purr, like that of a Latino rolling his r's. There were calls of cardinals and robins and blue jays, and across the pond the dry rasp of a red-tailed hawk, though I couldn't spot him. I did see two Carolina wrens flitting about the woodpile, and a single Baltimore oriole, a sight more rare than one might expect given the proximity of its baseball namesake, thrashing the leaves of the forest floor.

I climbed the steps to the cabin's back porch and stood in the drizzle, listening to this chorus, and Deirdre unpacked the car and made salmon for dinner. The rain kept coming, through the night and all the next day, though I slept through most of it. But the second morning dawned clear and bright and I awoke with the sun in my eyes.

italy

The changes came all at once, it seemed, a few waves amassed in a single tsunami. Hailey and the digi-chicks, among others, were now history, having resigned or been asked to leave. The magazine was still facing a tough market, and now the editor, Gerard McGee, was making major changes. Yet after the water receded, the photo department emerged stalwart, even strong in the broken places, to borrow a Hemingway saying. The de facto director of photography was now Romeo Cerecola, the picture editor of our World section, a congenial Italian who wore only black and who cut quite the picture commuting to our Georgetown offices atop his Scarabeo scooter, his black coat billowing behind him, a cigarette pinched between his lips. His management style was hands-off—do your job and don't bother me with the rest—which fit me well. We were still the *U.S. News* photo department, only now it was a place I longed to be, a place where all the collective stresses that accompany inner-office conflicts had been washed out to sea.

At home, too, things were turning around. Deirdre was pregnant yet again, her third time. And while we vowed not to indulge the urgent pleasures of expectation, the name games, the calendar math, the nursery layouts, fuck, they were impossible to resist. The day after Hailey's farewell fête, Deirdre and I flew to Sicily, a trip I'd planned as a belated thank-you for Iraq. We settled down for a few nights in Taormina, that ancient cliff-side city, with its purple bougainvillea and *pasta con le sarde,* me consuming everything in sight, her seeking sympathy for her dietary woes, for being in Italy without being able to drink wine or coffee. On the third day we again braved the Sicilian highways, where vehicles drive at two speeds, race car and donkey cart, and navigated our Fiat north to the port town of Milazzo, where we caught a car ferry to Salina, in the Aeolian islands.

Owing to its heights, this destination is visible from the Sicilian mainland. But only up close, as the ferry approaches its shores, can the drama of its topography be fully realized. Salina is a pair of volcanoes, molded together at their base like conjoined twins. The cones are green to their peaks with vegetation, being long extinct, and rise from the water at angles so sheer they call to mind a child's depiction of a volcano, minus the flowing lava. The few hamlets that brave this incline do so just above the coast, rewarding their residents, and occasional guests, with near-continuous views of the Ionian Sea. And to reach the beaches here, any of the beaches, one must descend a zigzag of steps carved into a cliff. The approach is more appealing than it may sound, as it offers an unlikely, aerial view of your destination, the thin strip of smooth, black rocks, like those in a Zen garden; the emerald water; the luxurious emptiness.

A single north-south road crosses the small hump of land between the two volcanoes, a hump long cultivated into vineyards,
and though the road is just wide enough for two cars to pass,
most people drive with their side mirrors folded inward. Entering one of the villages, Malfa, say, or Pollara, the road narrows
further, and most visitors park their vehicles and walk to the
town center, all distances here being quite short. The town's pi-
azzas are models of lethargy, with a few stores that open late and
close early, with dark, pretty people gliding by on bicycles and
feral cats lounging on small stoops, their eyes half closed. And
there is an abundance of gardens, which Salinians, like so many
Italians, appear to leave unrestrained, as if they are not gardens
at all but wild growth. If you turn down a garden path, which is,
in fact, the way to reach most of the homes, you are likely to pass
lemon and fig trees, shrubs of rosemary, thyme, and fennel, and
wooden arches roped with grapevines. The aroma of this well-
designed wilderness is both soothing and enlivening, like a coffee
shop, and somehow in keeping with the visual aesthetic of the island. Salina is the most beautiful place I've ever seen.

And that made it an inappropriate setting for a grave turn of
events. One night, coming to bed, Deirdre's body appeared different, just like that, as if someone had flipped a switch: her breasts
smaller, her skin pale, her expression deflated. She knew. I knew.
And we didn't say anything, afraid to break the spell of our surroundings. I turned out the light, and in the days that followed we
went about our vacation, climbing one of the volcanic cones and
snorkeling various beaches; then moved back to the mainland with
its Roman ruins and Greek temples, with its art galleries displaying painting after painting of the same scene, everywhere the
same goddamn scene, Madonna and child, Madonna and child,

Madonna and child. The ubiquity of that miracle made our fate seem all the more cruel, and in the dark hallways of Sicily's museums I held her hand a little tighter. Eventually there was bleeding, tears (from both of us), a search for the word "hospitals" in the index of our *Lonely Planet,* which advised not to seek medical treatment in Sicily if you could avoid it. And so we did avoid it, the trip nearing its end, and after landing in D.C. and getting a good night's sleep we drove to Sibley Hospital to face the music.

"Heart rate is 168," the ultrasound technician said. "The heart rate of what?" I almost asked, until we saw it on the screen, a blob of green pixels, fading in and out with her movements of the magic wand. And at its center an almost imperceptible flutter: its heart. It had a heart.

"So it's okay?" Deirdre asked

"Yep," she said, bored.

"The size is normal?"

"Yyy-ep."

"You're absolutely positive?" I interjected.

The technician twisted a volume knob and suddenly we could hear it. Boom. Boom. Boom. Deirdre put her palm over her mouth. That cardial soundtrack, it sounded like something from outer space, a life so distant and yet so close. Yes, it was in there, in the little dune that was Deirdre's belly. It was in there and it was doing fine.

I put my head on Deirdre's chest and stared at the image on the screen, our image. That heart, more visible now, firing with resolve. The technician printed out a thin screen shot for us to take home, and upon seeing the picture I wished I had asked to press the print button myself, so that I could take credit for such a surprising and lovely portrait.

nineteen

libya

"I was wondering if you want to go to Libya?" It was the kind of message that made me want to rip off my clothes and whirl them above my head. Though such an action would have landed me in handcuffs, and on the national news, as the president of the United States was standing ten feet away. I was at a Bush-Cheney Fundraiser in Santa Clara, California, sitting in the buffer while Dubya droned on about terrorists and their caves, about Senator Kerry and his flip-flopping. It seemed as good a time as any to check my voicemail, and there came Romeo's voice, that blunt question, one I had been waiting to hear for five years, if not more. I hung up the phone and stared at Bush.

"Because our coalition acted, Saddam's torture chambers are closed," he said. "Because we acted, Iraq's weapons programs are ended forever. Because we acted, nations like Libya have gotten the message and renounced their own weapons programs."

While I'm not sure who was concerned about Libya's weapons program prior to their giving it up, their action handed the Bush administration a PR victory. In return, a week before Romeo's message and one day after Moammar Gadhafi's government reaffirmed that it was indeed responsible for blowing up Pan Am flight 103 over Lockerbie, Scotland, the U.S. government lifted the twenty-three-year-old ban on travel there. That cleared the way for American businesses to tap Libya's vast oil wells, and American tourists to visit its unsung treasures. I knew the high-lights by heart. The medina in Tripoli, best shopping in the country, the Roman ruins at Leptis Magna, best preserved in the Mediterranean. And the Ubari Sand Sea, the country's mother draw, with its saffron dunes and salt lakes ringed by tall, wilting palms—the picture-perfect desert oasis, perhaps the prettiest site in all the Sahara. Though Bush was still speaking, I pulled out my cell phone and dialed Romeo. "Shit, yeah," I whispered.

Then I called Deirdre, left her a message that I was going, that we'd have to reschedule some childbirth classes we had com-ing up. I called back every five minutes, and finally she picked up. "Libya, huh?" she began. She had played the message but not called me back. Bush was wrapping up now, the scribblers pack-ing their computers, preparing to motorcade to Air Force One, then fly to Waco for the weekend.

"So what's the deal with those classes?"

"We can't reschedule. They book early." Her voice. It was all wrong, repressing anger, the I'm-upset-but-not-gonna-say-it tone.

"All right. Well. How important are they?" Silence. I was moving now, toward the vans, the phone pressed between my ear and my shoulder, my hands preventing my cameras from clanking together. "And when are they?" I should know this, I realized. Was quite certain I had just provided fodder for future arguments.

"The first weekend in April."

"And they're at GW Hospital?"

"Yes, Jim, they're at GW."

"I'll call 'em right now and try to reschedule." The motorcade to the airport lasted twenty minutes, which was enough time for me to learn that the classes were booked for months.

I tried again the next morning from the Waco Hilton, spent hours on the phone with Sibley, Georgetown, Holy Cross, with every hospital within a twenty-mile radius of D.C. All booked. And my aggravation took flight. People were in Waco for a clogging convention, of all things, and at least two of these visitors thought it appropriate to practice in their hotel room, directly above my head. Waco. I grabbed my keys and cameras and drove to the outskirts of Crawford, to a modest park I had been meaning to explore. Working my rental car along its backroads, looking for a quiet spot to think, I came to a halt before an unexpected site. The road ahead had been built across a dry wash, one that was now hidden beneath a foot of fast-moving water. The banks of this streamlet were blooming with short grasses, with things spongy and green. It had been raining for weeks before we got there.

I put the car in park and called Chip Stein of *Time,* who was also in Waco and who had two young children. "When Kyla was born, did you take those birthing classes?"

"We did La-something."

"Lamaze?"

"Yeah. Though it's still a sore subject. I missed like half of them."

"She didn't forgive you?"

"Put it this way. It came up again as recently as three weeks ago. Big mistake on my part." That wasn't the response I had hoped for.

I dialed the number of a more likely ally, a gay one: Sal Uffleman, managing editor of new media at *U.S. News,* and my best friend at the magazine. "Can I say something?" Uffleman interrupted me midsentence. "I know it seems like you don't have a son yet. But you do."

There was one more call to make, to tell either Deirdre or Romeo I was bagging. The longer I contemplated which number to dial, the higher my moral certitude that Deirdre, that my friends, that everyone was wrong but me. It didn't make sense, was sheer lunacy, to miss two weeks in Libya to attend a weekend of classes. Libya was second on my wish list, behind only North Korea. Certainly there were birthing books we could read instead, or videos we could rent. Of course there were. I stepped out of the car and stood on the banks of the wash. It was warm outside, the first warm day I had felt in four, maybe five months. Gazing upstream a hundred yards or so, I could see the source of the streamlet, where it was breaching the banks of a gushing river, and a hundred yards downstream the spot where they reunited. It was kind of beautiful, this divergence, how it brought life to a part of the basin long neglected.

▢ The oasis town of Ghat, a twenty-hour drive south from Tripoli, sits near the Libyan border with Algeria, a thin forest of date palms surrounding a giant, mud-walled hive. It looks like the early Indian dwellings of the American Southwest, like Chaco Canyon, the exterior walls cracked and sun-baked and on the verge of collapse. Yet Ghat is far from deserted, has in fact de-vised a clever and modern interpretation of its thousand-year history as a caravan center. From here it is possible to stock up on water, mint tea, and couscous, rent a pair of Land Cruisers with Tuareg drivers—the second car for towing out the first, and vice versa—and motor into the Murzuq Sand Sea. This is the real deal, as deserts go, the heart of the Sahara, no roads or villages or visible life, just dunes, tens of thousands of square miles of them, crested and serpentine. To lose oneself in its orangeness, to camp on its crests and stare out at the infinite, undulating yon-der, that seemed to me the most romantic experience—and one I vowed to make some day.

But for now I remained in Washington, D.C., sat on the floor of a basement classroom at GW Hospital, my arms around Deir-dre's belly and my legs straddling her waist, whispering words of encouragement as she practiced her breathing exercises. Those classes *were* absurd, but they were part of the experience, and she needed me there and the Murzuq Sand Sea wasn't going any-where. We might not have had a son yet, as my friend pronounced, but we did have each other, and if I didn't ante up now, then when?

He emerged a month later with his eyes wide open. Deirdre couldn't see him, her labor having yielded to an emergency C-section, with a green curtain blocking her view. But when they cut our son out of her, pried his slimy body loose from hers, his blue eyes darted wildly, a fish pulled from the sea. It would have been such a sight if the doctors hadn't betrayed their concern. They rushed him to a little table and pressed an oxygen mask to his mouth. "Respiratory distress," I heard one doctor say. A young black woman lifted his arms and let go; they dropped limply.

Deirdre was still strapped down in front of me, her arms outstretched while the doctors sewed her back together. "Has he cried? Is he okay?"

It took all my strength to respond with a smile. "They're working on him."

Our son had a full head of hair, and it was black and curly like mine, and my God, there he was. Right there. And something wasn't right and already I knew that this glimpse was all I would ever get, a single scene to replay over and over again for the rest of my broken life. That wet, frightened little boy, one I brought ill-prepared into the world, one that got further than the others but whose destiny was doomed because of my shit DNA. I did this to him. I ignored the doctors who told me I wouldn't be able to conceive and created this life, and in utero he had a valiant go of it, formed a brain and body, built ten fingers, ten toes, a bright red pee-pee, those blue eyes, and none of his construction mattered because it was built on a foundation of sand.

And then they got him started. He panted, made lots of little breaths, then bigger ones. He had fluid in his lungs and one of them hadn't inflated properly, but not to worry, the doctors assured me. He'd be fine by morning. The doctors kept him in intensive care, a little taco under a hot light. Deirdre was anxious and out of it, and when she fell asleep in her hospital bed, I went to his side. He was awake, alert, chewing on his finger. He was wearing only a diaper and had wires about his chest, and I held his little hand, let him hear my voice. I told him we loved him.

The next morning when I returned to see him, a doctor said she needed to speak with Deirdre and me together. I stared at her and she stared back, the kind of stare you don't want from a pediatrician. She and I walked to Deirdre's room, a long, silent march, the heavenly white hallways, the squeaky floors, the new moms pacing with their new babies, and when we arrived by her bedside and she read our expressions and asked what was wrong, the doctor said his lungs had cleared just fine and they were happy about that. But in the X-rays they noticed something else, that his heart appeared "malformed." It was round instead of oval, and he wouldn't be leaving the neonatal intensive care unit just yet. For two days I tried to figure out what that meant, a malformed heart, and so did they. But it was the weekend, and they said we'd have to wait until Monday, when they could bring in an echocardiogram machine from Children's Hospital. And when Monday came, they said the machine wasn't coming until Tuesday. By then I was out of my mind, jumping day and night between their bedsides, and when I ran home without my wife and child, a short trip to shower and grab the mail and papers, I went straight to the kitchen instead, poured myself a glass of Scotch. It was 11 a.m., but it felt a lot later.

The house was hot and silent, and I was soon refilling my glass and wandering outside. There was much activity in the side yard, the periodic cicadas having returned right on cue. Seventeen years after burrowing beneath the earth, they were crawling out all at once, a critter army crossing the grass, clinging to our white picket fence and shedding their old selves, their all-brown, underground armor for a long, brittle body, one with black skin, red eyes, and honey-colored wings. I watched them contemplate this new identity, drying out their many abdomens and making cautious movements of their wings. Those that didn't get swooped up by sparrows or pawed by Kitty, the neighborhood tabby, made a clumsy inaugural flight, reaching an altitude of maybe five or six feet before sputtering into the grass. But they were tenacious bugs and were soon airborne again, flitting among the treetops and securing mates, starting families, each whirring louder than the other, and what an impressive din, that alien sound, like the background noise of deepest, darkest Africa. Even inside the house with the windows closed there was an audible hum, a noise I had long forgotten, though now that I was hearing it again I remembered the feelings it had stirred those many years ago, the thrill of heading someplace else, and the unease—portentous emotions in the face of that first journey.

And now this. I was run through. My back ached. I hadn't slept well in ten years. After fifty states, sixty-four countries, and hundreds of thousands of miles, I wanted to stop, to put the brakes on this brilliant ride and redirect all my energy and emotion toward that which I seemed destined not to have. Malformed heart? Respiratory distress? You can't have children of your own? Don't they know what those words can do to a person? How they can render insignificant a lifetime of labor? How they can resign an already pessimistic person to the certitude of terrible loss? I was convinced that his heart would give out, that he would need a replacement and would suffer, and I had never wanted anything more than for him to be healthy and happy, for the three of us to be together, to pull myself from this orbit and help raise my son. That boy, the unbalanced force of which Newton spoke. *My* unbalanced force. My Carpathia. My redeemer. My flesh and blood. I loved him so much. To be a father and a better husband, a better man; yes, I can do this. I want this. I need this. I can and will be great at it. Just give me a fucking chance.

The next afternoon the attending physician sat Deirdre and me down, a consult that would shape the rest of our lives, I remember thinking. The outlook she offered wasn't among those I had envisaged. It wasn't even in the same ballpark. She said it had all been a big mistake, a resident misreading the X-rays. She said our son's heart looked just fine to her and there was no need for an echocardiogram and he could leave intensive care. I was too euphoric to demand any more details, to fume about what they had put us through. We reclaimed our boy and took him home.

▢ Summer in Washington is muggy and quiet. It is the time of year when the city reminds its citizens of the folly of their predecessors—hopeful men who built the capital of this nation on the grounds of a gurgling swamp. Summer heat in Washington seems not to roll in from the sky but to seep from the earth, the sewers, the cracks in the street. It lifts from the city like ghosts from a graveyard, punishing all the poor souls above, human or otherwise, for the centuries-old crime of being buried alive. Along Wisconsin Avenue the trees wilt lower each day, as if deflating. In Rock Creek Park, dog walkers make an exception for better judgment and allow their panting pets, for a few excited minutes, to wallow in the brown water that is Rock Creek. And on the Mall, the few tourists who knew nothing of this seasonal haunting sweat into their fanny packs and "Go DC" T-shirts, less interested now in summiting the Washington Monument than in learning why anyone in their right mind would live in such a place.

Like most native Washingtonians, I relish this season. It is an urban repellent, sending two of the three major tribes of Northwest D.C., the lawyers and the politicos, packing for elsewhere.

Washington is a city transformed; traffic is light and all the accompanying auto noise—the city's hum—is noticeably absent. The city has the feel of a college campus on summer break. And the third major tribe of Northwest, the one of which I am a member, can breath a sigh of relief, as there is nary a news story in sight.

Except every fourth year. The Kerry campaign was in full swing—and mine to have. The bus and train tours, the small-town rallies, the red, white, and blue. Presidential campaigns are hard work, but fun as hell, a moveable feast with newfound friends. And it was so easy to say no—not a guilty concession but what I truly wanted, could have no other way. Sorry. Can't do it. Find somebody else. On those days that I couldn't get out of it, had to fill in for just a few days and zip up to Ohio or down to Florida and join the press bubble, I felt as if I had nothing to offer. I couldn't make a picture to save myself because of how silly this effort was. This stress. Seventeen years of it. Not time wasted but time overplayed, trying to inflate a finite ability through sheer force of will. To be comfortable with one's limitations, for me the toughest challenge as a photojournalist, suddenly came naturally. So I wasn't a player in the pantheon of shooters. Who cared? In the field of fatherhood, to one little boy at least, I had a chance to become legend.

So for now all roads led home, led to my son's pudgy little landscapes—the rubber-band rolls of chub on his wrists, the bowed legs, the roly-poly belly and toes the size of tic tacs, those plump lips, the curly locks and his cookie-dough smell, the wiggle of his fingers, the flutter of his heart and the butterfly wings of his breath. A garden of so many Edens, this evidence of my existence, and I longed to discover each one. To relish his warm and nascent topography. To spend eternity in "tummy time," when you remove your shirt, his onesie, lie skin to skin, his body splayed atop yours and hearing the rhythm of your heart, breathing the scent of your skin, sleeping. After one such exposure, a humid June afternoon, in which I had left the AC off and the windows open, I stopped short before the bathroom mirror. On my chest was a perfect imprint of his body, red and totemic, his face in profile, the little arms and legs, the wide belly, a bear cub clinging for his life. And I cried for him, for his blind trust.

Our first family summer. I read him books in the afternoon and cooked us dinner in the evenings while Deirdre breast-fed him. In the mornings I went for walks with him hanging from my chest in a Baby Björn, early in the morning when it was still cool and the city slept. The cicadas were sluggish at that hour, and I could pluck them from the trees and guide his finger along their backs. We listened to the birds behind Fort Reno Reservoir, a forgotten field where finches and warblers gathered in the thrush. We saw rabbits there too, nibbling on wildflowers. I had read that babies dream about animals, and those early-morning safaris, the first and nearest of many to come, seemed a good way to give him things to dream about.